AFRICA

Teaching Resources

Prentice
Hall

Needham, Massachusetts
Upper Saddle River, New Jersey
Glenview, Illinois

ISBN 0-13-062992-8

1 2 3 4 5 6 7 8 9 10 06 05 04 03 02

Section Reading Support Transparencies

A Section Reading Support Transparency is provided for each section of the textbook. Each Section Reading Support Transparency provides a graphic organizer framework to help guide students in answering the Questions to Explore that begin each section. You may also use these transparencies to preview or review sections as you teach them.

Graphic organizers are classroom-tested learning tools for representing key pieces of information in a visual summary. The shape of the organizer shows the relationships between the pieces of information. Graphic organizers are especially useful to visual learners.

Each type of organizer in this transparency system represents a reading strategy that requires a critical thinking skill. You can reinforce the thinking skill as you show the graphic organizer.

Venn Diagram The overlapping circles of a Venn diagram are useful for comparing and contrasting similarities and differences.

Time Line The linear presentation of a time line helps students see a chronological sequence of events.

Flow Chart A flow chart visually represents the order of the steps in a process, or a sequence of events.

Concept Web The inner circle in a concept web contains the main idea, while the outer, smaller circles contain the supporting details.

Chart/Table The columns of a table facilitate classification and comparison.

Outline The structure of an outline makes clear the hierarchy of the information being presented—main idea, supporting details, and conclusions.

Cause/Effect Chart Whether showing a single cause and effect or multiple causes or effects, the chart format makes clear the causal connection between events and outcomes.

TABLE OF CONTENTS

AFRICA

CHAPTER 1 Africa: Physical Geography

Letter Home	3
SECTION 1 Classroom Manager, Guided Reading, and Quiz	4
SECTION 2 Classroom Manager, Guided Reading, and Quiz	7
SECTION 3 Classroom Manager, Guided Reading, and Quiz	10
Chapter Summary	13
Vocabulary Activity	14
Reteaching	15
Enrichment	16
Critical Thinking	17

CHAPTER 2 Africa: Shaped by Its History

Letter Home	18
SECTION 1 Classroom Manager, Guided Reading, and Quiz	19
SECTION 2 Classroom Manager, Guided Reading, and Quiz	22
SECTION 3 Classroom Manager, Guided Reading, and Quiz	25
SECTION 4 Classroom Manager, Guided Reading, and Quiz	28
SECTION 5 Classroom Manager, Guided Reading, and Quiz	31
Chapter Summary	34
Vocabulary Activity	35
Reteaching	36
Enrichment	37
Critical Thinking	38

CHAPTER 3 Cultures of Africa

Letter Home	39
SECTION 1 Classroom Manager, Guided Reading, and Quiz	40
SECTION 2 Classroom Manager, Guided Reading, and Quiz	43
SECTION 3 Classroom Manager, Guided Reading, and Quiz	46
SECTION 4 Classroom Manager, Guided Reading, and Quiz	49
Chapter Summary	52
Vocabulary Activity	53
Reteaching	54
Enrichment	55
Critical Thinking	56

CHAPTER 4 Exploring North Africa

Letter Home	57
SECTION 1 Classroom Manager, Guided Reading, and Quiz	58
SECTION 2 Classroom Manager, Guided Reading, and Quiz	61
Chapter Summary	64
Vocabulary Activity	65
Reteaching	66
Enrichment	67
Critical Thinking	68

CHAPTER 5 Exploring West Africa

Letter Home	69
SECTION 1 Classroom Manager, Guided Reading, and Quiz	70
SECTION 2 Classroom Manager, Guided Reading, and Quiz	73
SECTION 3 Classroom Manager, Guided Reading, and Quiz	76
Chapter Summary	79
Vocabulary Activity	80
Reteaching	81
Enrichment	82
Critical Thinking	83

CHAPTER 6 Exploring East Africa

Letter Home	84
SECTION 1 Classroom Manager, Guided Reading, and Quiz	85
SECTION 2 Classroom Manager, Guided Reading, and Quiz	88
SECTION 3 Classroom Manager, Guided Reading, and Quiz	91
Chapter Summary	94
Vocabulary Activity	95
Reteaching	96
Enrichment	97
Critical Thinking	98

Chapter 7 Exploring Central and Southern Africa

Letter Home	99
Section 1 Classroom Manager, Guided Reading, and Quiz	100
Section 2 Classroom Manager, Guided Reading, and Quiz	103
Chapter Summary	106
Vocabulary Activity	107
Reteaching	108
Enrichment	109
Critical Thinking	110
Answer Key	111

AFRICA
Physical Geography

Social Studies Hot Line

Dear Family,

For the next few weeks, our social studies class will be studying Africa. We will study the geography, history, and cultures of the continent. Some of our topics will include the four regions of Africa, the importance of location to each region, the great cultural diversity of this continent, and how life is changing for many African people.

In Chapter 1, we will learn about the main physical features of Africa, including the Great Rift Valley, the Sahara, the Sahel, the four main rivers, and Africa's high inland elevation. We will also find out how latitude, elevation, and distance from large bodies of water and landforms influence the African climate. As you travel around your area, you might encourage your child to talk about the climate: Is it wet or dry, hot or cold? How does climate influence how you live? Is it good for growing food? How does your child think it might compare with climates in Africa?

Looking at a map of the world can provide another springboard to discussing our studies. You might compare the latitude of your location with latitudes for different parts of Africa and predict how the change in latitude would affect the climate. You could also help your child find articles with photographs of Africa. Photos and articles will make great additions to our class's bulletin board display.

Look for more news about our class study of Africa. As we begin each new chapter, you will receive a letter from the social studies hot line. I hope you and your child will enjoy sharing our African studies.

Sincerely,

Land and Water

Lesson Objectives

Upon completion of this lesson, students will be able to:
- explain where Africa is located,
- describe climate zones and vegetation patterns found on the African continent,
- identify key geographic features and locate the major regions of Africa.

Engage Motivate Students to Learn

Warm-Up Activity Give each student a ball of modeling clay (or demonstrate the following activity yourself). Mold the clay inside a pie plate or a flat-bottomed bowl. Turn the resulting shape so that the flat side is on top. Explain that this shape approximates the contours of the African continent. Ask students what they can learn about Africa's lands from studying its contours. For example, how might water flow?

Activating Prior Knowledge Have students read Reach Into Your Background in the Before You Read box. Ask students to share with the class what they know about the geography of Africa. If necessary, prompt students with questions about rivers, mountains, deserts, and lakes. Record students' responses on the chalkboard.

Explore Develop Main Ideas

Help students understand Africa's geography by asking them to think about the following questions as they read the section: How might geographic factors influence how people live in different parts of Africa? In what ways might travel be difficult in Africa? Why are rivers an important physical feature?

Teach Solicit Student Participation

Have students create a table with four side labels: *North, West, East,* and *Central and Southern.* Top labels should be landforms such as *Plateaus, Rivers,* and *Mountains.* Students should check boxes to correlate side and top categories. Ask students to use their completed tables to write a summary of Africa's main geographic features. This activity should take about 30 minutes.

Assess Assess Evidence of Learning

See the answers to the Section Review questions. Students may also demonstrate evidence of learning by completing the Guided Reading and Review and the Section Quiz from the *Teaching Resources.* If students are doing a book project, that may also demonstrate evidence of learning by showing progress on project preparation.

CHAPTER 1

AFRICA
Physical Geography

Land and Water

A. As You Read

Directions: As you read Section 1, answer the following questions in the space provided.

1. Why is Africa often called the "plateau continent"?

_____

2. Near what landform are most of Africa's major lakes located?

_____

3. What are the names of the four major rivers in Africa?

_____

4. Why is it impossible for ships to sail all the way from Africa's interior to the sea?

_____

B. Reviewing Key Terms

Directions: Write the key term for each definition below.

5. a large, mostly flat area that rises above the surrounding land _____

6. the height of land above sea level _____

7. a long, steep cliff _____

8. a deep trench in the Earth _____

9. a rock-filled rapid _____

10. bits of rock and dirt on river bottoms _____

11. able to grow many plants _____

12. a small stream or river that flows into a larger river _____

SECTION QUIZ

Land and Water

A. Key Terms and Concepts

Directions: Read the statements below. If a statement is true, write T in the blank provided. If it is false, write F. Rewrite false statements to make them true.

_____ **1.** A large, raised area of mostly level land is called a plateau.

_____ **2.** Throughout Africa, the elevation, or height of land below sea level, is low.

_____ **3.** When soil is fertile, very few plants will grow in it.

_____ **4.** A small river or stream that flows into a larger river is called a tributary.

_____ **5.** In many parts of Africa, the coastal strip ends at a long escarpment, or steep cliff.

B. Main Ideas

Directions: Write the letter of the correct answer in each blank.

_____ **6.** Africa is often called the "plateau continent" because the land is generally
   a. flat.
   b. wet.
   c. high.
   d. dry.

_____ **7.** What is a major landform in East Africa?
   a. Mount Kilimanjaro
   b. the Sahara
   c. the Aswan Dam
   d. the Congo River

_____ **8.** Ships cannot sail all the way from Africa's interior to the sea because of
   a. cataracts in the rivers.
   b. monthly flooding of the rivers.
   c. too many rifts in the rivers.
   d. the shallowness of the rivers.

_____ **9.** What are three of the most important rivers in Africa?
   a. the Ghana, the Zambezi, and the Niger
   b. the Kilimanjaro, the Congo, and the Nile
   c. the Nile, the Congo, and the Niger
   d. the Guinea, the Zambezi, and the Sahara

_____ **10.** Why were people able to farm the land surrounding the Nile River?
   a. Frequent flooding deposited rich soil.
   b. Heavy rains provided water for the crops.
   c. Merchants established trading centers in the area.
   d. Farmers could buy different kinds of seeds from traders.

CHAPTER 1
AFRICA
Physical Geography

Climate and Vegetation

Lesson Objectives

Upon completion of this lesson, students will be able to:
- describe the major climate regions of Africa and the factors that influence climate,
- identify vegetation commonly found in Africa,
- explain the influence of climate and vegetation on African economic activities.

Engage Motivate Students to Learn

Warm-Up Activity Ask students to suppose that they have traveled two or three states' distance in any direction from your community. Have them describe the land and climate in the new location and then compare it with the land and climate in your community. Have students hypothesize about why any differences exist. Ask students whether they think both places are in the same climate region.

Activating Prior Knowledge Have students read Reach Into Your Background in the Before You Read box. After students have considered answers to the questions in the box, have them think about what the answers might be if the same questions were asked about Africa. Have students predict some answers for each question.

Explore Develop Main Ideas

As students read the section, encourage them to refer both to the map at the beginning of the chapter and to the climate map. Ask students to look for answers to questions such as the following: How does a place's location in relation to the Equator affect its seasons? What effect does elevation have on climate?

Teach Solicit Student Participation

Have students create picture postcards that show four distinct climate and/or vegetation regions of Africa. Students should include descriptive caption text with each postcard. This activity should take about 30 minutes.

Assess Assess Evidence of Learning

See the answers to the Section Review questions. Students may also demonstrate evidence of learning by completing the Guided Reading and Review and the Section Quiz from the *Teaching Resources.* If students are doing a book project, that may also demonstrate evidence of learning by showing progress on project preparation.

GUIDED READING AND REVIEW

Climate and Vegetation

A. As You Read

Directions: As you read Section 2, fill in the table below with information about climate and vegetation in Africa. Write supporting details for each main idea on the lines below.

Main Idea A
There are three major factors that influence climate in Africa.
1. _____
2. _____
3. _____
Main Idea B
There are three primary types of vegetation regions in Africa.
4. _____
5. _____
6. _____

B. Reviewing Key Terms

Directions: Complete each sentence by writing the correct term in the blank provided.

7. In very dry lands, farmers often must _____ their crops.

8. Sometimes in the middle of a desert, travelers may find a(n) _____ where there is water and some vegetation.

9. People who travel from place to place to make a living are called _____ .

CHAPTER 1
AFRICA
Physical Geography

Climate and Vegetation

A. Key Terms and Concepts

Directions: Fill in the blanks in Column I with the terms in Column II. Write the correct letter in each blank.

Column I

_____ 1. In countries with little rainfall, farmers must artificially water, or _____ , their crops.

_____ 2. A place in a dry region with springs and fresh underground water is called a(n) _____ .

_____ 3. A person who moves around to various places to make a living is called a(n) _____ .

_____ 4. The place where the southern edge of the Sahara meets the savanna is called the _____ .

_____ 5. Sometimes it doesn't rain for several years in a row in parts of the _____ in Southern Africa.

Column II

a. Sahel

b. nomad

c. irrigate

d. oasis

e. Namib Desert

B. Main Ideas

Directions: Write the letter of the correct answer in each blank.

_____ 6. A region's distance from the Equator, its elevation, amount of rainfall, and its closeness to large bodies of water and major landforms all influence its
   a. climate.
   b. soil.
   c. mineral resources.
   d. industry.

_____ 7. In Africa, how do farmers from dry regions prepare for the possible lack of rainfall?
   a. They plant only one crop.
   b. They plant a variety of crops.
   c. They do not irrigate their crops.
   d. They buy crops.

_____ 8. In Central Africa, much of the tropical rain forest region has been destroyed because people have
   a. cut down the trees.
   b. planted too many trees.
   c. used the land for fertile farmland.
   d. irrigated the land to water the trees.

_____ 9. Directly north and south of the rain forest, Africa is covered by
   a. desert.
   b. mountains.
   c. savanna.
   d. the Sahel.

_____ 10. Most of the nomads who live in the Sahara are
   a. artisans.
   b. merchants.
   c. manufacturers.
   d. herders.

Natural Resources

Lesson Objectives

Upon completion of this lesson, students will be able to:
- identify some of Africa's key natural resources,
- describe some ways in which Africans use natural resources,
- point out some challenges facing Africans in balancing the development and protection of their natural resources.

Engage Motivate Students to Learn

Warm-Up Activity Have students list hobbies and activities at which they excel. Discuss what each requires—for instance, time, money, equipment, or physical effort. Ask students whether they see any conflicts among the various interests. For example, there may be time conflicts or one activity may take the student away from home during an important family activity. Ask students how such conflicts might be resolved.

Activating Prior Knowledge Have students read Reach Into Your Background in the Before You Read box. Discuss students' interpretations of the saying and how they think the saying could apply to a country's economy.

Explore Develop Main Ideas

Direct students to read the section. Stop them at intervals to discuss the following questions: How is subsistence farming different from raising cash crops? Why might Africans want to raise cash crops? What are the benefits of a diversified economy?

Teach Solicit Student Participation

Have students work in small groups to create a cause-and-effect diagram concerning economic activities in Africa. Allow about 30 minutes for this activity.

Assess Assess Evidence of Learning

See the answers to the Section Review questions. Students may also demonstrate evidence of learning by completing the Guided Reading and Review and the Section Quiz from the *Teaching Resources*. If students are doing a book project, that may also demonstrate evidence of learning by showing progress on project preparation.

CHAPTER 1
AFRICA
Physical Geography

Natural Resources

A. As You Read

Directions: As you read Section 3, fill in the table below with information about the farming and mining products of Africa. Then complete the sentences that follow by filling in the blanks.

Products of Africa

Crops
1.
Minerals
2.

3. Most of Africa's workers are _____ .

4. African countries are now trying to diversify their _____ by developing new crops, raw materials, and manufactured goods.

5. In much of Africa, _____ mine the resources and take the profits.

6. Africa has few _____ to make products from its own raw materials.

B. Reviewing Key Terms

Directions: In the blanks provided, write the definitions for the following key terms.

7. subsistence farming

_____

8. cash crop

_____

9. economy

_____

10. diversify

_____

SECTION QUIZ

Natural Resources

A. Key Terms and Concepts

Directions: Match the definitions in Column I with the terms in Column II. Write the correct letter in each blank.

Column I

_____ 1. a system in which farmers raise crops to support their families

_____ 2. a crop, such as tea, coffee, or cocoa, which is raised by farmers to sell

_____ 3. to add variety to an economy

_____ 4. a substance, such as petroleum, gold, or diamonds, that is found in the land

_____ 5. all the things that people do to make a living in a particular place

Column II

a. economy

b. subsistence farming

c. mineral resource

d. diversify

e. cash crop

B. Main Ideas

Directions: Write the letter of the correct answer in each blank.

_____ 6. What is three fifths of Africa's farmland used for?
   a. cash crops
   b. subsistence farming
   c. large plantations
   d. planting hardwood trees

_____ 7. The major part of Africa's economy is
   a. manufacturing.
   b. harvesting trees.
   c. trading.
   d. farming.

_____ 8. Where in Africa do hardwood trees grow?
   a. only in East Africa
   b. only by the Nile
   c. only in Central and Southern Africa
   d. in all four regions of Africa

_____ 9. What happens in some African regions when cash crops fail?
   a. There are more jobs in manufacturing.
   b. There are enough imports to help people survive.
   c. There are food shortages.
   d. There are enough subsistence farms to produce food for the people.

_____ 10. In order to protect themselves in an uncertain world economy, many African countries are working to
   a. import all their manufactured goods.
   b. diversify their economies.
   c. borrow money from each other.
   d. produce only one important cash crop.

Name _____ Class _____ Date _____

AFRICA
Physical Geography

Guiding Questions:

- What are the main physical features of Africa?
- What factors influence the ways in which Africans make a living?

<u>Africa can be divided into four regions: North, West, East, and Central and Southern.</u> Each region contains different landforms and climates. North Africa is characterized by rocky mountains and huge deserts. West Africa consists mostly of grasslands, which are good for farming. East Africa has grasslands, hills, mountains, and plateaus. Central and Southern Africa is primarily flat or rolling grassland with some dense forests, mountains, and swamps.

<u>Much of the land of Africa is at a high elevation.</u> The tallest mountain, Mount Kilimanjaro in East Africa, is 19,341 feet (5,895 m) high. The interior of the continent forms a large plateau. Along most of the edges of Africa lies a narrow coastal plain, which is marshy or arid in different locations. In East Africa, there is a huge valley that stretches for 4,000 miles (6,400 km). It was formed millions of years ago and is called the Great Rift Valley. The four major rivers of Africa are the Nile, the Congo, the Zambezi, and the Niger, all of which flow from the mountains to the sea.

<u>Much of Africa lies between the Tropic of Capricorn and the Tropic of Cancer. Because of this, many parts of Africa are tropical and hot.</u> However, other factors, including amount of rainfall, elevation and distance from large bodies of water and landforms, influence the climate. Higher elevations are cooler. Close to the Equator are dense, hot forests where it rains most of the time. North and south of the Equator are grasslands. These grasslands have both wet and dry seasons. Past the grassland regions are deserts, including the Sahara to the north and the Namib and the Kalahari to the south.

<u>The majority of African workers are farmers.</u> Three fifths of them are subsistence farmers who grow grains, fruits, and vegetables. Others grow cash crops, such as tea, coffee, and cacao, or harvest hardwood trees. In North and West Africa, there are large petroleum deposits. In other locations people mine copper, silver, uranium, and diamonds, which are exported. Africa's economies are especially dependent on weather conditions, particularly rainfall, and on the price of crops. In recent times, many countries have been trying to diversify their economies with new crops, raw materials, and manufactured goods.

VOCABULARY ACTIVITY

CHAPTER 1

AFRICA
Physical Geography

Directions: Match the definitions in Column I with the key terms in Column II. Write the correct letter in each blank. If necessary, look up the terms in your textbook glossary.

Column I

_____ 1. a person who moves from place to place to make a living

_____ 2. a fertile place in a desert where there is water and vegetation

_____ 3. a rock-filled rapid or waterfall

_____ 4. the height of land above sea level

_____ 5. a small stream or river that flows into a larger river

_____ 6. a large, mostly flat area that rises above the surrounding land

_____ 7. bits of rock and dirt deposited by rivers

_____ 8. a crop that is raised for sale

_____ 9. rich soil that is able to grow many plants

_____ 10. a deep trench in the Earth

_____ 11. a long, steep cliff

_____ 12. to artificially water crops

_____ 13. all the things people do to make a living in a particular place

_____ 14. raising crops to support one's family

_____ 15. to add variety

_____ 16. a region where tall grasses grow

Column II

a. cataract

b. cash crop

c. diversify

d. economy

e. elevation

f. escarpment

g. fertile

h. irrigate

i. nomad

j. oasis

k. plateau

l. rift

m. savanna

n. silt

o. subsistence farming

p. tributary

AFRICA
Physical Geography

Directions: Use the information in your textbook to complete the chart. Briefly describe the land, climate, vegetation, and natural resources of each region of Africa.

Region	Land	Climate	Vegetation	Natural Resources
North Africa				
West Africa				
East Africa				
Central and Southern Africa				

Name _____ Class _____ Date _____

CHAPTER 1

Africa
Physical Geography

The Great Rift Valley

Directions: Read the passage below and answer the questions.

The Great Rift Valley is a giant split in the continent of Africa. It is not the only such split in the Earth's surface. But the 4,000-mile- (6,400-km-) long rift is the largest one that can be seen. The other huge rifts lie below the sea.

The Great Rift Valley has some of Africa's most spectacular scenery. Most of the valley ranges from 30 to 40 miles (48 to 64 km) wide. Steep, clifflike walls form the sides of the valley. The walls look like giant steps carved into the rock. In some places, the walls rise more than 6,000 feet (1,800 m). Two of the world's deepest lakes—Lake Tanganyika and Lake Nyasa—are in the Great Rift Valley. The area also has many volcanoes.

The Great Rift Valley was not created in the same way as the Grand Canyon of the United States. The Colorado River carved out the Grand Canyon. The Great Rift Valley, on the other hand, was created when plates in the Earth's crust pulled apart. Earth's plates have been moving for millions of years and continue to move today. The Great Rift Valley spreads as earthquakes happen and volcanoes erupt.

Volcanoes in the Great Rift Valley have erupted so often that some areas have almost filled up with lava and ash. Over time, the volcanic ash turns into rich farmland. Volcanic ash has also preserved many fossils, including the bones of early human beings. In fact, the Great Rift Valley has yielded some of the oldest human fossils ever found.

1. How is the Great Rift Valley unique?

_____

2. How is the Great Rift Valley like the Grand Canyon?

_____

3. How is it different from the Grand Canyon?

_____

_____

_____

_____

AFRICA
Physical Geography

Identifying Central Issues

How Plants Survive in the Sahara

Directions: Read the passage. Then, under the correct heading below, list the ways in which plants adapt to the dry conditions of the Sahara.

Although plant life is scarce in the Sahara, it does exist. But how do plants survive in a place where years can pass without rain?

Many Saharan plants have long root systems. Some have roots that reach deep enough to tap underground water. Other plants have long horizontal roots that absorb all the water available over a broad area. Still other plants have "rain roots." These fine roots grow as soon as rain falls. In addition, some plants take in moisture through their leaves as well as their roots.

Saharan plants also have adapted to hold the water they do get. The roots of some desert grasses are covered with mucus to which sand sticks. The mucus and sand protect the roots from drying out. Other grasses have leaves that roll up during dry spells. When the leaf is coiled, little moisture evaporates.

Still other plants have different ways of surviving desert conditions. Some desert plants live short lives. Their seeds lie on the ground until a rain falls. When rain does fall, the seeds grow rapidly. The plants complete their life cycle in a few weeks and again leave seeds.

Ways of Increasing the Amount of Water Absorbed

1. _____

2. _____

3. _____

4. _____

Ways of Keeping Moisture

5. _____

6. _____

Ways of Making the Most Use of Rainfall

7. _____

LETTER HOME

CHAPTER 2

AFRICA
Shaped by Its History

Social Studies Hot Line

Dear Family,

During the next few days, our social studies class will focus on the history of Africa. We will learn about the earliest people, the growth of civilizations and kingdoms, the coming of Europeans, and the struggle for independence, as well as important issues for Africa today.

To help your child learn about the early African peoples and civilizations, look for museum exhibits about ancient African cultures. If there are no exhibits available, you might find articles in magazines about topics such as the earliest people in Africa; ancient Egypt, Nubia, Mali, Songhai, Aksum, Zimbabwe, or Ghana; or early African farming methods and tools.

We will also be studying the effects of Europeans on Africa and the African slave trade. We will learn how Europeans created colonies and took away the power of Africans to rule themselves. Ask your child to talk about how it would feel to have people from another country suddenly take over the government and impose their laws, customs, and beliefs. Talking about how you might react could lead to a discussion of the struggle for freedom in many African countries.

Look for more information to support our class exploration of Africa. In the coming weeks, we will study the cultures of each region, and then look at a few countries in greater depth. I hope you and your child are enjoying learning more about this very diverse continent.

Sincerely,

CHAPTER 2
AFRICA
Shaped by Its History

Africa's First People

Lesson Objectives

Upon completion of this lesson, students will be able to:
- explain how early humans lived and got food,
- summarize the achievements of the civilizations along the Nile River,
- describe the possible causes and the effects of the Bantu migrations.

Engage Motivate Students to Learn

Warm-Up Activity Ask students to imagine that a thousand years from now, archaeologists are studying some of the items in your classroom. Challenge students to speculate on what the scientists might learn about them by studying various items, such as pencils, a globe, student desks, a U.S. flag, and so on.

Activating Prior Knowledge Have students read Reach Into Your Background in the Before You Read box. Ask students to think about how they know about events that occurred when they were too young to remember. Have they heard them described by family members? Have they seen photographs or home videos? Discuss with the class why people need to remember past events, and the different methods for doing so.

Explore Develop Main Ideas

Ask students to consider the following questions as they read: What have scientists learned about the daily lives of early humans? Why did early Africans begin to farm? What were some characteristics of the civilizations along the Nile? What were some of the results of the Bantu migrations?

Teach Solicit Student Participation

Organize the class into five teams to compose some answers to the questions given in the Explore part of the Lesson Plan. Observe individual participation. After teams have completed their discussions, call on a member from each team to share their answer to one of the questions. Invite other teams to contribute additional ideas to the class discussion. This activity should take about 20 minutes.

Assess Assess Evidence of Learning

See the answers to the Section Review questions. Students may also demonstrate evidence of learning by completing the Guided Reading and Review and the Section Quiz from the *Teaching Resources*. If students are doing a book project, it may also demonstrate evidence of learning by showing progress on project preparation.

Africa's First People

A. As You Read

Directions: As you read Section 1, fill in the table below with information about Africa's first people.

Africa's First People

How did they obtain food?	1.
What allowed them to settle?	2.
What civilizations grew up along the Nile?	3.
What were the Bantu migrations?	4.
What were some of the effects of these migrations?	5.

B. Reviewing Key Terms

Directions: Write the key term for each definition below.

6. a person who gathers wild food and hunts animals to survive _____

7. to adapt wild plants and animals for human use _____

8. more than is needed _____

9. a society with cities, a government, social classes, art, and architecture
_____

10. to move from one place to another _____

11. a group that shares a language, a religion, and customs _____

CHAPTER 2
AFRICA
Shaped by Its History

Africa's First People

A. Key Terms and Concepts

Directions: Read the statements below. If a statement is true, write T in the blank provided. If it is false, write F. Rewrite false statements to make them true.

_____ **1.** A person who survives by gathering wild fruits, nuts, and roots is called a hunter-gatherer. _____

_____ **2.** When early communities produced a food surplus, they had less food than they needed. _____

_____ **3.** Many Stone Age farming groups eventually became civilizations, which are societies with no cities, no government, and no social classes.

_____

_____ **4.** Groups of people who spoke Bantu languages decided to migrate, or remain, in West Africa. _____

_____ **5.** People who have different languages, religions, and customs form ethnic groups.

_____

B. Main Ideas

Directions: Write the letter of the correct answer in each blank.

_____ **6.** How did the first people who lived in East Africa get food?
    a. by farming and mining   **c.** by hunting and gathering
    b. by herding   **d.** by trading

_____ **7.** After early people began domesticating plants and animals, they were able to
    a. trade with foreign countries.   **c.** conquer their neighbors.
    b. settle in one place.   **d.** travel from one place to another looking for food.

_____ **8.** In ancient Egypt, people created hieroglyphics, which were
    a. iron tools.   **c.** picture-writings.
    b. statues.   **d.** boats.

_____ **9.** When West Africans learned to work with iron, their population
    a. conquered others.   **c.** began a period of peace.
    b. increased.   **d.** decreased.

_____ **10.** Over the years, Bantu-speakers eventually moved from their homelands and settled in
    a. North Africa.   **c.** East and West Africa.
    b. West Africa.   **d.** Central and Southern Africa.

Kingdoms and Empires

Lesson Objectives

Upon completion of this lesson, students will be able to:
- describe the Egyptian, Nubian, and Aksum civilizations that grew up along the Nile,
- summarize the rise and fall of the kingdoms and city-states of ancient Africa.

Engage Motivate Students to Learn

Warm-Up Activity Ask students to look carefully at a physical map of Africa and to identify places on the map where they think ancient civilizations might have arisen. Suggest that they begin by listing the things that are needed to build a civilization, such as water and fertile land. Explain that they will be reading about some ancient African civilizations in this section. Encourage them to check their accuracy in predicting where civilizations were established.

Activating Prior Knowledge Have students read Reach Into Your Background in the Before You Read box. Combine students' lists and record the most frequently mentioned items on the chalkboard. Encourage students to explain their choices.

Explore Develop Main Ideas

As students read the section, urge them to look for specific reasons for the success of each of the kingdoms and empires. Ask them to name some achievements of each, to explain which depended upon trade, and to identify which lasted the longest.

Teach Solicit Student Participation

Have students create a chart that lists the six kingdoms and city-states in rows. Have them label three columns as follows: *Time Period, Location,* and *Characteristics.* Encourage students to use the chart to compare and contrast the kingdoms and city-states. This activity should take about 25 minutes.

Assess Assess Evidence of Learning

See the answers to the Section Review questions. Students may also demonstrate evidence of learning by completing the Guided Reading and Review and the Section Quiz from the *Teaching Resources.* If students are doing a book project, that may also demonstrate evidence of learning by showing progress on project preparation.

CHAPTER 2

AFRICA
Shaped by Its History

Kingdoms and Empires

A. As You Read

Directions: As you read Section 2, answer the following questions in the space provided.

1. What religion traveled to Aksum along the trade routes?

_____

2. What items were traded between West African kingdoms and North Africa?

_____

3. What effect did traders have on the culture of West Africa?

_____

4. What helped the African city-states develop?

_____

5. Across which ocean did the trade network that began in East Africa stretch?

_____

B. Reviewing Key Terms

Directions: Complete each sentence by writing the correct term in the blank provided.

6. The _____ is the holy book of the religion of Islam.

7. One of the Five Pillars of Islam is for Muslims to make a(n) _____ to Mecca.

8. The African language that mixes Arabic words and a Bantu language is called

_____ .

9. Kilwa, Mombasa, and Malindi were powerful East African _____ .

SECTION QUIZ

Kingdoms and Empires

A. Key Terms and Concepts

Directions: Read the statements below. If a statement is true, write T in the blank provided. If it is false, write F. Rewrite false statements to make them true.

_____ **1.** Mecca is the holy book of the religion of Islam.

_____

_____ **2.** Aksum used to be an important trade center in East Africa.

_____

_____ **3.** Mansa Musa, the king of Mali, made a pilgrimage, or religious journey, in 1324.

_____

_____ **4.** The Bantu language, a mix of Arab and African words, developed in East Africa.

_____

_____ **5.** A city that has no government but controls much of the surrounding land is a city-state.

_____

B. Main Ideas

Directions: Write the letter of the correct answer in each blank.

_____ **6.** The importance of the early West African kingdoms was based on
   a. the manufacture of cloth.
   b. the trade of gold for salt.
   c. the conquest of Aksum.
   d. the rule of the king of Mali.

_____ **7.** Trade across West Africa was originally controlled by
   a. Mali.
   b. Ghana.
   c. Egypt.
   d. Ethiopia.

_____ **8.** How was Islam spread into many parts of Africa?
   a. by Chinese merchants
   b. by Christian missionaries
   c. by the Egyptian pharaohs
   d. by Muslim traders

_____ **9.** Why did Songhai become West Africa's most powerful kingdom?
   a. It traded with China and India.
   b. It controlled important trade routes and trading cities.
   c. It manufactured bronze.
   d. It established farming settlements along the Nile.

_____ **10.** In general, what helped West African and East African city-states to develop?
   a. farming
   b. manufacturing
   c. forestry
   d. trade

CHAPTER 2
AFRICA
Shaped by Its History

The Conquest of Africa

Lesson Objectives

Upon completion of this lesson, students will be able to:
- trace the progress of European exploration of Africa,
- explain the origin and effects of the slave trade,
- describe the process of the colonization of Africa by European nations.

Engage Motivate Students to Learn

Warm-Up Activity Ask students what they would like to do when they grow up. Then ask how they would feel if they were told that they couldn't do any of these things. Instead, they would be assigned a job. It would probably be working in a field or cleaning a house. If they refused to do what they were told, they could be severely punished. Urge students to discuss how they would feel about this future.

Activating Prior Knowledge Have students read Reach Into Your Background in the Before You Read box. Record students' ideas without judgment or comment. Then open a discussion about the fairness of some of the methods proposed.

Explore Develop Main Ideas

Have students read the section. Tell them to look for answers to these questions as they read: What did Europeans learn as they began exploring Africa? In what ways did contact with Europeans change Africa? Why did the slave trade develop?

Teach Solicit Student Participation

Have students create a concept web for each of these terms: *European contact* and *slavery*. Have them complete the webs with facts from the section. Have students use their webs to contribute to a follow-up class discussion. You may wish to create master webs on the chalkboard. This activity should take about 25 minutes.

Assess Assess Evidence of Learning

See the answers to the Section Review questions. Students may also demonstrate evidence of learning by completing the Guided Reading and Review and the Section Quiz from the *Teaching Resources*. If students are doing a book project, that may also demonstrate evidence of learning by showing progress on project preparation.

Name _____ Class _____ Date _____

The Conquest of Africa

A. As You Read

Directions: As you read Section 3, fill in the table below with information about European trade with, and colonization of, Africa.

Main Idea A
Three factors caused European contact with Africa to increase.

1. Inventions: _____

_____

2. Trade: _____

_____

3. Slave trade: _____

_____

Main Idea B
The results of European contact with Africa were as follows.

4. Slavery: _____

_____

5. Resources: _____

_____

6. Government: _____

_____

7. Land: _____

_____

8. People: _____

_____

B. Reviewing Key Terms

Directions: In the blank provided, write the definition for the following key term.

9. colonize

_____

The Conquest of Africa

A. Key Terms and Concepts

Directions: Fill in the blanks in Column I with the terms in Column II. Write the correct letter in each blank.

Column I

_____ 1. A museum called the House of Slaves is located on the island of ____ .

_____ 2. Sailors in the 1400s used new instruments such as the ____ to help them navigate at sea.

_____ 3. The horrors of the slave crossings were described in a book by ____ .

_____ 4. Dutch explorers established a trading post at the ____ on Africa's southern tip.

_____ 5. European nations wanted to ____ , or settle, Africa and take over its governments.

Column II

a. astrolabe

b. Cape of Good Hope

c. colonize

d. Gorée

e. Olaudah Equiano

B. Main Ideas

Directions: Write the letter of the correct answer in each blank.

_____ 6. The first contact between Europeans and Africans began in the 1400s through
   a. slavery.
   b. trade.
   c. conquest.
   d. settlement.

_____ 7. Why did Portuguese ships travel to Africa's east coast?
   a. to seize the riches of the city-states
   b. to establish farming communities
   c. to improve the lives of the villagers
   d. to support the rulers

_____ 8. By the late 1600s, the European traders were exchanging
   a. ivory for cassava and yams.
   b. guns for enslaved Africans.
   c. enslaved Africans for diamonds.
   d. copper and brass for African clothing.

_____ 9. Which statement best describes the effect of the slave trade on Africa?
   a. It enabled African countries to trade as equals with European nations.
   b. It strengthened the rule of local village rulers.
   c. It was an important way of spreading African culture to the Americas.
   d. It resulted in the loss of many healthy and capable workers.

_____ 10. What is one important result of the Europeans' rush for territory in Africa?
   a. They improved life for many Africans.
   b. They drew new political boundaries.
   c. They grew many new crops.
   d. They encouraged peace.

Independence and Its Challenges

Lesson Objectives

Upon completion of this lesson, students will be able to:
- explain the growth of nationalism in Africa,
- describe Africa's role during World Wars I and II,
- identify the paths to independence taken by Ghana, Tanzania, Morocco, and Angola.

Engage Motivate Students to Learn

Warm-Up Activity Encourage students to talk about why they like local teams better than teams from other places. Point out that feeling loyalty to local teams is natural. Ask students whether they have these kinds of feelings for other things that are not associated with sports, such as their school, community, state, and country. Tell students that this feeling of pride and loyalty has motivated people in many countries to seek independence.

Activating Prior Knowledge Have students read Reach Into Your Background in the Before You Read box. Allow students to express their ideas about independence. You may wish to record the most frequent responses on the chalkboard.

Explore Develop Main Ideas

Direct students to read the section. Tell them to look for the causes that lay behind the African independence movements. Discuss the different means each nation used to achieve independence and why nations followed different paths toward it.

Teach Solicit Student Participation

Write the following outline heads on the chalkboard.

   I. Nationalism
  II. Events Leading to Independence Movements
 III. Independence

Have students complete an outline of the section as they read, using the listed heads. Ask students to use their outlines in a class discussion. This activity should take about 25 minutes.

Assess Assess Evidence of Learning

See the answers to the Section Review questions. Students may also demonstrate evidence of learning by completing the Guided Reading and Review and the Section Quiz from the *Teaching Resources*. If students are doing a book project, that may also demonstrate evidence of learning by showing progress on project preparation.

CHAPTER 2

AFRICA

Shaped by Its History

Independence and
Its Challenges

A. As You Read

Directions: As you read Section 4, answer the following questions. If necessary, use a separate sheet of paper.

1. What effect did the European borders have on African ethnic groups?

_____

_____

2. What did African leaders realize would have to be done to be rid of colonial rule?

_____

_____

3. What was Pan-Africanism and when did it begin?

_____

_____

4. What was the effect of World War II on the Africans who fought?

_____

5. How did the Algerians gain independence from France?

_____

6. Why was it difficult for some newly independent African countries to govern themselves?

_____

B. Reviewing Key Terms

Directions: Complete each sentence by writing the correct term in the blank provided.

7. A feeling of pride in one's homeland is called _____ .

8. The movement that stressed African unity and cooperation was known as

_____ .

9. When Africans in the Gold Coast wanted to protest against the British, they

staged a _____ of certain products and services.

10. Some African countries have had a long history of _____ , in which the government is controlled by the people.

SECTION QUIZ

Independence and Its Challenges

A. Key Terms and Concepts

Directions: Match the definitions in Column I with the terms in Column II. Write the correct letter in each blank.

Column I

_____ 1. a feeling of pride in one's homeland

_____ 2. a political movement that stressed African unity.

_____ 3. countries that fought the armies of Germany, Italy, and Japan in World War II

_____ 4. an organized protest in which people refuse to buy or use certain products or services

_____ 5. a form of government in which citizens help to make government decisions

Column II

a. Allies

b. boycott

c. democracy

d. nationalism

e. Pan-Africanism

B. Main Ideas

Directions: Write the letter of the correct answer in each blank.

_____ 6. What was the slogan for the Pan-African movement?
    a. One continent, one language.
    b. Africa for Africans.
    c. Food for Zimbabwe.
    d. No independent rule.

_____ 7. What is one way that World War II affected the African independence movement?
    a. It inspired Africans to continue European rule.
    b. It weakened the African countries.
    c. It encouraged other countries to speak out in favor of colonialism.
    d. It weakened colonial powers.

_____ 8. After independence, the colony of Gold Coast changed its name to
    a. Nigeria.
    b. Egypt.
    c. Ghana.
    d. Somalia.

_____ 9. The ways in which Ghana and Algeria won independence show that
    a. some African colonies won independence peacefully.
    b. African colonies were not willing to fight with European armies.
    c. colonial powers let go easily.
    d. colonial powers never let go of a colony peacefully.

_____ 10. One challenge faced by many newly independent African countries was creating
    a. stable governments.
    b. new monetary systems.
    c. new national languages.
    d. new trade routes.

CHAPTER 2
AFRICA
Shaped by Its History

Issues for Africa Today

Lesson Objectives

Upon completion of this lesson, students will be able to:
- describe the economic issues facing African nations,
- summarize the social issues encountered by African countries,
- explain the challenges posed by Africa's environment.

Engage Motivate Students to Learn

Warm-Up Activity Ask students to suppose that they have graduated from school and are out on their own for the first time. Tell them that they are excited about their new independence, but also uncertain. Have students write a paragraph about some of the decisions they will have to make and some of the responsibilities that come with independence. Invite volunteers to read their paragraphs aloud. Discuss students' ideas using the context of a newly independent nation.

Activating Prior Knowledge Have students read Reach Into Your Background in the Before You Read box. Encourage discussion of the challenges they face and the ways in which they address those challenges.

Explore Develop Main Ideas

Ask students to read the section and, as they do so, to think about the historic origins of the challenges facing modern Africa. Do all of modern Africa's problems stem from historic causes? Which ones? How did the problems develop? How are African nations solving these problems?

Teach Solicit Student Participation

Write these words on the chalkboard: *farming, minerals, education, health,* and *environment.* Remind students that these are key topics discussed in this section. Ask students to write a sentence stating the main idea about each topic and then to write at least one detail about it. Have students use their main ideas and details during class discussion. This activity should take about 20 minutes.

Assess Assess Evidence of Learning

See the answers to the Section Review questions. Students may also demonstrate evidence of learning by completing the Guided Reading and Review and the Section Quiz from the *Teaching Resources.* If students are doing a book project, that may also demonstrate evidence of learning by showing progress on project preparation.

Name _____ Class _____ Date _____

Issues for Africa Today

A. As You Read

Directions: As you read Section 5, fill in the table below with information about Issues for Africa Today.

Issues and Actions

Economy	1.
Action Taken	2.
Education	3.
Action Taken	4.
Environment	5.
Action Taken	6.

B. Reviewing Key Terms

Directions: For each definition below, write the correct term in the blank provided.

7. raising crops to support one's family _____

8. large-scale production of crops for sale _____

9. a plant combined from two or more types of the same plant _____

10. the ability to read and write _____

11. the length of time an average person will live _____

CHAPTER 2

AFRICA

Shaped by Its History

Issues for Africa Today

5

A. Key Terms and Concepts

Directions: Read the statements below. If a statement is true, write T in the blank provided. If it is false, write F. Rewrite false statements to make them true.

_____ 1. The small-scale production of crops such as coffee, cocoa, and bananas is called commercial farming.

_____ 2. The ability to read and write, or literacy, differs from country to country in Africa.

_____ 3. When farmers combine two or more types of different kinds of plants, a hybrid results.

_____ 4. African countries are working to overcome health problems and increase life expectancy, or the length of time an average person is expected to live.

_____ 5. By developing fishing, fish processing, and mining, the country of Senegal has diversified its economy.

B. Main Ideas

Directions: Write the letter of the correct answer in each blank.

_____ 6. Most African economies are based on
   a. farming and herding.
   b. farming and mining.
   c. forestry and manufacturing.
   d. manufacturing and farming.

_____ 7. About three fourths of the workers in Africa are
   a. merchants.
   b. manufacturers.
   c. farmers.
   d. traders.

_____ 8. What are African countries doing in order to depend less on the sale of one export?
   a. They are importing more goods.
   b. They are diversifying their economies.
   c. They are borrowing large sums of money from other countries.
   d. They are selling fewer exports.

_____ 9. What is one important educational goal in African countries today?
   a. to send fewer students to village schools
   b. to send all students to foreign schools
   c. to improve the literacy rate
   d. to discourage students from studying their own cultures

_____ 10. One serious environmental problem facing African countries today is
   a. the decrease in soil erosion.
   b. the loss of desert land.
   c. the increase in soil erosion.
   d. the increase in the number of forests.

CHAPTER SUMMARY

AFRICA
Shaped by Its History

Guiding Questions:

- How have Africa's cultures changed?

The earliest humans may have lived in Africa. They survived by hunting and gathering food. Over thousands of years, people in Africa learned to herd animals and farm. Farming allowed them to settle in one place. In time, some of these farming groups evolved into civilizations—societies with cities, governments, writing, art, and social classes. Over 6,000 years ago, civilizations arose in Egypt and Nubia. About 2,500 years ago, West Africans learned to heat and shape iron into weapons and tools. Over hundreds of years, kingdoms grew up in East and West Africa. These included Aksum and Kilwa in the east; Ghana, Mali, and Songhai in the west; and Zimbabwe in the south. By the 1300s, Islam had become an important religion in Mali and other kingdoms.

Europeans had established a slave trade in Africa by the 1500s. Twelve million Africans were enslaved and taken to North America, never to return. The youngest, healthiest, and most able workers were taken from their homelands. The result was a disaster for the enslaved people and for their homelands.

The slave trade ended in the 1800s. Then Europeans began to raid Africa for resources. Having better weapons, the Europeans stopped the fierce African resistance. By the late 1800s, Europeans had set up colonies in many parts of Africa. They used Africa as a source for raw materials and a place to sell their own products. They did not build factories in Africa, where there is still little industry. African people lost the power to run their own governments. Europeans took the best land, created new borders, and forced the Africans to work for them.

While Europeans were colonizing Africa, many Africans continued to work and fight for independence. Pan-Africanism was a movement that began in the 1920s that stressed unity among all Africans. In the decades after World War II, countries such as Great Britain began to give up their African colonies. Most African nations had great difficulties after independence. They had had little experience in government. Conflicts arose among ethnic groups, and economic conditions were often bad.

Today, many African countries are working to keep their traditions alive while adapting to the modern world. They are dealing with issues such as strengthening their economies, feeding and educating growing populations, and preserving the environment.

AFRICA
Shaped by Its History

Directions: Below is a list of key terms from Chapter 2. Write one sentence or phrase on a separate sheet of paper that describes the meaning of each term. If necessary, look at Chapter 2 to see how the terms are used.

1. boycott
2. city-state
3. civilization
4. colonize
5. commercial farming
6. democracy
7. domesticate
8. ethnic group
9. hunter-gatherer
10. hybrid
11. life expectancy
12. literacy
13. migrate
14. nationalism
15. Pan-Africanism
16. pilgrimage
17. Quran
18. surplus
19. Swahili

Name _____ Class _____ Date _____

CHAPTER
2

AFRICA
Shaped by Its History

Directions: Use the information in your textbook to match the events from the list with the correct time frames. Two events fit under one of the time frames.

Major Events in African History
- Muslim traders spread Islam to West and East Africa.
- Africa loses its most capable workers to the European slave trade.
- Great civilizations arise in Egypt and Nubia.
- Bantus migrate from West Africa to Central and Southern Africa, spreading farming, herding, and iron tools.
- Africans unite to gain independence from European rule.
- Trade gives rise to wealthy West African kingdoms and East African city-states.
- Europeans colonize Africa, causing divisions among ethnic groups.

1. about 6000 B.C. to the A.D. 300s

_____

_____

2. beginning about 2,000 years ago

_____

_____

3. from the 600s through the 1500s

_____

_____

4. from the 1500s through the 1800s

_____

_____

5. in the late 1800s

_____

_____

6. in the 1900s

_____

_____

Africa: Shaped by Its History

AFRICA
Shaped by Its History

Sundiata, the Lion King of Mali

Directions: Read about the life of Sundiata, the first ruler of Mali. Then write a paragraph telling how Sundiata overcame obstacles.

Sundiata founded the kingdom of Mali. He was the son of a Mandingo king. It was hard for Sundiata to learn to walk. At the age of seven, he was still crawling instead of walking. Finally, a blacksmith made braces for him, and he learned to walk. Sundiata exercised and worked hard until he grew very strong. He became an especially good archer. Sundiata's mother taught him to respect Mandinka traditions and laws, which helped him become as wise as he was fit.

While Sundiata was still young, his father died. A Susu king took over his kingdom and exiled Sundiata and his mother. During this time, Sundiata became a warrior and hunter. He raised an army and defeated the Susu king. Because of his courage, Sundiata was chosen to rule Mali.

Sundiata built a strong, peaceful kingdom. People loved him for his kindness and sense of humor. Sundiata greatly valued friendship. According to legend, he sent his sons and daughters to live in distant courts and invited the children of other rulers to stay at his court. He believed that children who grow up together are less likely to fight one another as adults.

Sundiata's clan was named the Keita. Their symbol was the lion. As a result, Sundiata is sometimes called the Lion King of Mali.

_____

_____

_____

_____

_____

_____

CRITICAL THINKING

CHAPTER 2

AFRICA
Shaped by Its History

Making Comparisons

Traditional African Village Government

Directions: Throughout African history, most people have lived in small villages. How did these villages govern themselves? The chart below describes one of the typical patterns. Study the chart and complete the activities that follow. Answer the questions on the back of this page or on another sheet of paper.

One Pattern of African Village Government

Who Serves as Leader(s)	a council consisting of elders of the village
How Leaders Are Chosen	by age
How Decisions Are Made	by discussing an issue until a *consensus*, or a common agreement, is reached

1. Complete this chart by describing how your city or town is governed.

Government in My City or Town

Who Serves as Leader(s)	
How Leaders Are Chosen	
How Decisions Are Made	

2. What are the major differences between these two patterns of government?

3. What do you think are the main advantages of each form of government?

4. What do you think are the main disadvantages of each form of government?

CHAPTER 3

Cultures of Africa

Social Studies Hot Line

Dear Family,

Our social studies class will now explore the cultures of Africa. We will look at the four major geographic regions: North, West, East, and Central and Southern Africa. We will learn how North Africa's location along the Mediterranean Sea has invited trade and the exchange of cultural ideas in the region. We will study the great diversity of cultures and languages in West and East Africa, and find out how South Africa has influenced life in the Central and Southern region. If you have any firsthand knowledge of African ways of life or know people who do, you could add greatly to our study by sharing these with your child.

As you read the newspaper or watch or listen to the news, look for reports about African cultures. These could include news stories on politics, music, art, work, health, or changing ways of life. You might like to talk about what you find with your child. If you have access to the Internet, you and your child might find information about African cultures there. As you find information about life in Africa, encourage your child to compare it to life in your community.

You'll be receiving more information during the coming weeks about the cultures of the different African regions. Have fun as you and your child share the exciting exploration of Africa.

Sincerely,

The Cultures of North Africa

Lesson Objectives

Upon completion of this lesson, students will be able to:
- define the term *culture* and explain how it unites people in North Africa,
- describe some beliefs of Islam and its effect on life in North Africa,
- explain how North Africa's Mediterranean location has influenced its culture.

Engage Motivate Students to Learn

Warm-Up Activity Ask students to name a cultural characteristic that they think most Americans share. For example, most Americans speak English. List and discuss some of the students' ideas, leading them to the conclusion that Americans have very diverse cultural characteristics. Ask students what they think it would be like to live in a place where almost everyone shares the same religion and many people share the same heritage.

Activating Prior Knowledge Have students read Reach Into Your Background in the Before You Read box. Ask students to consider how they get to school, the subjects they study, their extracurricular activities, and so forth.

Explore Develop Main Ideas

As students read the section text, pause to discuss and answer the following questions: What is the main religion of North Africa and what are some important aspects of that religion? How can the influences of different cultures be seen in North Africa? What are some of the ways North Africans make a living? What effect has North Africa's location on the Mediterranean Sea had on the culture of the region?

Teach Solicit Student Participation

Invite students to create a web with *Culture of North Africa* at the center. Secondary circles can contain details about the culture, and tertiary circles can identify cultural influences. Students may explain these influences using supporting facts from the section. This activity should take about 20 minutes.

Assess Assess Evidence of Learning

See the answers to the Section Review questions. Students may also demonstrate evidence of learning by completing the Guided Reading and Review and the Section Quiz from the *Teaching Resources*. If students are doing a book project, that may also demonstrate evidence of learning by showing progress on project preparation.

CHAPTER 3
**Cultures
of Africa**

The Cultures of North Africa

A. As You Read

Directions: As you read Section 1, fill in the table below with details about the cultures of North Africa.

Facts About North African Cultures

Religion	1.
Islamic Law	2.
Ethnic Groups	3.
Cultural Changes	4.
Mediterranean Influence	5.

B. Reviewing Key Terms

Directions: Fill in the blank in each sentence below with one of the key terms from Section 1.

6. A region's _____ includes its food, clothing, homes, jobs, language, world view, and religion.

7. Islamic law is based on the _____ .

8. The Berbers are a(n) _____ who live in North Africa.

9. The movement of customs and ideas is called _____ .

SECTION QUIZ

The Cultures of North Africa

A. Key Terms and Concepts

Directions: Fill in the blanks in Column I with the terms in Column II. Write the correct letter in each blank.

Column I

_____ 1. North Africa's cultures have been influenced by its location along the _____ .

_____ 2. The way of life of a group of people who share similar beliefs and customs is a(n) _____ .

_____ 3. _____ is the religion that unites the people of North Africa.

_____ 4. The Tuareg travel across the _____ with their herds of camels, goats, and other livestock.

_____ 5. When people travel, they spread customs and ideas from one place to another through _____ .

Column II

a. cultural diffusion

b. culture

c. Mediterranean Sea

d. Islam

e. Sahara

B. Main Ideas

Directions: Write the letter of the correct answer in each blank.

_____ 6. All aspects of daily life in North Africa, including business, government, and family life, are governed by
 a. national law.
 b. Islamic law.
 c. Buddhist teachings.
 d. Old Testament law.

_____ 7. The different peoples of North Africa are unified by
 a. government and Islam.
 b. Islam and the French language.
 c. the Arabic language and Islam.
 d. Buddhism and Islam.

_____ 8. What are the largest ethnic groups in North Africa?
 a. Yoruba and Arab
 b. Arab and Ethiopian
 c. Berber and Arab
 d. Berber and Tuareg

_____ 9. How did the mixing of cultures in North Africa occur?
 a. through conquest and religion
 b. through government decree and trade
 c. through trade and conquest
 d. through religion and trade

_____ 10. What is one of the more recent influences on North Africa?
 a. ancient African traditions
 b. Western culture
 c. cultural diffusion
 d. Eastern ideas

CHAPTER 3
Cultures
of Africa

The Cultures of West Africa

Lesson Objectives

Upon completion of this lesson, students will be able to:
- explain aspects of cultural diversity in West Africa,
- describe the role of the family in West African culture,
- summarize how West Africans preserve cultural traditions.

Engage Motivate Students to Learn

Warm-Up Activity Have students imagine that they are creating a community newspaper. Ask them what languages should be represented in order to reach most readers. Elicit ideas for articles to help readers speaking different languages live, work, and communicate together.

Activating Prior Knowledge Have students read Reach Into Your Background in the Before You Read box. Invite students to share their lists and ideas with the class. Pool students' contributions to make a class fact sheet about ethnic groups and their cultures, languages, and customs.

Explore Develop Main Ideas

Have students read the section. Ask students to keep the following questions in mind as they read: Why is West Africa so culturally diverse? Why are young men going to the cities to work? How is life in West African cities different than life in the villages? What problems may result from West Africa's cultural diversity and changing family lives?

Teach Solicit Student Participation

Encourage students to develop an ad inviting people to visit West Africa for business and pleasure. Ads may include artwork, poetry, or mock quotations or testimonials if their content is plausible. Post the ads in the classroom and use them to begin a discussion about the cultures of West Africa. This activity should take about 30 minutes.

Assess Assess Evidence of Learning

See the answers to the Section Review questions. Students may also demonstrate evidence of learning by completing the Guided Reading and Review and the Section Quiz from the *Teaching Resources*. If students are doing a book project, that may also demonstrate evidence of learning by showing progress on project preparation.

GUIDED READING AND REVIEW

The Cultures of West Africa

A. As You Read

Directions: As you read Section 2, fill in the table below with information about the cultures of West Africa. Under each main idea, write two supporting statements.

Main Idea A
West Africa has a great variety of cultures.

I. _____

_____

2. _____

_____

Main Idea B
Family ties have a powerful effect on West African culture.

3. _____

_____

4. _____

_____

B. Reviewing Key Terms

Directions: For each definition below, write the correct term in the blank provided.

5. a wide variety of cultures _____

6. a family relationship _____

7. a family that consists of parents and children _____

8. a family that includes relatives other than parents and children _____

9. a group of families with a common ancestor _____

10. a group of lineages that trace their descent back to a common ancestor

_____

11. African storyteller, who passes on oral traditions _____

CHAPTER 3
Cultures
of Africa

The Cultures of West Africa

A. Key Terms and Concepts

Directions: Match the definitions in Column I with the terms in Column II. Write the correct letter in each blank.

Column I

_____ **1.** having a wide variety of cultures

_____ **2.** family consisting of parents and their children

_____ **3.** family that includes other relatives besides parents and children

_____ **4.** group of families with a common ancestor

_____ **5.** several groups of families with roots going back to a very early ancestor

Column II

a. clan

b. culturally diverse

c. extended family

d. lineage

e. nuclear family

B. Main Ideas

Directions: Write the letter of the correct answer in each blank.

_____ **6.** West Africa has a wide variety of cultures because it has
   a. a steady climate.
   b. many ethnic groups.
   c. a variety of vegetation.
   d. only one religion.

_____ **7.** Which statement is true of West Africa's ethnic groups?
   a. They do not conduct business with one another.
   b. They are all farmers.
   c. They speak different languages.
   d. They live in separate villages.

_____ **8.** What is one important way that kinship affects life in West Africa?
   a. There is a strong sense of community.
   b. There is a great deal of jealousy between different clans.
   c. There are no extended families in many villages.
   d. There isn't a strong sense of family relationships.

_____ **9.** The trend of villagers moving to cities in West Africa is called
   a. patrilineage.
   b. ruralism.
   c. urbanization.
   d. colonization.

_____ **10.** By telling traditional stories, the griot helps to preserve
   a. farming techniques.
   b. lineage.
   c. African languages.
   d. West African traditions.

The Cultures of East Africa

Lesson Objectives

Upon completion of this lesson, students will be able to:
- describe the influence of East Africa's location on its cultures,
- summarize the role of the Swahili language in East African cultures,
- explain how ideas about land ownership have changed.

Engage Motivate Students to Learn

Warm-Up Activity Ask students who "owns" the Mississippi River, the Rocky Mountains, or the neighborhood parks in your community. Discuss who can use these places. Then ask students who owns the building in which they live and who can use it. Compare the different kinds of ownership. Tell students that in East Africa, traditional views about land ownership are similar to American views about public lands.

Activating Prior Knowledge Have students read Reach Into Your Background in the Before You Read box. You may want to make available a dictionary that gives word origins so students can compile a list of words that have come from other languages.

Explore Develop Main Ideas

Instruct students to read the section. Discuss with students why peoples from India, Europe, and Southwest Asia came together in East Africa. Ask: *What is Swahili culture? How does it unify countries in East Africa? How did European ideas about land use differ from those of the East Africans?*

Teach Solicit Student Participation

Ask students to create three bookmarks commemorating a lecture series about East Africa. Students should use information from the section to add text or illustrations to the bookmarks that provide information about issues facing the region. This activity should take about 35 minutes.

Assess Assess Evidence of Learning

See the answers to the Section Review questions. Students may also demonstrate evidence of learning by completing the Guided Reading and Review and the Section Quiz from the *Teaching Resources*. If students are doing a book project, that may also demonstrate evidence of learning by showing progress on project preparation.

CHAPTER 3
Cultures
of Africa

The Cultures of East Africa

A. As You Read

Directions: As you read Section 3, answer the following questions in the space provided.

1. What is the primary cause of cultural diversity in East Africa? Why?

_____

_____

2. Who are the Swahili people? Where do they live?

_____

3. Why do Kenya and Tanzania promote the use of the Swahili language?

_____

4. What two religions have large followings in East Africa?

_____

5. What ideas did Africans have about land before the arrival of Europeans?

_____

6. Who introduced the idea of privately owned land to Africa?

_____

7. What happened to the old plantations when many African countries became independent?

_____

8. How do most East Africans feel about the land where they grew up?

_____

9. If asked where home is, what will most East Africans say?

_____

B. Reviewing Key Terms

Directions: Complete the sentence below by writing the correct term in the blank provided.

10. The British set up _____ in East Africa where they grew cash crops.

Name _____ Class _____ Date _____

CHAPTER 3
Cultures of Africa

The Cultures of East Africa

A. Key Terms and Concepts

Directions: Match the definitions in Column I with the terms in Column II. Write the correct letter in each blank.

Column I

_____ 1. culture of Africans who have mixed African and Arab ancestry

_____ 2. large farm where cash crops are grown

_____ 3. country in East Africa

_____ 4. former president of Tanzania

_____ 5. capital of Tanzania

Column II

a. Dar es Salaam

b. Julius Nyerere

c. Kenya

d. plantation

e. Swahili

B. Main Ideas

Directions: Write the letter of the correct answer in each blank.

_____ 6. Why are so many different languages spoken in East Africa?
   a. because everyone attends school
   b. because most people have to trade with other countries
   c. because many ethnic groups live here
   d. because the region was originally conquered by different European countries

_____ 7. East Africa has great cultural diversity because of its
   a. location.
   b. climate.
   c. geography
   d. transportation.

_____ 8. Two important religions with large memberships in East Africa are
   a. Islam and Buddhism.
   b. Christianity and Confucianism.
   c. Christianity and Buddhism.
   d. Islam and Christianity.

_____ 9. When Europeans first settled East Africa, they introduced the idea of
   a. the right to farm plots of land.
   b. privately owned land.
   c. subsistence farming.
   d. herding livestock.

_____ 10. For many East Africans, their homes in rural villages are
   a. not important to them.
   b. forgotten when they move to the cities.
   c. considered their true homes.
   d. sold to purchase apartments in the cities.

The Cultures of Central and Southern Africa

Lesson Objectives

Upon completion of this lesson, students will be able to:
- describe the influence of South Africa on the entire region of Central and Southern Africa,
- explain Central Africa's cultural diversity and link it to cultural diversity in other parts of Africa.

Engage Motivate Students to Learn

Warm-Up Activity Tell students that during the 1960s, black Americans joined together to win full political and civil rights. Ask students how they think this fight for rights affected black Americans' sense of community.

Activating Prior Knowledge Have students read Reach Into Your Background in the Before You Read box. Invite volunteers to share with the class some of their methods for achieving goals.

Explore Develop Main Ideas

Draw a cause-and-effect diagram on the chalkboard. After students read the section, have volunteers fill in the diagram. You may prompt students by having them think of causes for these effects: *blacks began to view themselves as citizens; transportation links were built in South Africa; migrant workers forged a group identity; Congolese live both very traditional and very modern lives.* Urge students to answer the question "why" as they identify corresponding causes.

Teach Solicit Student Participation

After students have read the section, have them develop a Venn diagram showing what things are traditional, modern, and a combination of modern and traditional. This activity should take about 20 minutes.

Assess Assess Evidence of Learning

See the answers to the Section Review questions. Students may also demonstrate evidence of learning by completing the Guided Reading and Review and the Section Quiz from the *Teaching Resources.* If students are doing a book project, that may also demonstrate evidence of learning by showing progress on project preparation.

Name _____ Class _____ Date _____

The Cultures of Central and Southern Africa

A. As You Read

Directions: As you read Section 1, fill in the table below with details about the cultures of Central and Southern Africa.

	Making a Living	Changes to Tradition
Southern Africa	1.	2.
Central Africa	3.	4.

B. Reviewing Key Terms

Directions: In the blanks provided, write the definition for each key term.

5. nationalism

_____

_____

6. migrant worker

_____

_____

CHAPTER 3
Cultures
of Africa

The Cultures of Central and Southern Africa

A. Key Terms and Concepts

Directions: Read the statements below. If a statement is true, write T in the blank provided. It if is false, write F. On a separate sheet of paper, rewrite false statements to make them true.

_____ **1.** An important political party in South Africa is the African Party.

_____ **2.** The country of South Africa has had little influence on the region.

_____ **3.** The Mbuti, who live in the rain forests of Congo, have a culture more than 3,000 years old.

_____ **4.** People who stay in one place to work are called migrant workers.

_____ **5.** The country of Congo in Southern Africa has few ethnic groups.

B. Main Ideas

Directions: Write the letter of the correct answer in each blank.

_____ **6.** How did the struggle of black South Africans for political rights affect their identity?
   a. They thought of themselves as colonial rulers.
   b. They thought of themselves as members of their country.
   c. They considered themselves connected to North Americans.
   d. They considered themselves the political leaders of Africa.

_____ **7.** How did the struggle for self rule in South Africa affect other African countries?
   a. It encouraged them to remain colonies of European countries.
   b. It inspired similar movements in nearby countries.
   c. It encouraged them to become part of South Africa.
   d. It encouraged them to establish monarchies in their countries.

_____ **8.** In order to get enough workers for its mines, South African companies used
   a. only South African workers.
   b. workers from throughout Southern Africa.
   c. workers from North America.
   d. workers from the villages of North Africa.

_____ **9.** Why was the National Union of Mineworkers important to South Africa's history?
   a. It forced members to obey government laws.
   b. It elected the first president of South Africa.
   c. It played an important role in the struggle for equal rights.
   d. It encouraged members not to strike in support of their causes.

_____ **10.** The Mbuti of Congo live
   a. in the shantytowns of the cities.
   b. in apartments in the cities.
   c. in rural villages.
   d. in the rain forests.

Name _____ Class _____ Date _____

CHAPTER
3

Cultures of Africa

Guiding Questions:
- How have Africa's cultures changed?
- What factors influence the ways in which Africans make a living?

Each of the four regions of Africa has its own unique cultures. Within each region, there exist many ways of life: traditional and modern, urban and rural, rich and poor.

North Africans are united by Islam and the Arabic language. More than 95 percent of the people are Muslims. Muslims believe in one God and that Muhammad was God's messenger. The Quran is the sacred book of Islam. It teaches about God and provides a guide to life. The Quran forbids stealing, murder, gambling, and drinking alcohol. Islamic law is based on the Quran and governs all aspects of Muslim life.

In contrast to North Africa, West Africa has no single unifying cultural element. The region has 17 countries, hundreds of ethnic groups, and many people speak several languages. Most West Africans are farmers in rural areas. Many who live in the Sahel herd animals, while people along the Atlantic Coast fish. Kinship is a strong bond in West African cultures. West African culture has influenced American culture because many enslaved Africans came from this region.

Because East Africa is located along the Indian Ocean, it has been affected by Arab, Asian, and other African cultures. It is a region of many ethnic groups and languages. A unifying element in East Africa has been the Swahili language, the official language of Kenya and Tanzania. It serves as a second language for millions of East Africans. In East Africa, both Islam and Christianity have large followings. East Africans feel a strong bond to the land where they grew up. Most people consider home to be the village of their family or clan.

In denying rights to black South Africans, South Africa forced them to struggle for basic freedoms. This struggle produced a strong sense of nationalism, which inspired other countries in the region. South Africa is the richest and most industrialized country in Africa. Migrant workers have come from throughout the region to work here. These workers became a strong force for political change in the region.

There are areas of Central Africa where people still live in small forest camps. Others in the region live in crowded shantytowns in order to work in urban areas. The region includes many religions: Christianity, traditional African beliefs, and Islam.

Cultures of Africa

Directions: Match the definitions in Column I with the key terms in Column II. Then write the correct letter in each blank. If necessary, you can look up the terms in your textbook glossary.

Column I

_____ **1.** a group of families with a common ancestor

_____ **2.** a family that consists of parents and children

_____ **3.** a feeling of pride in one's homeland or nation

_____ **4.** a group of lineages that trace their descent back to a common ancestor

_____ **5.** a large farm where cash crops are grown

_____ **6.** the movement of customs and ideas from one culture to another

_____ **7.** a family relationship

_____ **8.** a wide variety of cultures

_____ **9.** a family that includes relatives other than parents and children

_____ **10.** an African storyteller who passes on oral traditions

_____ **11.** the way of life of people who share similar customs and beliefs

_____ **12.** a person who moves from place to place to work

Column II

a. clan

b. cultural diffusion

c. cultural diversity

d. culture

e. extended family

f. griot

g. kinship

h. lineage

i. migrant worker

j. nationalism

k. nuclear family

l. plantation

RETEACHING

Cultures of Africa

Directions: Use the information in your textbook to fill in the outline. Write a brief description for each subheading in the outline.

I. Cultures of North Africa

    A. The Influence of Islam

    _____

    _____

    B. Location's Influence on Cultural Change

    _____

II. Cultures of West Africa

    A. The Cultural Diversity of West Africa

    _____

    _____

    B. Family Ties in West Africa

    _____

III. Cultures of East Africa

    A. The Development of Swahili Culture

    _____

    _____

    B. Ideas About Land and Home

    _____

IV. Cultures of Central and Southern Africa

    A. South Africa's Influence on the Region of Southern Africa

    _____

    _____

    B. Central Africa's Similarity to Other Regions of Africa

    _____

Cultures of Africa

West African Sculpture

Directions: The following pictures show sculpture from West Africa. These types of sculpture influenced many modern Western artists. Study the pictures. Then use them to answer the questions. If necessary, write your answers on another sheet of paper.

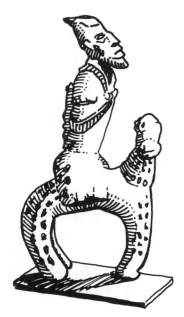

Clay rider on horseback, Mali

Wooden mask, Sierra Leone

Brass figure of a king, Nigeria

1. From what materials were West African sculptures made?

_____

2. What is the main subject of these sculptures?

_____

3. Is the style of the sculptures very realistic or somewhat abstract?

_____

4. How do you think these sculptures might be used?

_____

5. What do you like most about these sculptures?

_____

CRITICAL THINKING

Cultures of Africa

Drawing Conclusions

Age Sets in African Culture

Directions: Read the passage and the sentences that follow it. Decide whether or not each sentence states a conclusion that could be drawn from the passage. Place an X before those sentences that do state a reasonable conclusion.

In many African communities, all the people belong to age sets. An age set is made up of people who are close in age, much like a grade in school. People belong to their age sets for life. As children grow up, become adults, and get older, they move through their life stages with other members of their age set.

In the village of Ohafia, Nigeria, members of the younger age sets share certain duties. For example, they might keep the paths cleared. To pass into the adult age set, members of a young age set must do an important community project. They might build a library or have electricity brought to a remote village. Members of the adult age set guard the village and make sure that people follow the rules. When adults become elders, they become leaders of the community.

_____ **1.** Elders in a traditional African community hold positions of respect.

_____ **2.** In a traditional African village, a young man would be considered a good chief.

_____ **3.** A great deal of conflict occurs between different age sets.

_____ **4.** Even the young in traditional African villages have duties.

_____ **5.** At each stage in life, an African in a traditional village is expected to fulfill certain responsibilities.

_____ **6.** Rule by elders is common in traditional African villages.

_____ **7.** Girls and women do all the work in African villages.

_____ **8.** Age ranking is a way of organizing the work and responsibilities of a community.

_____ **9.** Boys and men do most of the physical labor in African villages.

_____ **10.** Age sets are disappearing in Africa.

Exploring North Africa

Social Studies Hot Line

Dear Family,

As our social studies class continues its study of Africa, we will look at each of the four regions in more detail. During the next few days we are going to learn about two countries in North Africa: Egypt and Algeria. In our study, we will examine the contrast of rural and urban life in both places, find out about the importance of Islam, and learn about the two main ethnic groups in Algeria: the Arabs and the Berbers.

One of the most fascinating aspects of life in North Africa is the way in which traditions thousands of years old exist alongside modern life. Villages of mud and stone are found not far from modern cities. Even within cities, there are sections built many hundreds of years apart. To help your child better understand this, you might identify the oldest and newest buildings where you live. You might also encourage your child to speculate about what life was like a thousand years ago in your area. How has it changed? How might the pressures of modern life affect someone living in a traditional rural village not far away? How are rural life and urban life different in the United States?

As you read or watch news reports, look for information about life in modern Egypt or Algeria. You can use these reports to stimulate discussion with your child about our class studies. If you have access to the Internet, you may be able to find more information and stories online.

I hope you and your child will enjoy this closer look at North Africa.

Sincerely,

Egypt: Hearing the Call of Islam

Lesson Objectives

Upon completion of this lesson, students will be able to:
- explain the influence of Islam on Egyptian culture,
- compare and contrast the lives of urban and rural Egyptians.

Engage Motivate Students to Learn

Warm-Up Activity Have students list the differences between living in a city and living in a rural area in the United States. Ask them to compare and contrast the kinds of jobs and the types of housing found in the two areas. Record students' responses on the chalkboard.

Activating Prior Knowledge Have students read Reach Into Your Background in the Before You Read box. Then ask volunteers to name their favorite holidays, and to tell how they celebrate them. Discuss whether the holidays named are shared by most Americans or are specific to certain groups of Americans.

Explore Develop Main Ideas

Have students read the section and ask them to explore questions such as these: What are some important teachings and practices of Islam? How has Islam affected the way Egyptians live? Why do some Egyptian women wear veils? Why have many people moved from rural areas to cities? What is life like in rural areas of Egypt?

Teach Solicit Student Participation

Ask students to write a letter from the point of view of a rural Egyptian visiting Cairo for the first time. Tell students to include in their letters observations of things that a rural person would find unfamiliar as well as things familiar. This activity should take about 20 minutes.

Assess Assess Evidence of Learning

See the answers to the Section Review questions. Students may also demonstrate evidence of learning by completing the Guided Reading and Review and the Section Quiz from the *Teaching Resources.* If students are doing a book project, that may also demonstrate evidence of learning by showing progress on project preparation.

Egypt: Hearing the Call of Islam 1

A. As You Read

Directions: As you read Section 1, answer the following questions on a separate sheet of paper.

1. What do Muslims do during the month of Ramadan?

2. What do Muslims believe about the Quran?

3. How often do devout Muslims pray?

4. What is the Sharia and on what is it based?

5. What has led to disagreements among Egyptian Muslims? How does this affect women?

6. Which is the largest city in Egypt? How would you describe life here?

7. Where are most of the rural villages in Egypt?

8. What are the homes of the fellaheen like?

9. What one thing unifies most of the people in Egypt?

B. Reviewing Key Terms

Directions: Complete the sentences below by writing the correct terms in the blanks provided.

10. Egyptian _____ hope that renewing their faith in Islam every day will help them maintain traditional values in a modern age.

11. Most _____ do not own land.

12. In Cairo, many people shop for food in a _____ , or open-air market.

Name _____ Class _____ Date _____

Egypt: Hearing the Call of Islam

A. Key Terms and Concepts

Directions: Complete each sentence in Column I by writing the letter of the correct term in Column II. Write the correct letter in each blank.

Column I

_____ 1. During the holiday of _____ , people fast from dawn to dusk and think of those who are less fortunate than themselves.

_____ 2. People in Cairo still shop in a traditional open-air market, or _____ .

_____ 3. Islamic law, or _____ , is based on the Quran and on the words and deeds of Muhammad.

_____ 4. _____ is the capital and largest city of Egypt.

_____ 5. Egypt's rural farmers are known as _____ .

Column II

a. bazaar

b. Ramadan

c. Sharia

d. fellaheen

e. Cairo

B. Main Ideas

Directions: Write the letter of the correct answer in each blank.

_____ 6. The official religion of Egypt is
   a. Christianity.
   b. Buddhism.
   c. Confucianism.
   d. Islam.

_____ 7. What is one way that religion has affected Egyptian daily life?
   a. People now follow the teachings of Buddha.
   b. Most national laws are in agreement with Islamic law.
   c. National laws are generally different from those in the Sharia.
   d. All citizens follow Islamic law rather than the laws of Egypt.

_____ 8. Originally, Islam spread from
   a. Egypt to Nigeria.
   b. Saudi Arabia to North Africa.
   c. Egypt to Southern Africa.
   d. Mesopotamia to Cairo.

_____ 9. Why do people in Egypt move to the cities from rural areas?
   a. Housing is plentiful.
   b. They want jobs and a better education.
   c. The cities are less crowded than the villages.
   d. It's easy to drive in the cities.

_____ 10. Where do most of the people in Egypt's rural areas live?
   a. in the north
   b. around Cairo or Alexandria
   c. along the Nile or by the Suez Canal
   d. in the mountains

Algeria: The Casbah and the Countryside

Chapter and Section Support

Lesson Objectives

Upon completion of this lesson, students will be able to:
- describe the differences and similarities between the Berbers and the Arabs of Algeria,
- compare and contrast rural and city life in Algeria.

Engage Motivate Students to Learn

Warm-Up Activity Ask students to brainstorm a list of the many ethnic groups that have come to the United States. Encourage students to think of foods, music, dances, art, words, and other contributions various ethnic groups have made to American culture.

Activating Prior Knowledge Have students read Reach Into Your Background in the Before You Read box. Ask students to brainstorm some ideas about clothing and other items people would need to survive in a desert climate.

Explore Develop Main Ideas

As students read the section, have them consider questions such as the following: Where do most Algerians live? What is a typical Berber household like? How do most people who live in Berber villages make their livings? How have the Arabs influenced Berber life? What are some features of Algerian cities?

Teach Solicit Student Participation

Ask students to work in groups of four to make a Venn diagram showing similarities and differences between the Berbers and the Arabs of Algeria. Use the diagrams as a basis for a discussion of the section. This activity should take about 20 minutes.

Assess Assess Evidence of Learning

See the answers to the Section Review questions. Students may also demonstrate evidence of learning by completing the Guided Reading and Review and the Section Quiz from the *Teaching Resources*. If students are doing a book project, that may also demonstrate evidence of learning by showing progress on project preparation.

GUIDED READING AND REVIEW

Algeria: The Casbah and the Countryside

A. As You Read

Directions: As you read Section 2, fill in the table below with details about Algeria. Write at least two facts in the spaces provided.

Facts About Algeria

Berbers	1. 2.
Arabs	3. 4.
Rural Life	5. 6.
City Life	7. 8.

B. Reviewing Key Terms

Directions: In the blanks provided, write the definitions for the following key terms.

9. terrace _____

10. souq _____

11. casbah _____

CHAPTER 4
Exploring
North Africa

Algeria: The Casbah
and the Countryside

A. Key Terms and Concepts

Directions: Match the definitions in Column I with the terms in Column II. Write the correct letter in each blank.

Column I

_____ **1.** the name of the ethnic group that has lived in North Africa since at least 3000 B.C.

_____ **2.** a social group that includes more relatives than just a mother, a father, and their children

_____ **3.** a platform cut into the mountainside for crops

_____ **4.** the name of the ethnic group that spread across North Africa in the A.D. 600s

_____ **5.** an open-air marketplace

Column II

a. Arab

b. Berber

c. extended family

d. souq

e. terrace

B. Main Ideas

Directions: Write the letter of the correct answer in each blank.

_____ **6.** In Algeria, more than 85 percent of the land is difficult to live on because it is
 a. too mountainous.
 b. part of the Sahara.
 c. covered by rain forests.
 d. too crowded.

_____ **7.** The two main ethnic groups in Algeria are
 a. Chinese and Arab.
 b. Arab and Muslim.
 c. Arab and Berber.
 d. Muslim and Hindu.

_____ **8.** Berbers adapted to Arab rule by following the central government as well as
 a. their native Christianity.
 b. their village governments.
 c. a farming lifestyle.
 d. an urban lifestyle.

_____ **9.** How are Berbers and Arabs similar?
 a. Both speak French and Chinese.
 b. Both live only in large cities.
 c. Both live in extended families.
 d. Both live only in rural areas.

_____ **10.** Which statement best describes the cities of Algeria?
 a. The people have little in common with one another.
 b. The cities are all completely modernized.
 c. Few of Algeria's people live in the cities.
 d. The cities are a mix of modern buildings and traditional open-air marketplaces.

Name _____ Class _____ Date _____

Exploring North Africa

Guiding Questions:
- How have historical events affected the cultures and nations of Africa?
- What factors influence the ways in which Africans can make a living?

Egypt is located in the eastern part of North Africa, across the Red Sea from Saudi Arabia, where Islam began. Egyptians are unified by their faith in Islam. Egyptian Muslims, like others, pray five times a day. The teachings of the Quran, or Muslim holy book, stress the importance of honesty, honor, giving to others, and loving and respecting families. Many Egyptian Muslims are renewing their faith by trying to live each day according to Sharia, or Islamic law.

About half of all Egyptians live in cities. Cairo is the largest city and is very crowded. Some parts of the city are over 1,000 years old, while others contain modern high-rise buildings. Many people have moved from rural areas to the cities to find work. Those who stay in rural areas live mostly along the Nile River. These villagers are primarily farmers living in homes built of mud bricks or stones. Traditions in rural villages have changed little during the past 4,000 years.

Algeria lies to the west of Egypt and is dominated by the Sahara. Algeria borders the Mediterranean Sea to the north. Most Algerians live in this coastal area. The two main ethnic groups in Algeria are Berbers and Arabs. The Berbers have lived here for thousands of years. The majority live in rural villages, where they farm and herd animals. Family is very important to the Berbers. Their village governments are made up of the heads of each family.

The Arabs came to North Africa in the A.D. 600s, bringing Islam to the region. This event changed the traditional Berber way of life. The Arabs created a central government based on Islam. Over time, the Berbers have adapted by keeping their own village governments along with obeying the central government. The Arabs who conquered North Africa were nomads. Some Berbers were influenced by them and changed from a farming to a nomadic way of life. Berbers and Arabs who live in the cities have the most in common. Like Egypt's cities, Algeria's contain both old and modern sections.

Exploring North Africa

Directions: Match the key terms in the box with the definitions below. Write the correct letter in each blank. Then write a sentence in the space provided that uses that term or the plural form of the term. If necessary, look up the terms in your textbook glossary, or see how they are used in Chapter 4.

> **a.** bazaar
> **b.** fellaheen
> **c.** terrace

_____ **1.** an open-air market often found in North Africa

_____

_____

_____

_____ **2.** a platform of earth that is cut into the side of a mountain for growing crops

_____

_____

_____

_____ **3.** Egypt's rural farmers

_____

_____

_____

_____

RETEACHING

CHAPTER 4

Exploring North Africa

Directions: Use the information in your textbook to complete each statement.

1. The religion of most Egyptians is _____ .

2. Muslims in Egypt disagree about

   _____ .

3. Because Cairo is so crowded, people live in _____ .

4. The fellaheen live in _____ .

5. The Berbers of Algeria base their village government on _____ .

6. In Berber villages, most families make their living by _____ .

7. Both Muslim Arabs and non-Muslim Berbers traditionally live with

   _____ .

8. Muslim Arabs based their central government in Algeria on _____ .

9. Due to Arab influence, many Berbers changed from a _____ .

   to a _____ lifestyle.

10. Algeria's cities contain both old sections with _____ and new sections

    with _____ .

Name _____ Class _____ Date _____

Exploring North Africa

Architecture of a Mosque

Directions: Study the diagram and captions. Then write a paragraph describing the parts of a typical mosque.

Parts of a Mosque

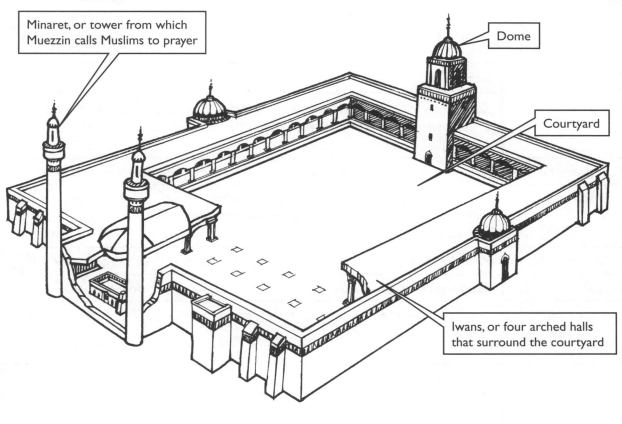

Minaret, or tower from which Muezzin calls Muslims to prayer

Dome

Courtyard

Iwans, or four arched halls that surround the courtyard

_____

_____

_____

_____

_____

Name _____ Class _____ Date _____

Exploring North Africa

Making Comparisons

Daily Life of a Tuareg Family

Directions: The Tuareg are a group of Berbers who live in North Africa. Some Tuareg are nomads who tend herds of livestock in the Sahara and the Sahel. The chart below tells what their daily life is like. Study the chart and then make a similar chart describing your day. On a separate sheet of paper, list ways in which your life is similar to and different from theirs.

Time	Activities
Sunrise	Day begins. Milk the goats and sheep, which are kept in a pen near the tents. Let animals out to graze. Eat breakfast. (Men and women eat separately. Children eat after their parents.)
Morning hours	Women clean the tent and grind grain. Men tend the camels and cattle.
Noon	Second main meal of the day (millet, rice, wheat, or wild grain porridge; milk; millet or wheat bread; goat meat and mutton on special occasions; game animals; and wild plants).
Afternoon hours	Rest during the heat of the day. Brew and drink tea several times a day.
Toward sunset	Tend the goats and sheep, who return from grazing on their own.
After sunset	Eat supper. Gather in tents for games, songs, music, stories or for listening to the radio.

Time	Activities

Exploring West Africa

Social Studies Hot Line

Dear Family,

We are now studying the cultures of West Africa. During the next few days, we will learn about the countries of Nigeria, Ghana, and Mali. We will learn how West Africa was the center of the African slave trade that brought millions of Africans to the United States and other places. West Africans carried with them a rich cultural heritage of ideas, music, and stories that has strongly influenced American culture.

You might listen with your child to examples of African musical influence, such as jazz and blues (elements of which are found in much of pop music). You could also read stories like Joel C. Harris's *Uncle Remus Stories* or *The People Could Fly* by Virginia Hamilton (NY: Knopf, 1985). You might also try to find examples of West African traditional or pop music, such as King Sunny Ade, Ali Farka Toure, Youssou N'Dour, and Baba Mal.

As you read the newspaper or watch the news, look for reports about Nigeria, Ghana, and Mali. Discuss what you find with your child, comparing political, social, environmental, and other issues with similar ones in the United States.

The problem of growing deserts, or desertification, in Mali might stimulate discussion about water supplies in the United States, particularly in the Southwest. Or, you might talk about how your lives would change if the climate or land conditions suddenly changed. What might happen if the soil in your state became unusable, the average temperature rose or fell five degrees, or the average amount of rainfall changed?

You will be receiving more reports about our study of Africa in coming weeks as we study East and Central and Southern Africa. I hope you are continuing to enjoy sharing with your child what she or he is learning.

Sincerely,

Nigeria: One Country, Many Identities

Lesson Objectives

Upon completion of this lesson, students will be able to:
- identify Nigeria's three main ethnic groups,
- describe the different ways of life of Nigeria's three main ethnic groups.

Engage Motivate Students to Learn

Warm-Up Activity Have students suppose that they are visiting a country where people speak a different language and have different customs. Ask students to consider what difficulties they might encounter. Would they feel like outsiders? Would they try to find someone who spoke their language? Would they avoid contact with the residents, or would they try to communicate in some way?

Activating Prior Knowledge Have students read Reach Into Your Background in the Before You Read box. Have students estimate the number of people they have communicated with so far today. Then have them consider whether and how they would have communicated with these people if many of them did not share their language.

Explore Develop Main Ideas

Ask students to keep the following questions in mind as they read the section: What are Nigeria's three main ethnic groups? What changes occurred when Europeans arrived? How did the three main ethnic groups and other ethnic groups form the country of Nigeria, and how do their ways of life differ?

Teach Solicit Student Participation

Have students create a chart with three rows labeled: *Igbo, Hausa-Fulani,* and *Yoruba,* and three columns labeled: *region, culture*, and *history.* Ask students to fill in the chart with facts from the section. Use the completed chart as the basis for a discussion of the differences and similarities among these groups. This activity should take about 20 minutes.

Assess Assess Evidence of Learning

See the answers to the Section Review questions. Students may also demonstrate evidence of learning by completing the Guided Reading and Review and the Section Quiz from the *Teaching Resources.* If students are doing a book project, that may also demonstrate evidence of learning by showing progress on project preparation.

CHAPTER 5
Exploring West Africa

Nigeria: One Country, Many Identities

A. As You Read

Directions: As you read Section 1, answer the following questions in the space provided.

1. Who ruled Nigeria before the Europeans arrived?

_____

2. When did Nigeria achieve independence and from whom?

_____

3. How did Nigeria change its capital and why?

_____

_____

4. How have the Hausa-Fulani made their living for hundreds of years?

_____

5. What is the oldest city in West Africa? How long has it been a center of trade?

_____

6. What is the name of the city in which many Yoruba live? In the 1800s, what was it a center of?

_____

7. How do the Yoruba and Igbo make their living?

_____

8. How do the Igbo rule themselves?

_____

9. How was the 1991 census in Nigeria unusual?

_____

10. Why was the census so important to the people of Nigeria?

_____

B. Reviewing Key Terms

Directions: In the blanks provided, write the definitions for the following key terms.

11. multiethnic

_____

12. census

_____

Name _____ Class _____ Date _____

Nigeria: One Country, Many Identities

A. Key Terms and Concepts

Directions: Read the statements below. If a statement is true, write T in the blank provided. If it is false, write F. Rewrite false statements to make them true.

_____ **1.** Nigeria is multiethnic, which means that many ethnic groups live within its borders.

_____

_____ **2.** In 1991, the Nigerian government moved the nation's capital to Lagos in the south.

_____

_____ **3.** The Hausa and the Yoruba together make up about 32 percent of Nigeria's people.

_____

_____ **4.** In Nigeria, a census determines which ethnic group has the most power.

_____

_____ **5.** The Igbo rule themselves with a system of monarchy.

_____

B. Main Ideas

Directions: Write the letter of the correct answer in each blank.

_____ **6.** What are Hausa, Yoruba, and Igbo?
  a. the major cities in Nigeria
  b. ethnic groups in Nigeria
  c. the largest markets in Nigeria
  d. the most important rivers in Nigeria

_____ **7.** Which statement is true of Nigeria?
  a. Few ethnic groups live here.
  b. About one out of every five Africans live here.
  c. It is the smallest country in Africa.
  d. People have been living in Nigeria since 1900.

_____ **8.** In the late 1400s, the Portuguese first came to Nigeria in order to buy
  a. cloth.
  b. food.
  c. slaves.
  d. timber.

_____ **9.** The capital of Nigeria was moved in order to be closer to
  a. the Sahara.
  b. more ethnic groups.
  c. the major rivers.
  d. the major trade routes.

_____ **10.** The Hausa-Fulani people in Nigeria have made their living for hundreds of years by
  a. farming.
  b. mining.
  c. manufacturing.
  d. trading.

CHAPTER 5
Exploring
West Africa

Ghana: First in Independence

Lesson Objectives

Upon completion of this lesson, students will be able to:
- identify the circumstances that led to Ghana's gaining its independence,
- describe economic and political setbacks and successes following Ghana's independence.

Engage Motivate Students to Learn

Warm-Up Activity Ask students to think about what an ideal form of government would be. Have them consider what kind of person or persons would lead the government and make decisions.

Activating Prior Knowledge Tell students that a turning point is an event or a situation that triggers change. Then have students read Reach Into Your Background in the Before You Read box.

Explore Develop Main Ideas

As students read the section, ask them to keep the following questions in mind: Why did Kwame Nkrumah believe that his country should seek independence? How did the British benefit from controlling the Gold Coast's economy? What are some features of Ghana's economy and culture today?

Teach Solicit Student Participation

Have students make a time line that shows the main events in Nkrumah's life. Important moments in Ghana's history should also be included. This activity should take about 20 minutes.

Assess Assess Evidence of Learning

See the answers to the Section Review questions. Students may also demonstrate evidence of learning by completing the Guided Reading and Review and the Section Quiz from the *Teaching Resources*. If students are doing a book project, that may also demonstrate evidence of learning by showing progress on project preparation.

Name _____ Class _____ Date _____

Ghana: First in Independence

A. As You Read

Directions: As you read Section 2, write four supporting ideas or facts for each main idea listed below.

Main Idea A
Kwame Nkrumah had many beliefs and goals for Ghana.

1. _____
_____

2. _____
_____

3. _____
_____

4. _____

Main Idea B
Life has changed in many ways since independence in Ghana.

5. _____
_____

6. _____
_____

7. _____
_____

8. _____

B. Reviewing Key Terms

Directions: Complete the sentences below by writing the correct terms in the blanks provided.

9. Nigeria achieved _____ , or political independence, in 1957.

10. The government of Kwame Nkrumah was overthrown by a military
_____ nine years after independence in Ghana.

Ghana: First in Independence

A. Key Terms and Concepts

Directions: Fill in the blanks in Column I with the terms in Column II. Write the correct letter in each blank.

Column I

_____ 1. Many African countries wanted their ____ .

_____ 2. Cocoa was an important ____ of the Gold Coast.

_____ 3. The first leader of Ghana was overthrown by a military ____ .

_____ 4. The first president of Ghana was ____ .

_____ 5. In the 1980s, Ghana's president, ____ , tried to reform the country's politics and economy.

Column II

a. coup

b. export

c. Jerry Rawlings

d. Kwame Nkrumah

e. sovereignty

B. Main Ideas

Directions: Write the letter of the correct answer in each blank.

_____ 6. Kwame Nkrumah encouraged the people of his country to
   a. expand their trade routes with other countries.
   b. stop importing food.
   c. seek independence from Great Britain.
   d. become a colonial power.

_____ 7. Why did the British colonize the Gold Coast?
   a. to control its economy
   b. to control its government
   c. to control its religious life
   d. to control its educational system

_____ 8. Army officers threw Nkrumah out of office because they blamed him for
   a. reforming the country's politics.
   b. the country's economic problems.
   c. not helping his fellow citizens.
   d. not trying to unify the country.

_____ 9. How did Jerry Rawlings change life in Ghana?
   a. He encouraged the citizens to adopt Western cultural values.
   b. He constructed a dam.
   c. He tried to reform Ghana's politics and economy.
   d. He built a large conference center.

_____ 10. When the British ruled the Gold Coast, the people grew fewer food crops because
   a. cash crops were more profitable.
   b. the land wasn't fertile enough.
   c. farmers spent more time on crafts.
   d. imported food was very cheap.

CLASSROOM MANAGER

Mali: The Desert Is Coming

CHAPTER 5
Exploring
West Africa

Lesson Objectives

Upon completion of this lesson, students will be able to:
- identify the relationship between Mali's environment and the way people make their livings,
- describe the effects of desertification,
- explain how Mali is coping with the problem of desertification.

Engage Motivate Students to Learn

Warm-Up Activity Remind students that pollution from automobiles is a problem throughout the world. In some cities, air pollution has become so serious that there are regulations to discourage people from driving. Ask students what steps the United States has taken to help the air stay clean.

Activating Prior Knowledge Ask students to describe how a person in Minnesota would dress during December compared with how a person in Hawaii would dress. Then have students read Reach Into Your Background in the Before You Read box.

Explore Develop Main Ideas

Tell students to read the section. Ask them to keep in mind the following questions: What used to be different about life in the Sahel? What is desertification? Why is it important to understand the causes of desertification?

Teach Solicit Student Participation

Ask students to write a paragraph explaining how desertification has affected the way Malians make their livings. Have them include information about the business community of Tombouctou and the Tuaregs.

Assess Assess Evidence of Learning

See the answers to the Section Review questions. Students may also demonstrate evidence of learning by completing the Guided Reading and Review and the Section Quiz from the *Teaching Resources*. If students are doing a book project, that may also demonstrate evidence of learning by showing progress on project preparation.

CHAPTER 5
Exploring
West Africa

Mali: The Desert Is Coming

A. As You Read

Directions: As you read Section 3, fill in the table below with details about Mali. Write at least three facts in the spaces provided.

Facts About Mali

Environment	1.
	2.
	3.
The Sahel	4.
	5.
	6.
Desertification	7.
	8.
	9.

B. Reviewing Key Terms

Directions: Complete the sentences below by writing the correct terms in the blanks provided.

10. The people in the Sahel are greatly affected by _____ , or the process by which fertile land becomes desert.

11. Some environmentalists believe that the growing desert in the Sahel is caused by many

years of _____ .

12. Many people think that when animals overgraze an area, they _____ the soil.

SECTION QUIZ

Mali: The Desert Is Coming

A. Key Terms and Concepts

Directions: Match the definitions in Column I with the terms in Column II. Write the correct letter in each blank.

Column I

_____ **1.** a zone between the desert and the forest stretching through the middle of Mali

_____ **2.** to wear away slowly

_____ **3.** the change of fertile land into land that is too dry or damaged to support life

_____ **4.** a period of time when there is little or no rain

_____ **5.** the desert that covers much of West Africa

Column II

a. desertification

b. drought

c. erode

d. Sahara

e. Sahel

B. Main Ideas

Directions: Write the letter of the correct answer in each blank.

_____ **6.** The Sahara, Sahel, and savanna are the
   a. most important rivers of Mali.
   b. most important cities of Mali.
   c. major vegetation zones of Mali.
   d. main languages of Mali.

_____ **7.** People who live in the Sahel make their living mainly by
   a. manufacturing.
   b. raising livestock.
   c. weaving.
   d. mining.

_____ **8.** What is the greatest threat to the economy of Mali?
   a. the spread of the Sahara
   b. the increase in the amount of rain
   c. the end of all trade with other African countries
   d. the unstable world market for goods made in the country

_____ **9.** What is one explanation for the desertification of the Sahel?
   a. long periods of rain
   b. too many floods
   c. too little sun
   d. long periods of drought

_____ **10.** The spread of the Sahara is threatening the way of life of the
   a. Saudi Arabians.
   b. Berbers.
   c. Tuareg.
   d. Egyptians.

Name _____ Class _____ Date _____

Exploring West Africa

Guiding Questions:

- How have historical events affected the cultures and nations of Africa?
- What factors led to the development of different governments across Africa?

<u>There are 17 countries in West Africa and hundreds of ethnic groups and languages.</u> Three of these countries are Nigeria, Ghana, and Mali.

<u>Nigeria has more people than any other African country. More than 400 languages are spoken in Nigeria.</u> The three most common are Hausa, Yoruba, and Igbo, the languages of its three main ethnic groups. Nigeria was created by Europeans. It includes ethnic groups that were used to ruling only their own people. The Hausa-Fulani live in the north and are primarily herders and traders. The Yoruba live near the coast and farm their lands. The city of Lagos is traditionally a Yoruban city. The Igbo live in the southeast and are farmers who have not built cities.

<u>Europeans ruled Ghana, which they called the Gold Coast, for many years.</u> Under colonial rule, the British encouraged farmers to grow cocoa as a cash crop. People grew less food and became dependent on imported food and factory items. Kwame Nkrumah was a leader who worked to make his land independent. In 1957, Ghana became independent, and Nkrumah became the leader of the new country. Nine years later, Nkrumah was replaced by a military government. During the 1980s, Jerry Rawlings led the country by stressing the traditional African values of hard work and sacrifice. Under his leadership, Ghana's economy grew stronger and its cultural heritage was preserved.

<u>Mali lies in the northern part of West Africa.</u> About one third of the country is in the Sahara, where few people live. Another portion is in the semiarid Sahel, and a third is savanna, the only area that gets enough rain to grow crops. Most people in Mali make their living by trading, farming, and herding. However, the growth of desert land, called deser-tification, is threatening all of these occupations. The grasslands of the Sahel are gradually disappearing. Some people think that overgrazing by animals is the cause. Others say that long periods of drought have caused the problem. <u>Today, the government is working with the United Nations to find solutions to the problem of desertification.</u>

Name _____ Class _____ Date _____

Exploring West Africa

Directions: Read the following sentences. The words in bold type make each sentence false. Rewrite each sentence to make it true. Use your textbook if you need help. Key terms from your textbook are underlined. If necessary, look up the terms in your textbook glossary.

1. Nigeria is an example of a <u>multiethnic</u> country because there are many **types of plants** living here.

   _____

2. A <u>census</u> is taken to count the number of **rain days each month.**

   _____

3. In 1957, Great Britain agreed to grant <u>sovereignty</u> to the people of Ghana, who were given **money.**

   _____

4. After the military <u>coup</u>, the government **stayed the same.**

   _____

5. <u>Desertification</u> has been changing **desert into fertile land** for years.

   _____

6. Animals may help to <u>erode</u> the soil by **walking on it.**

   _____

7. An <u>ethnic group</u> contains people who have **many different languages and religions.**

   _____

8. A <u>drought</u> takes place when there is **too much rainfall.**

   _____

Exploring West Africa

Directions: Use the information in your textbook to write each sentence from the box under the country it relates to.

- Trading, herding, and farming are threatened by desertification.
- It was called the Gold Coast.
- The Sahara and Sahel cover most of the country.
- It includes Hausaland, Yorubaland, and Igboland.
- Here the Igbo traditionally rule themselves with a democratic council of elders.
- Its capital was moved to Abuja to be closer to different ethnic groups.
- It has the Kurmi Market in Kano, one of the largest trading centers in Africa.
- Its economy has improved with the promotion of the traditional African values of hard work and sacrifice.
- Tombouctou, once a wealthy center of learning and business, is slowly being covered in sand.
- It was the first African colony south of the Sahara to become independent.

1. Nigeria

_____

_____

_____

_____

2. Ghana

_____

_____

_____

_____

3. Mali

_____

_____

_____

_____

Exploring West Africa

Yoruba Proverbs

Directions: The following proverbs come from the Yoruba, who live in Nigeria, Benin, and Togo. Explain what you think each proverb means.

1. The Lord of Heaven has created us with different natures.

_____

_____

2. One who waits for chance may wait a year.

_____

_____

3. One who does not understand the yellow palm-bird says the yellow palm-bird is noisy.

_____

_____

4. You sleep like the Opere (a bird noted for its sleepiness).

_____

_____

5. One who eats the sweet should also eat the sour.

_____

_____

6. One who forgives gains the victory in the dispute.

_____

_____

7. The person who has bread to eat does not appreciate the severity of a famine.

_____

_____

8. A hunchback is never asked to stand upright.

_____

_____

Exploring West Africa

Recognizing Bias

Successful West African Farms

Directions: Read this excerpt from a newspaper article about a farming community in Nigeria. Then complete the activities that follow.

Rural areas, where most Africans live, make headlines chiefly when famines occur. . . . readers should know that this is not all there is to Africa. . . .

Our focus has been on African agriculture. . . . An excellent example [is] the Kofyar people of Nigeria. The Kofyar themselves may not be the stuff of headlines, but they are part of an African landscape that is just as real. . . .

. . . in 1905, the Kofyar lived and farmed in the hills of Jos Plateau near the center of Nigeria. . . . They had developed a highly intensive farming system. . . .

Each family [kept] its own small herd of goats to provide fertilizer. Using broad hoes, the Kofyar worked the fields into "waffle" ridges that prevented erosion and captured rainfall for crops. Terraces were constructed on hillsides otherwise too steep for cultivation. . . .

Although most [Kofyar] have stayed on the farm, a significant number have taken an education and careers in the city. There are Kofyar teachers, judges, bankers and university administrators, but even the most successful maintain homes on the farm, and many continue to grow crops.

1. According to the authors of this article, what bias do most newspaper articles on Africa reflect?

_____

_____

2. What activities in your community are likely to be ignored by newspaper reporters?

3. Find a newspaper article about Africa that shows the kind of bias these authors are referring to.

4. Find another newspaper article about Africa that presents a different slant on life here.

—From "Out of Africa: Hope and Progress," by Glenn Davis Stone and M. Priscilla Stone, *St. Louis Post-Dispatch,* November 11, 1996. Reprinted by permission.

LETTER HOME

Exploring East Africa

Social Studies Hot Line

Dear Family,

We are continuing our study of Africa by focusing on East Africa. We will study three countries in the region in detail: Ethiopia, Tanzania, and Kenya. We will begin by learning about the history of Ethiopia and how a unique form of Christianity developed here. We will then look at how Tanzanians and Kenyans have dealt with political and economic challenges while preserving peace. Finally, we will study how life is changing in East Africa as more people move from the country to the city.

If you can find magazine articles about any of these countries, they can provide your child with a helpful addition to our studies. You might have your child cut out photographs to share with the class.

Looking with your child at a map of the area can stimulate discussion about the influence of location on people's way of life. You might note the coastal areas and talk about how such a location would stimulate trade and the exchange of ideas and customs.

As your child reads about the contrast in East Africa between city and country life, you might like to talk about how they are different in the United States. If you have moved recently or know other people who have, you could use the experience as a focus for discussion about the challenges of moving away from home.

In our next section, the last on Africa, we will learn more about Central and Southern Africa. Thank you for your help and support of our studies.

Sincerely,

CHAPTER 6
Exploring
East Africa

Ethiopia
Churches and Mosques

1

Lesson Objectives

Upon completion of this lesson, students will be able to:
- describe how Christianity and Islam reached Ethiopia,
- compare and contrast rural and urban life in Ethiopia.

Engage Motivate Students to Learn

Warm-Up Activity Display a large world map. Tell students that Ethiopia once included the present-day countries of Eritrea, Djibouti, and Somalia, and have students locate these countries and Ethiopia on the map. Have students identify some possible land or sea routes that people from surrounding regions or countries could have taken to travel to ancient Ethiopia.

Activating Prior Knowledge Ask students to consider what they have learned since first grade. What skills do they have that first graders have not yet acquired? Then have students read Reach Into Your Background in the Before You Read box.

Explore Develop Main Ideas

Have students read the section. Discuss with them the two main religions of Ethiopia. Ask students to consider the following questions as they read: How did Christianity spread to Ethiopia? How did Islam come to Ethiopia? How do the lives of rural Ethiopians differ from the lives of urban Ethiopians?

Teach Solicit Student Participation

Have students write a five-question true-or-false quiz about the material covered in the section. Ask students to also make an answer key. For additional reinforcement, have students exchange quizzes. Alternately, you might read selected statements and have the class say whether each is true or false. This activity should take about 20 minutes.

Assess Assess Evidence of Learning

See the answers to the Section Review questions. Students may also demonstrate evidence of learning by completing the Guided Reading and Review and the Section Quiz from the *Teaching Resources.* If students are doing a book project, that may also demonstrate evidence of learning by showing progress on project preparation.

GUIDED READING AND REVIEW

Ethiopia
Churches and Mosques

A. As You Read

Directions: As you read Section 1, fill in the table below with information about Ethiopia.

Information About Ethiopia

Christianity	1.
	2.
	3.
Islam	4.
	5.
Lalibela	6.
	7.
	8.
Addis Ababa	9.
	10.

B. Reviewing Key Terms

Directions: Fill in the blank in the sentence below.

11. When young people wished to study music and painting in ancient Ethiopia, they could

    enter a Christian _____ .

CHAPTER 6
Exploring
East Africa

Ethiopia:
Churches and Mosques

A. Key Terms and Concepts

Directions: Read the statements below. If a statement is true, write T in the blank provided. If it is false, write F. On a separate sheet of paper, rewrite false statements to make them true.

_____ 1. A place where priests live, work, and study is called a mosque.

_____ 2. One of the oldest languages in the world is called Geez.

_____ 3. Somalia was the capital of Christian Ethiopia for about 300 years.

_____ 4. The capital of Ethiopia is Eritrea.

_____ 5. Most Ethiopians live in rural areas.

B. Main Ideas

Directions: Write the letter of the correct answer in each blank.

_____ 6. Ethiopian Christians were isolated from Christians in other parts of the world because they were
    a. separated by the Red Sea.
    b. trading with Egypt.
    c. surrounded by Islamic countries.
    d. living in rural areas.

_____ 7. How did early Arab traders affect the culture of Ethiopia?
    a. Some Ethiopians adopted the Muslim faith.
    b. The Ethiopians went to Arab schools.
    c. All Ethiopians adopted the Arab language.
    d. The Ethiopians conquered the Arabs.

_____ 8. Today, the religions practiced by most Ethiopians are
    a. Christianity and Islam.
    b. Judaism and Christianity.
    c. Islam and Buddhism.
    d. Christianity and Buddhism.

_____ 9. Few of the people who live in Lalibela have
    a. food.
    b. religious beliefs.
    c. cars.
    d. farmland.

_____ 10. Which statement is true of Ethiopia's capital city?
    a. It looks similar to a country village.
    b. Most people here make a living by manufacturing products.
    c. Most Ethiopians live in the capital.
    d. It's a mix of modern and traditional ways of living.

Tanzania: When People Cooperate

Lesson Objectives

Upon completion of this lesson, students will be able to:
- identify the peoples who ruled Tanzania prior to independence,
- explain the changes instituted by Julius Nyerere during his presidency,
- describe the current economic, political, and social issues facing Tanzania.

Engage Motivate Students to Learn

Warm-Up Activity Write the following statement on the chalkboard: "Only hard work can end poverty." Allow students a few minutes to react to the statement and then ask them whether they think the statement is true. Have students explain their ideas. Tell students that as they read this section, they will discover how Tanzania fared under a policy that promoted hard work and self-reliance.

Activating Prior Knowledge Ask students to think of one or two recent changes in their lives. Then have them read Reach Into Your Background in the Before You Read box.

Explore Develop Main Ideas

Have students read the section. Prompt discussion with questions such as these: What were the reasons behind such policies as the one-party political system and *ujamaa?* What improvements came about as a result of Nyerere's policies? Why did some of Nyerere's ideas fail? Why was the idea of a multiparty government a cause for celebration?

Teach Solicit Student Participation

Ask students to make a chart with two headings: *One-Party System* and *Multiparty System.* Have students record the features, both positive and negative, of the two systems. This activity should take about 20 minutes.

Assess Assess Evidence of Learning

See the answers to the Section Review questions. Students may also demonstrate evidence of learning by completing the Guided Reading and Review and the Section Quiz from the *Teaching Resources.* If students are doing a book project, that may also demonstrate evidence of learning by showing progress on project preparation.

Tanzania: When
People Cooperate

A. As You Read

Directions: As you read Section 2, answer the following questions in the space provided.
If necessary, use a separate sheet of paper.

1. How did Julius Nyerere help all ethnic groups feel that they were part of Tanzania?

_____

2. What did Nyerere do to avoid conflict among ethnic groups in political elections? Why?

_____

3. What did Nyerere say to Tanzanians about the meaning of independence? What did he
mean?

_____

4. What is *ujamaa?* What were ujamaa villages?

_____

5. What were some of Nyerere's successes?

_____

6. How did the ujamaa program end?

_____

7. How did the new leaders change farming practices in Tanzania?

_____

8. How did the election system change in Tanzania after Julius Nyerere left office?

_____

B. Reviewing Key Terms

Directions: Complete each sentence by writing the correct term in the blank provided.

9. Julius Nyerere was proud to increase the _____ rate in Tanzania.

10. Tanzania has a huge _____ because it has had to borrow money.

11. A country that has two or more political parties has a _____ .

Name _____ Class _____ Date _____

Tanzania: When People Cooperate

A. Key Terms and Concepts

Directions: Fill in the blanks in Column I with the terms in Column II. Write the correct letter in each blank.

Column I

_____ 1. Much of Tanzania was once ruled by the British, who called it ____ .

_____ 2. The capital of Tanzania is ____ .

_____ 3. Tanzania is working to pay off its ____ , or money owed to other countries.

_____ 4. Part of Tanzania is an island called____ .

_____ 5. The first president of Tanzania was ____ .

Column II

a. Dar es Salaam

b. foreign debt

c. Julius Nyerere

d. Zanzibar

e. Tanganyika

B. Main Ideas

Directions: Write the letter of the correct answer in each blank.

_____ 6. Why has Tanzania always been a center of trade?
  a. The country is located on the coast of West Africa.
  b. The country has a strong army.
  c. The country surrounds the Nile River.
  d. The country is located on the coast of East Africa.

_____ 7. The nation of Tanzania was formed when Tanganyika joined with the island of
  a. Kaliban.
  b. Dar es Salaam.
  c. Zanzibar.
  d. Zambia.

_____ 8. What is one change that the first president brought to Tanzania's political system?
  a. He created a one-party system of government.
  b. He refused to hold elections.
  c. He created a two-party system of government.
  d. He ended the monarchy.

_____ 9. In an effort to improve the economy, the president asked farmers to move to
  a. large cities.
  b. the coast of the country.
  c. ujamaa villages.
  d. the mountains of the country.

_____ 10. How did Tanzania's new leaders try to improve the country's economy?
  a. They increased the taxes.
  b. They borrowed money from foreign countries.
  c. They asked farmers to stop producing cash crops.
  d. They refused to trade with other African countries.

CHAPTER 6
Exploring
East Africa

Kenya: Skyscrapers
in the Savanna

3

Lesson Objectives

Upon completion of this lesson, students will be able to:
- identify the ways people make their livings in rural areas of Kenya,
- describe why Kenyans are moving to cities,
- explain how people who have moved to cities maintain family ties.

Engage Motivate Students to Learn

Warm-Up Activity Ask students to think of ways in which groups sometimes "pull together" to achieve a common goal, such as organizing a neighborhood cleanup or raising funds for a charitable purpose. Record students' ideas on the chalkboard. Then ask them why teamwork and organization are necessary for these activities to be successful.

Activating Prior Knowledge Have students read Reach Into Your Background in the Before You Read box. Then ask them to consider how they would stay in contact with people if they did not have telephones or computers.

Explore Develop Main Ideas

Have students read the section and then discuss questions such as the following: What are the features of rural and urban life in Kenya? What is *harambee,* and what are some examples of it? What kinds of work do women do? Why do men leave their families to find work in Nairobi?

Teach Solicit Student Participation

Have students begin two concept webs. They should label one web *Females* and the other *Males.* Encourage students to suggest words or phrases that describe differences and similarities between the ways men and women in Kenya live. Aspects common to both sexes can be connected to both webs. This activity should take about 25 minutes.

Assess Assess Evidence of Learning

See the answers to the Section Review questions. Students may also demonstrate evidence of learning by completing the Guided Reading and Review and the Section Quiz from the *Teaching Resources.* If students are doing a book project, that may also demonstrate evidence of learning by showing progress on project preparation.

GUIDED READING AND REVIEW

Kenya: Skyscrapers
in the Savanna

A. As You Read

Directions: As you read Section 3, answer the following questions in the space provided.

1. From what backgrounds are the people of Kenya?

_____

2. What do the people of Kenya have in common?

_____

3. What is an example of harambee?

_____

4. Who are most of Kenya's farmers?

_____

5. What are some of the children's responsibilities in a Kenyan farming village?

_____

6. What do village children do for fun?

_____

7. How is Kenyan life changing?

_____

8. Who usually moves to the city? What are the effects of this move?

_____

9. How do women help themselves in rural Kenya?

_____

10. In cities, what do men from the same ethnic group do for each other?

_____

11. What does Moses Mpoke say about who he is?

_____

B. Reviewing Key Terms

Directions: Complete the sentence by writing the correct key word in the blank provided.

12. The Swahili word that means "let's pull together" is _____ .

CHAPTER 6
Exploring East Africa

Kenya: Skyscrapers in the Savanna

A. Key Terms and Concepts

Directions: Match the definitions in Column I with the terms in Column II. Write the correct letter in each blank.

Column I

_____ 1. a small farm owned and run by a Kenyan family

_____ 2. the highest mountain in Kenya

_____ 3. a Swahili word that means "let's pull together"

_____ 4. the first president of Kenya

_____ 5. the capital of Kenya

Column II

a. harambee

b. Jomo Kenyatta

c. Mount Kenya

d. Nairobi

e. shamba

B. Main Ideas

Directions: Write the letter of the correct answer in each blank.

_____ 6. Most of Kenya's people work as
   a. merchants.
   b. teachers.
   c. farmers.
   d. manufacturers.

_____ 7. Which statement is true of Kenya's people?
   a. They belong to only two ethnic groups.
   b. They belong to many ethnic groups.
   c. They speak one language.
   d. They are mostly of European descent.

_____ 8. How is the way of life for many Kenyans changing?
   a. Most women are moving to large villages to find work.
   b. Most men and women are leaving the rural areas.
   c. Many men are going to the cities to find work.
   d. Many men are becoming the primary caretakers for the children.

_____ 9. In order to solve community problems, women in rural areas all over Kenya work together to create
   a. large farms.
   b. educational centers.
   c. new open-air markets.
   d. self-help groups.

_____ 10. Most newcomers to the city are made welcome by
   a. teachers from local schools.
   b. social workers.
   c. government officials.
   d. members of the same ethnic group.

Name _____ Class _____ Date _____

Exploring East Africa

Guiding Questions:

- How have historical events affected the cultures and nations of Africa?
- What factors influence the ways in which Africans make a living?

Ethiopia once included the countries of Eritrea, Djibouti, and Somalia. It contains one of the sources of the Nile River. Its history has been recorded by monks for centuries. It was an ancient center of trade. Egyptian Christians spread their religion into Ethiopia. Roughly 200 years later, the Arabs conquered North Africa but spared Ethiopia. In time, Muslim traders controlled trade in the region and settled along Ethiopia's coast. The Christians became more isolated as they moved inland. Ethiopian Muslims and Christians have lived together peacefully for the most part. Lalibela was the capital of Christian Ethiopia for about 300 years. It is a rural town without electricity or running water. Addis Ababa is the capital and largest city. It has modern conveniences.

Tanzania, to the south of Ethiopia, has long been a center of trade. Tanzania became independent in 1961. Its president, Julius Nyerere, worked to help Tanzania become self-reliant. He made Swahili the national language, so that diverse ethnic groups would all feel part of the new country. To avoid problems between ethnic groups, Nyerere insisted that there be only one political party. He kept peace in Tanzania and greatly improved education. However, he was unable to boost the economy. New leaders changed some of his programs and created a multiparty political system.

Kenya is changing rapidly today. Located in central East Africa, it has areas of good farmland, dry grasslands, and deserts. Most of the people are farmers who live in rural villages. The nation includes more than 40 different ethnic groups, who are primarily Christian or Muslim. Kenya's people value both land and family. In farming villages, most of the women farm for food, while men usually raise cash crops. In order to find work, however, many men are moving to the city. The women left at home must do twice as much work. Women in rural locations have started self-help groups, in which they work together to solve problems in their communities. Men in the city often live with relatives, friends, or members of their ethnic group. Their friendships can make life away from home bearable.

Exploring East Africa

Directions: The underlined words in the following passages are important terms from Chapter 6. Use the space provided to write sentences of your own using the terms or forms of the terms. If necessary, look up the terms in your textbook glossary.

1. Iyasus Moa entered a <u>monastery</u> in Ethiopia to learn about art and become a Christian monk.

_____

_____

_____

2. Swahili is the <u>lingua franca</u> of Tanzania. Two people who speak different first languages can speak Swahili to one another.

_____

_____

_____

3. Many countries borrow money from other countries and create a <u>foreign debt</u>.

_____

_____

_____

4. <u>Harambee</u> was a campaign begun by Jomo Kenyatta to help pull the people of Kenya together.

_____

_____

_____

5. The first elections in Tanzania that were held under the <u>multiparty system</u> occurred in 1995.

_____

_____

_____

Name _____ Class _____ Date _____

Exploring East Africa

Directions: Use the information in your textbook to write one important fact about each topic.

1. The chief religions of Ethiopia

_____

2. Why Ethiopian Christianity developed in a unique way

_____

_____

3. Differences between rural and city life in Ethiopia

_____

_____

4. Nyerere's programs for Tanzania

_____

_____

5. Changes made in Tanzania after Nyerere retired

_____

_____

6. What Kenyans have in common

_____

7. Life in a Kenyan farming village

_____

8. Migration to the cities in Kenya

_____

9. Women's self-help groups in Kenya

_____

10. The life of men in the cities in Kenya

_____

Exploring East Africa

The Kikuyu of Kenya

Directions: Read the following passage about the history of the Kikuyu of Kenya. Then, choose one of the other East African ethnic groups listed below and investigate their history, traditions, or way of life. Write a short summary of your findings.

The Kikuyu, the largest ethnic group in Kenya, have a long history. According to an ancient story, the group was founded by a man named Gikuyu, whose wife had nine daughters. The nine clans of the present-day Kikuyu were named for these daughters.

The Kikuyu had begun to settle in what is now Kenya by the 1400s. During the 1500s, they spread throughout central Kenya. As the Kikuyu clans grew larger, they organized communities that traded with other groups in Kenya. In the 1700s, the Maasai, another East African ethnic group, began moving into Kikuyu territory. However, the Kikuyu maintained control of their land.

In 1895, the British took control of Kenya and began to take away Kikuyu land. The Kikuyu could not defend themselves against the military might of the British. Still, they refused to give up their way of life. In the 1920s, they set up their own independent schools. Students were expected to work hard and achieve high grades. The Kikuyu soon were considered among the best-educated people in Africa.

After World War II, the Kikuyu tried to gain their independence. In the 1950s, they formed armed bands and rebelled against the British. Thousands of Kikuyu were killed or imprisoned. The uprising, however, forced the British to give Kenya self-rule, and finally independence in 1963. Jomo Kenyatta, a prominent Kikuyu leader, became the country's first prime minister. At his prompting, the new Kenyan government began to give land back to the Kikuyu.

Today, the Kikuyu have the most powerful political party in Kenya, the Kenya African Union. Making up about 20 percent of the country's population, they are the largest ethnic group in Kenya. They are also one of the best educated and most prosperous. Many teachers, lawyers, and doctors in Kenya today are Kikuyu.

Other East African Ethnic Groups

Amhara of Ethiopia
Baggara of Sudan
Dinka of Sudan and Ethiopia
Kamba of Tanzania and Kenya
Maasai of Kenya and Tanzania

Chapter and Section Support

Name _____ Class _____ Date _____

Exploring East Africa

Identifying Central Issues

African Music and Dance

Directions: Read the passage. Then list the four main ideas of the passage.

Although African music and dance varies among ethnic groups, there are some common features. One special characteristic of African music and dance is that it is polyrhythmic. *Polyrhythms* are complex combinations of different rhythms played at the same time. Western music typically has two rhythms, and rarely three. African music commonly has five and sometimes as many as twelve. In African dancing, the moves accompany the music. The dancer's body reproduces the polyrhythms of the music. Thus, the head may move in one rhythm, the shoulders in a second, the arms in a third, the trunk in a fourth, and the feet in a fifth.

In most parts of Africa, music is much more a part of daily life than it is in the United States. For example, the Kamba, who live in Kenya and Tanzania, sing while they work at home and in the fields. They often make background music with drums, bells, rattles, and gourds. Choral singing is also widespread in Africa. Singing often takes the pattern of the call-and-response song. A solo singer raises the song and a chorus responds.

The music of East Africa shows distinct Arab and Islamic influences. One sign of this influence is the greater use of stringed instruments in East Africa. The one-string fiddle, for example, was introduced by Arabs.

Main Ideas

1. _____

   _____

2. _____

   _____

3. _____

   _____

4. _____

   _____

Exploring Central and Southern Africa

Social Studies Hot Line

Dear Family,

As our social studies class completes its study of Africa, we will look at the Democratic Republic of Congo and South Africa, two nations in the central and southern region of the continent. We will learn about the importance of mining in Congo, how the country became independent, and what has taken place since independence. In South Africa, we will look at the European influence, particularly that of Dutch settlers, or Afrikaners, and the British. We will study how the small white population held all the power and created the system of apartheid. Finally, we will see how apartheid came to an end in the 1990s.

The changing countries of Congo and South Africa are in the news almost daily. Finding and discussing news reports with your child will add a great deal to our explorations. A trip to the library might help your child find out more about this African region. If you have access to the Internet, you should be able to locate news and other information on-line.

As you find out more, encourage your child to compare life in your community with what you are learning about the region. What things are similar? What are different? You might also talk about the changes that are taking place in these two countries. What are some reasons that change might be so difficult?

Now that we are ending our exploration of Africa, I hope you and your child have enjoyed learning more about this diverse and fascinating continent.

Sincerely,

Democratic Republic of Congo: Rich but Poor

Lesson Objectives

Upon completion of this lesson, students will be able to:
- describe Congo's physical geography and the significance of its natural resources,
- describe Congo's economic and political history.

Engage Motivate Students to Learn

Warm-Up Activity Tell students that developing countries have little in the way of cash resources and rely upon loans from wealthier countries to finance the building of much-needed transportation systems, communications systems, hospitals, and other services. Help students understand that paying back large loans severely strains a developing country's economy.

Activating Prior Knowledge Have students read Reach Into Your Background in the Before You Read box. Ask students to decide which resources on their lists are the most essential. Suggest that students rank each resource according to its importance.

Explore Develop Main Ideas

As students read the section, have them look for answers to the following questions: What are Congo's most important natural resources? How have Congo's abundant natural resources affected the lives of the Congolese? How do other countries benefit from Congo's resources? What have been some of the results of rebellion and changes in leadership?

Teach Solicit Student Participation

Ask students to make time lines that describe important dates and time periods in the economic and political histories of Congo. This activity should take about 25 minutes.

Assess Assess Evidence of Learning

See the answers to the Section Review questions. Students may also demonstrate evidence of learning by completing the Guided Reading and Review and the Section Quiz from the *Teaching Resources.* If students are doing a book project, that may also demonstrate evidence of learning by showing progress on project preparation.

CHAPTER 7
Exploring Central and Southern Africa

Democratic Republic of Congo: Rich but Poor

A. As You Read

Directions: As you read Section 1, fill in the table below with information about Congo.

Facts About Congo

Mining	1. 2. 3.
Physical Features	4. 5.
Natural Resources in History	6. 7. 8.
Mobutu's Rule	9. 10.

B. Reviewing Key Terms

Directions: Fill in the blanks in each sentence below with the correct key term.

11. When Mobutu came to power in Congo, he set up an _____ government, in which he alone had the power to govern.

12. One of the ways in which Mobutu tried to cut all ties with Congo's colonial past was to _____ foreign industries.

Name _____ Class _____ Date _____

Democratic Republic of Congo: Rich but Poor

A. Key Terms and Concepts

Directions: Read the statements below. If a statement is true, write T in the blank provided. If it is false, write F. Rewrite false statements to make them true.

_____ **1.** Congo has huge copper deposits in the southern province of Swahili.

_____

_____ **2.** King Leopold II of Belgium was a brutal ruler of Congo.

_____

_____ **3.** Congo won its independence from France in 1960.

_____

_____ **4.** In a democratic government, a single leader has all the power.

_____

_____ **5.** In Congo, industries that had been owned by foreign companies were nationalized.

_____

B. Main Ideas

Directions: Write the letter of the correct answer in each blank.

_____ **6.** Although most of Congo's people are farmers, most of the country's wealth comes from
    a. forestry.
    b. textiles.
    c. mining.
    d. manufacturing.

_____ **7.** The Europeans first came to what is now Congo because they wanted the country's
    a. gold.
    b. cocoa.
    c. cultural history.
    d. forests.

_____ **8.** What happened to Congo when the price of copper dropped sharply in the late 1970s?
    a. The country's foreign debt decreased.
    b. The prices of many farm exports rose.
    c. The country earned more money from the sale of its major export.
    d. The country's economy collapsed.

_____ **9.** What did Congo's president do when people protested against government cutbacks?
    a. He resigned.
    b. He put his opponents into prison.
    c. He called for a new election.
    d. He changed government policies.

_____ **10.** As many Congolese citizens grew poorer, some middle-class people decided to
    a. leave the country.
    b. form a new political party.
    c. stop paying taxes.
    d. establish a monarchy.

South Africa
The End of Apartheid

Lesson Objectives

Upon completion of this lesson, students will be able to:
- describe the policies and legacy of apartheid,
- identify the challenges that face post-apartheid South Africa.

Engage Motivate Students to Learn

Warm-Up Activity Ask students how many of them are right-handed. Then ask students how they would react to a new school policy that says all right-handed people can occupy only the basement of the school and must always carry special passes. The best learning resources and sports equipment are reserved for left-handed people. Ask students whether they think such a policy would be fair. What would they do to oppose it?

Activating Prior Knowledge Have students read Reach Into Your Background in the Before You Read box. You might invite students to write in their journals about an experience of being unfairly left out.

Explore Develop Main Ideas

Have students read the section. Ask them to consider questions such as the following: What was apartheid? During apartheid, why did black families and white families live so differently? Why was it difficult for black families to improve their lives? What changes were made in South Africa after Nelson Mandela became president?

Teach Solicit Student Participation

Have students create a chart with three columns: *Life Under Apartheid, Life After Apartheid,* and *Reasons for Change.* Ask students to fill in the chart with facts from the section. Use the completed charts as the basis for a discussion of predictions about South Africa's future. This activity should take about 25 minutes.

Assess Assess Evidence of Learning

See the answers to the Section Review questions. Students may also demonstrate evidence of learning by completing the Guided Reading and Review and the Section Quiz from the *Teaching Resources.* If students are doing a book project, that may also demonstrate evidence of learning by showing progress on project preparation.

Name _____ Class _____ Date _____

South Africa
The End of Apartheid

A. As You Read

Directions: As you read Section 2, answer the following questions in the space provided.

1. When did the ancestors of most of today's black South Africans first settle in Southern Africa?

_____

2. What was the name that Dutch settlers used for themselves? What language did they speak?

_____

3. What was the result of British and Dutch wars for control of South Africa?

_____

4. What was stated in the Natives Land Act of 1913?

_____

5. Who created the system of apartheid?

_____

6. What effect did apartheid have on blacks?

_____

7. When blacks protested peacefully, how did the police respond?

_____

8. What leader supported the laws that brought down the apartheid system? Who became South Africa's first elected president?

_____

9. After the end of apartheid, how did jobs for whites and blacks compare?

_____

B. Reviewing Key Terms

Directions: On a separate sheet of paper, write the definition for each key term listed below.

10. apartheid

11. discriminate

12. homeland

CHAPTER 7
Exploring Central and
Southern Africa

South Africa:
The End of Apartheid

A. Key Terms and Concepts

Directions: Fill in the blanks in Column I with the terms in Column II. Write the correct letter in each blank.

Column I

_____ 1. The political system that legalized racial discrimination in South Africa is called _____ .

_____ 2. To treat others unfairly because of race, religion, or gender is to _____ against them.

_____ 3. An area of land where South African blacks were forced to live is called a(n) _____ .

_____ 4. In 1990, the president of South Africa, _____ , helped to change its political system.

_____ 5. On May 5, 1994, _____ was elected president.

Column II

a. apartheid

b. discriminate

c. F. W. de Klerk

d. homeland

e. Nelson Mandela

B. Main Ideas

Directions: Write the letter of the correct answer in each blank.

_____ 6. The Afrikaners are the descendants of
   a. Portuguese settlers in South Africa.
   b. American settlers in South Africa.
   c. Dutch settlers in South Africa.
   d. English settlers in South Africa.

_____ 7. What happened when diamonds and gold were discovered in the Transvaal?
   a. Afrikaners began mining the area.
   b. British prospectors pushed Afrikaners off their farms.
   c. Americans settled in South Africa.
   d. South Africa became a colony of Great Britain.

_____ 8. After 1910, laws passed by the white-led government of South Africa were intended to
   a. keep land and wealth under white control.
   b. help black South Africans work for higher wages.
   c. divide the land equally between white and black citizens.
   d. improve the living conditions of all workers in the country.

_____ 9. How did laws passed by the National Party in 1948 affect the country?
   a. They increased the power of black citizens.
   b. They made discrimination illegal.
   c. They divided South Africans into categories according to race.
   d. They made South Africans rich.

_____ 10. Nelson Mandela's government finally ended
   a. legal discrimination on the basis of race.
   b. economic discrimination.
   c. the political system in South Africa.
   d. laws that affected trade.

Name _____ Class _____ Date _____

Exploring Central and Southern Africa

Guiding Questions:

- What factors led to the development of different governments across Africa?
- What factors influence the ways in which Africans make a living?

The Democratic Republic of Congo, located in west Central Africa, is Africa's third-largest country and one of the world's main sources of copper. Congo has four physical regions: the Congo Basin, the Northern Uplands, the Eastern Highlands, and the Southern Uplands. The landscape includes dense rain forests, savanna, and wooded areas. About two thirds of Congo's people make a living by farming, but most of the nation's wealth comes from mining copper, gold, and diamonds. For hundreds of years, Europeans (primarily Belgians) controlled the country to obtain its resources for profit. In 1960, Congo became an independent nation. After five years of political problems and fighting, Mobutu Sese Seko took control. He set up an authoritarian government and renamed the country Zaire. Mobutu nationalized foreign-owned industries. Poor management and a drop in the world price of copper brought about a collapse in Congo's economy in the late 1970s. The government cut spending, which was especially hard on poor people.

South Africa lies at the southern tip of Africa. The ancestors of today's black South Africans first came to the area about 1,500 years ago. In 1652, Dutch settlers set up a colony in Cape Town. They called themselves Afrikaners. Later, other Europeans settled and fought with the black Africans and with the Dutch. By the late 1800s, the Europeans had forced black Africans off the best land. In 1910, the British gained control of the country and declared it independent. The government of the new nation was entirely white.

In 1948, the Afrikaners won control of the country and began the system of apartheid, or "separateness." Laws divided people into categories by race. Racial discrimination became legal. Apartheid denied nearly all rights to blacks. During the 1950s and 1960s, blacks protested. Many protesters were killed or jailed. The protests continued. Other countries joined the movement against apartheid. Finally, the country began to tear down apartheid. In 1994, all South Africans received the right to vote. Most voted to make Nelson Mandela their president. A black South African, Mandela had spent 28 years in prison for fighting apartheid. Legal discrimination ended. However, real change is coming slowly. Whites still control most of the country's biggest businesses. South Africans are faced with a huge challenge: giving blacks equality while reassuring whites that they will not lose their rights in the process.

Exploring Central and Southern Africa

Directions: Match the key terms in the box with the definitions below. Write the correct letter in each blank. Then write a sentence in the space provided that uses that term or the plural form of the term. If necessary, look up the terms in your textbook glossary or see how they are used in Chapter 7.

a. apartheid	**c.** discriminate	**e.** nationalize
b. authoritarian	**d.** homeland	

_____ **1.** South African area where blacks were forced to live, in the driest and least fertile parts of the country

_____

_____

_____ **2.** ruled by one leader or a small group

_____

_____

_____ **3.** to put under government control

_____

_____

_____ **4.** the South African system in which racial groups were separate; it made racial discrimination legal

_____

_____

_____ **5.** to treat people unfairly based on race, religion, or gender

_____

_____

Name _____ Class _____ Date _____

Exploring Central and Southern Africa

Directions: Use the information in your textbook to complete each statement.

1. Most of Congo's wealth comes from

_____

_____.

2. Foreign companies helped put the military leader Mobutu Sese Seko in power in Congo because

_____

_____.

3. Mobutu took charge by

_____

_____.

4. After Congo's economy collapsed, Mobutu responded by

_____

_____.

5. In South Africa, land and wealth were kept in white hands by

_____

_____.

6. Apartheid affected the lives of blacks by

_____

_____.

7. Apartheid was finally ended because

_____

_____.

8. Despite the end of apartheid, South Africa remains a divided society because

_____

_____.

Exploring Central and Southern Africa

Traditional Zulu Housing

Directions: Read the paragraph and study the diagram. Then answer the questions.

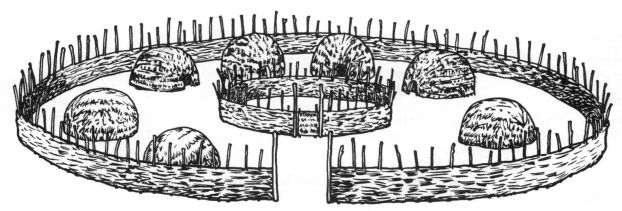

The Zulu make their home in South Africa. Like many other African ethnic groups, the Zulu have long lived in extended families. Traditionally, family members did not live together in one building, however. They had separate, one-room buildings for each person. These buildings were small, with doorways that were not as tall as many people. The houses were dome-shaped and made of straw and grass. They were arranged in a circle around a central pen for the livestock. The entire homestead was surrounded by a fence.

1. What do you think are some of the advantages of the traditional Zulu housing style?

_____

_____

_____

_____

2. From studying their housing, would you think that the Zulu spent a great deal of time outdoors? Why or why not?

_____

_____

_____

_____

CRITICAL THINKING

CHAPTER

7

Exploring Central and Southern Africa

Distinguishing Fact From Opinion

Views of Youth in South Africa

Directions: In the following passages, teenagers in South Africa give their views on the changes in their country since apartheid ended. Read the passages. Then identify the statements that follow as fact or opinion. Write *Fact* or *Opinion* next to each sentence.

Tulani Xakekile
"Not much has changed since the end of apartheid. Change will come, but I don't see it yet. There have been a lot of promises."

Agrineth Lekalakala
"I'd like to go to college. I just finished my exams and I'm waiting for the results. . . . I'll need a scholarship to go.

I'm looking for work while I wait for my test results. I want to work so I can help my family. We have no money. My mother was a nurse, but she had an accident. My father was working but he lost his job. They have to support me, one brother, two sisters—and my mother adopted two children who lost their parents.

Even if I don't get into university, nothing is impossible for me. I feel I can do whatever I feel like doing."

Marianneke Zondstra
"My school used to be all white. Now, it's open to all races. The school is two-thirds white and one-third other races. Most of the others are colored. There are a few blacks. Now I have friends from all races. Three years ago, you were never around them; you didn't even know about them. Now you learn not to judge someone just by how they look."

Carmen Fernandis
"We're able to go to better schools now that apartheid has been abolished. They have far better equipment and far better teaching. The classes are smaller, and teachers can spend time with each student."

_____ **1.** Everything is better in South Africa since apartheid ended.

_____ **2.** People of different races mix more in South Africa since apartheid ended.

_____ **3.** Some blacks in South Africa still lack jobs and enough money.

_____ **4.** The most important thing to South Africans is jobs.

_____ **5.** The most important thing to South Africans is education.

—From *Scholastic Update,* February 25, 1994 issue. Copyright © 1994 by Scholastic Inc. Reprinted by permission of Scholastic Inc.

Answer Key

Chapter 1

Section 1 Guided Reading

1. because the elevation of much of the land is high
2. the Great Rift Valley
3. Nile, Congo, Niger, and Zambezi
4. because the rivers are broken by cataracts, or rock-filled rapids
5. plateau
6. elevation
7. escarpment
8. rift
9. cataract
10. silt
11. fertile
12. tributary

Section 1 Quiz

1. T
2. F; Throughout Africa, the elevation, or height of land above sea level, is high.
3. F; When soil is fertile, many plants will grow in it.
4. T
5. T
6. c   7. a   8. a   9. c   10. a

Section 2 Guided Reading

1. latitude or distance from the Equator
2. elevation
3. unpredictable rainfall
4. tropical rain forests
5. tropical savannas
6. deserts
7. irrigate
8. oasis
9. nomads

Section 2 Quiz

1. c   2. d   3. b   4. a   5. e
6. a   7. b   8. a   9. c   10. d

Section 3 Guided Reading

1. cacao, coffee, barley, wheat, dates, yams, cassava, corn, rice, tea, hardwood trees
2. petroleum, gold, copper, silver, uranium, titanium, diamonds
3. farmers
4. economies
5. foreign companies
6. factories
7. raising crops to support one's family
8. a crop that is raised for sale
9. all the things that people do to make a living in a particular place
10. to add variety

Section 3 Quiz

1. b   2. e   3. d   4. c   5. a
6. b   7. d   8. d   9. c   10. b

Vocabulary Activity

1. i   2. j   3. a   4. e   5. p
6. k   7. n   8. b   9. g   10. l
11. f   12. h   13. d   14. o   15. c   16. m

Reteaching

North Africa
    rocky mountains, Sahara
    Mediterranean, arid, semiarid
    mostly desert and desert scrub
    farmland, petroleum, iron, cobalt, copper
West Africa
    grasslands
    arid, semiarid, tropical wet, tropical wet and dry
    desert, savanna, and rain forest
    farmland, hardwood trees, petroleum, gold, iron

Answer Key

East Africa

   grasslands, hills, mountains, plateaus

   arid, semiarid, tropical wet and dry, highlands

   desert, savanna, and rain forest

   farmland, uranium, hydroelectric power, coal, diamonds

Central and Southern Africa

   flat or rolling grasslands, forests, mountains, swamps, deserts

   tropical wet, tropical wet and dry, arid, semi-arid, marine west coast

   savanna, rain forest, and desert

   farmland, tin, copper, gold, diamonds, coal, iron, hydroelectric power

Enrichment

1. It is the largest split in the Earth's surface that can be seen.

2. It is a deep, long split in the Earth's surface.

3. It was not created by water erosion. It was created by the pulling apart of the Earth's plates. Unlike the Grand Canyon, it is the site of volcanic eruptions and earthquakes. It also has rich farmland, unlike the Grand Canyon.

Critical Thinking

1. deep roots that tap the groundwater

2. long horizontal roots that absorb water over a broad area

3. "rain roots" that grow in response to a shower or to dew

4. leaves that absorb water

5. roots that are covered in mucus and sand to prevent drying out

6. leaves that roll up to reduce evaporation

7. seeds wait for rainfall and then complete their life cycle quickly

Chapter 2

Section 1 Guided Reading

1. hunting animals and gathering food

2. farming and herding, domesticating plants and animals

3. Egypt and Nubia

4. Groups speaking Bantu languages moved from West Africa to find new land in Central and Southern Africa.

5. They brought with them their iron tools, the ideas of farming and herding, and Bantu languages.

6. hunter-gatherer

7. domesticate

8. surplus

9. civilization

10. migrate

11. ethnic group

Section 1 Quiz

1. T

2. F; When early communities produced a food surplus, they had more food than they needed.

3. F; Stone Age farming groups eventually became civilizations, which are societies with cities, governments, and social classes.

4. F; Groups of people who spoke Bantu languages decided to migrate, or move, from West Africa.

5. F; People who share the same language, religion, and customs form an ethnic group.

6. c   7. b   8. c   9. b   10. d

Section 2 Guided Reading

1. Christianity

2. gold for salt

3. Many Muslims traveled here and introduced the religion of Islam.

4. trade

5. the Indian Ocean

Answer Key

6. Quran
7. pilgrimage
8. Swahili
9. city-states

Section 2 Quiz

1. F; The holy book of the religion of Islam is the Quran.
2. T
3. T
4. F; A new language called Swahili, which was a mix of Arab words and a Bantu language, developed in East Africa.
5. F; A city that has its own government and controls much of the surrounding land is a city-state.
6. b   7. b   8. d   9. b   10. d

Section 3 Guided Reading

Answers may vary. Sample answers are given.

1. lateen sail, astrolabe
2. European traders set up trading posts and traded for gold, ivory and other products in Ghana, Mali, East Africa, and other coastal areas.
3. Europeans enslaved Africans to work in colonies in the Americas.
4. The youngest, healthiest, and most capable African workers were taken away.
5. Europeans took African resources for their own profit.
6. Europeans did not allow Africans to participate in government.
7. Europeans colonized many parts of the continent and took the best farmland.
8. Europeans forced Africans to work. Europeans drew new political boundaries that divided some ethnic groups and forced some differing groups to live together, creating conflict.
9. to settle an area and take over or create a government

Section 3 Quiz

1. d   2. a   3. e   4. b   5. c

6. b   7. a   8. b   9. d   10. b

Section 4 Guided Reading

1. The borders forced some old rivals to live in the same country.
2. They would have to build a spirit of togetherness among all groups.
3. a movement that stressed unity among all Africans that began in the 1920s
4. After fighting for freedom in Europe, they returned home wanting their own freedom.
5. They won a war that lasted for eight years.
6. The colonial powers had rarely allowed Africans to share in government; new leaders were not prepared.
7. nationalism
8. Pan-Africanism
9. boycott
10. democracy

Section 4 Quiz

1. d   2. e   3. a   4. b   5. c
6. b   7. d   8. c   9. d   10. a

Section 5 Guided Reading and Review

1. Many countries depend on exporting one or two products; many have little industry; some may have difficulty feeding growing populations.
2. Countries are diversifying their economies and helping farmers to grow more.
3. Many children must work to help their families; there is not always enough money to build schools; schools are often overcrowded.
4. Families sacrifice so their children can go to school; families help build new schools; students take turns attending schools.
5. Problems include a growing desert, decreasing forests, and soil erosion.
6. Countries are planting trees and vegetables, developing irrigation projects, and trying new crops.
7. subsistence farming

Answer Key

8. commercial farming

9. hybrid

10. literacy

11. life expectancy

Section 5 Quiz

1. F; The large-scale production of crops such as coffee, cocoa, and bananas is called commercial farming.

2. T

3. F; When farmers combine two or more types of the same plant, a hybrid results.

4. T

5. T

6. b 7. c   8. b   9. c   10. c

Vocabulary Activity

Answers: Sentences will vary. Sample answers are given.

1. The angry citizens staged a boycott and would not buy any foreign products.

2. There were several powerful city-states in East Africa that controlled large areas of land.

3. About 5,000 years ago, a civilization with cities and a government arose on the Nile River.

4. During the 1800s, Europeans thought they had the right to colonize, or take over, African lands.

5. Commercial farms often produce crops such as bananas, cocoa, and coffee for export.

6. Many African countries have a long history of democracy, while others do not allow citizens many rights.

7. When people learned to domesticate plants and animals, they could begin farming.

8. In Africa, there are hundreds of ethnic groups that share languages, religions, and customs.

9. The earliest humans were hunter-gatherers and had not yet learned to plant crops.

10. Scientists try to help farmers by developing hybrids of plants to increase crops.

11. Life expectancy differs among countries, depending upon health care and living conditions.

12. The literacy rate, or the ability to read and write, has greatly increased in Tanzania, .

13. When people want a better life, they may migrate to a new location.

14. Many Africans had strong feelings of nationalism when subjected to foreign rule.

15. The slogan of Pan-Africanism during the 1920s was "Africa for Africans."

16. One of the five important parts of Islam is to take a pilgrimage to Mecca.

17. Muslims base their laws on the teachings found in the Quran.

18. When farmers have surplus crops, they can sell or trade what they do not need.

19. Many people in East Africa speak Swahili today.

Reteaching

1. Great civilizations arise in Egypt and Nubia.

2. Bantus migrate from West Africa to Central and Southern Africa, bringing with them farming, herding, and iron tools.

3. Trade gives rise to wealthy West African kingdoms and East African city-states; Muslim traders spread Islam to West and East Africa.

4. Africa loses its most capable workers to the European slave trade.

5. Europeans colonize Africa, causing divisions among ethnic groups.

6. Africans unite to gain independence from European rule.

Enrichment

Students' paragraphs will vary, but should focus on how Sundiata overcame his physical handicap, developed his strength, fought back to regain his father's kingdom, and ruled with wisdom.

Critical Thinking

Answers will vary. Sample answers are given.

Answer Key

1. a mayor and council; The public votes. Candidates with the most votes win positions. The council votes and a majority wins. The mayor makes some decisions with the advice of aides.

2. One major difference is that traditional African villages were ruled by elders, while American cities and towns have elections to choose leaders. Another difference is that the African system emphasizes a consensus in reaching decisions, while the American system operates under majority rule.

3. African—elders would probably make wise and reasonable leaders because of their life experience, and people would tend to follow through on their decisions because they were reached by consensus; American—system accommodates a larger number of people and allows for younger, perhaps more change-oriented leaders.

4. African—decisions might take a long time to reach and elders might tend to follow tradition and resist change; American—system is less personal, may lack continuity because of frequent change of leaders, and may not value tradition enough.

Chapter 3

Section 1 Guided Reading

1. More than 95 percent of North Africans are Muslims.
2. Based on the Quran, Islamic law governs all aspects of life, including family life, business, banking, and government.
3. Most are Arabs; other groups include Berbers.
4. Cultural ideas move around with travelers and through conquest.
5. North Africa's location on the Mediterranean makes it a hub of trade and allows influences from cultures of Europe, Asia, and Africa.
6. culture
7. Quran
8. ethnic group
9. cultural diffusion

Section 1 Quiz

1. c   2. b   3. d   4. e   5. a
6. b   7. c   8. c   9. c   10. b

Section 2 Guided Reading

Answers may vary. Possible answers are given. Accept all thoughtful and factual answers.

1. West Africa contains 17 countries and hundreds of different ethnic groups.
2. There is no single religion or language for the people of West Africa.
3. Many West Africans live in extended families.
4. Many West African families share common ancestors and have kinship ties with others in clans and lineages.
5. cultural diversity
6. kinship
7. nuclear family
8. extended family
9. lineage
10. clan
11. griot

Section 2 Quiz

1. b   2. e   3. c   4. d   5. a
6. b   7. c   8. a   9. c   10. d

Section 3 Guided Reading

1. its location, because it has a long coastline on the Indian Ocean, which connects it with Arabs and Asians
2. Africans who have mixed Bantu and Arab ancestry. They live along the East African coast from Somalia to Mozambique.
3. They are trying to preserve their African heritage.
4. Islam and Christianity
5. They used the land but did not own it; nobody bought or sold land.
6. European settlers

Answer Key

7. They were broken up and sold to individual Africans.

8. They feel a strong bond to it.

9. They will name the village of their family or clan.

10. plantations

Section 3 Quiz

1. e   2. d   3. c   4. b   5. a
6. c   7. a   8. d   9. b   10. c

Section 4 Guided Reading

1. migrating to South Africa to work in the mines

2. struggle for majority rule

3. hunting and gathering in some rural areas; working in factories, offices, and hotels

4. living in cities

5. a group's identity as members of a particular nation

6. a person who moves from place to place to work

Section 4 Quiz

1. F; An important political party in South Africa is the African National Congress.

2. F; The country of South Africa has had a great impact on the region.

3. T

4. F; People who move from place to place to work are called migrant workers.

5. F; The country of Congo in Central Africa has many ethnic groups.

6. b   7. b   8. b   9. c   10. d

Vocabulary Activity

1. h   2. k   3. j   4. a   5. l   6. b
7. g   8. c   9. e   10. f   11. d   12. i

Reteaching

Answers will vary. Sample answers are given.

A. Most North Africans are Muslims, and Islam forms a common bond of culture among the people.

B. Because of its Mediterranean location, North Africa has been a hub of trade as well as a place of conquest, both of which have caused the mixing of cultures.

A. West Africa has hundreds of ethnic groups that speak different languages. West Africans also have many ways of making a living.

B. West Africans maintain strong kinship bonds with their extended families and sometimes with their clans, though urbanization is changing family life.

A. Arab traders settled in East Africa, and their culture mixed with various African cultures, producing Swahili culture. Swahili serves as the second language of millions of East Africans.

B. Africans did not know the concept of land ownership until Europeans introduced it in the 1800s. Now land is privately owned. East Africans, no matter where they live, consider the village of their family or clan as home.

A. The long struggle for majority rule in South Africa inspired similar movements in nearby countries. To meet its economic needs, South Africa drew migrant workers from nearby countries and built a transportation system throughout the region. The migrant workers formed a new group identity and took political action.

B. Central Africa is culturally diverse, with a mixture of traditional and modern ways of life.

Enrichment

1. brass, wood, clay

2. people

3. somewhat abstract

4. Answers will vary. Most are decorative, but some could be used in ceremonies.

5. Answers will vary.

Critical Thinking

Students should mark an X before sentences 1, 4, 5, 6, and 8.

Answer Key

Chapter 4

Section 1 Guided Reading

1. They fast from dawn to dusk, think about those who are less fortunate, and try not to get angry when things go wrong.

2. that it contains the words of God, which were revealed to Muhammad during the month of Ramadan

3. five times a day

4. The Sharia is Islamic law. It is based on the Quran, on the words and deeds of Muhammad, and on comments written by Muslim scholars and lawmakers.

5. Egyptian Muslims disagree over whether most or all of Egypt's laws should match Islamic law. Some people believe that women are required by Islamic law to wear a veil over their faces; others do not.

6. Cairo is very crowded, with much traffic and housing shortages; some people live in tents or on rowboats on the Nile, others in huge graveyards.

7. along the Nile

8. Most are made of mud bricks or stones and are small, with one to three rooms and flat roofs.

9. their faith in Islam

10. Muslims

11. fellaheen

12. bazaar

Section 1 Quiz

| 1. b | 2. a | 3. c | 4. e | 5. d |
| 6. d | 7. b | 8. b | 9. b | 10. c |

Section 2 Guided Reading

Answers may vary. Sample answers are provided. Accept all thoughtful and accurate answers.

1. Most live in rural villages in extended families.

2. They base their government on families, farm and herd, and build terraces to increase farmland.

3. They came to North Africa in the A.D. 600s and slowly conquered the area.

4. They live in extended families, have a central Islamic government, and traditionally were nomads.

5. Some people are farmers; some are nomads.

6. There is a mix of Berbers and Arabs; most are Muslims; some Berbers have kept their ways, others have mixed Islam and African religions.

7. Berbers and Arabs in the cities have the most in common with each other.

8. There are mosques and markets (souqs); older parts of cities are called casbahs, which have narrow winding streets; there are also modern sections.

9. an earthen platform cut into the side of a mountain, used for growing crops in steep places

10. open-air marketplace

11. older parts of the cities

Section 2 Quiz

| 1. b | 2. c | 3. e | 4. a | 5. d |
| 6. b | 7. c | 8. b | 9. c | 10. d |

Vocabulary Activity

Answers will vary. Sample answers are given.

1. a; In Egypt, many people shop for food and clothing at the bazaar.

2. c; In Algeria, mountain farmers use terraces to grow crops on steep slopes.

3. b; Some fellaheen farm small, rented plots of land, and others work in the fields of rich landowners.

Reteaching

1. Islam

2. whether or not all Egyptian laws should be based on Islamic law

3. apartment buildings, tents on rowboats on the Nile, and homes built on graveyards

4. one- to three-room homes of mud bricks or stones with a courtyard that is shared with animals

5. family. The head of each family is a member of the village assembly.

Answer Key

6. farming and herding

7. extended families

8. Islam

9. farming; nomadic

10. houses and stores close together on narrow streets; tall buildings and wide streets

Enrichment

Descriptions will vary. A sample response is given.

A typical mosque has one or more minarets, or towers. From a minaret, a muezzin calls Muslims to prayer. At the center of a mosque is a courtyard. Around the courtyard are four arched halls called iwans, and several entrances. One entrance is topped by a dome.

Critical Thinking

Answers will vary.

Chapter 5

Section 1 Guided Reading

1. many ethnic groups, including the Hausa, the Fulani, the Yoruba, and the Igbo

2. 1960; Great Britain

3. The capital was moved from the city of Lagos in the south to Abuja in the central portion of the country. The new location was close to more than one ethnic group; the government was trying to help unify the country.

4. by trading

5. Kano; for over a thousand years

6. Lagos; the European slave trade

7. by farming

8. with a democratic council of elders

9. For three days, no one could enter or leave the country or change location between the hours of 7:00 A.M. and 7:00 P.M.

10. Because the ethnic group with the largest population would have the most political power.

11. containing many ethnic groups

12. a count of all the people in a country

Section 1 Quiz

1. T

2. F; In 1991, the Nigerian government moved the nation's capital from Lagos, in the south, to Abuja, in central Nigeria.

3. F; The Hausa and the Fulani together make up about 32 percent of Nigeria's people.

4. T

5. F; The Igbo rule themselves with a democratic council of elders.

6. b   7. b   8. c   9. b   10. d

Section 2 Guided Reading

Answers will vary. Sample answers are given. Accept all thoughtful and accurate answers.

1. He believed in independence from Great Britain.

2. He thought that the people of Ghana should benefit from their own wealth.

3. He believed that the people of Ghana could rule themselves.

4. He led his people to independence.

5. introduction of new technology

6. political change

7. economic problems, then a growing economy

8. renewal of traditional culture

9. sovereignty

10. coup

Section 2 Quiz

1. e   2. b   3. a   4. d   5. c
6. c   7. a   8. b   9. c   10. a

Section 3 Guided Reading

Answers may vary. Accept all thoughtful and accurate answers.

1. The Sahara covers one third of Mali.

2. The desert is growing.

3. Few people live in the Sahara, more in the Sahel, and some in the savanna grasslands.

Answer Key

4. a zone between desert and savanna, stretches through the middle of Mali and 11 other African countries

5. Its grasslands have supported grazing for thousands of years.

6. is home to the trading center for salt caravans in the city of Tombouctou

7. possibly caused by overgrazing, drought, or both

8. destroying usable land through soil erosion

9. causing people to leave their homelands and change how they survive

10. desertification

11. drought

12. erode

Section 3 Quiz

1. e   2. c   3. a   4. b   5. d
6. c   7. b   8. a   9. d   10. c

Vocabulary Activity

1. Nigeria is an example of a multiethnic country because there are many ethnic groups living there.

2. A census is taken to count the number of people in a country.

3. In 1957, Great Britain agreed to grant sovereignty to the people of Ghana, who were given independence.

4. After the military coup, the government changed hands.

5. Desertification has been changing fertile land into desert for years.

6. Animals may help to erode the soil by overgrazing.

7. An ethnic group contains people who have the same language and religion.

8. A drought takes place when there is too little or no rainfall.

Reteaching

1. It includes Hausaland, Yorubaland, and Igboland.

Its capital was moved to Abuja to be closer to different ethnic groups.

It has the Kurmi Market in Kano, one of the largest trading centers in Africa.

Here the Igbo traditionally rule themselves with a democratic council of elders.

2. It was called the Gold Coast.

It was the first African colony south of the Sahara to become independent.

Its economy has improved with the promotion of the traditional African values of hard work and sacrifice.

3. The Sahara and Sahel cover most of the country.

Trading, herding, and farming are threatened by desertification.

Tombouctou, once a wealthy center of learning and business, is slowly being covered in sand.

Enrichment

Answers will vary. Sample responses are given.

1. People are naturally different and should not be expected to be the same.

2. A person may wait a long time for chance, or luck, to bring good things; one has to go after or work for good things.

3. People criticize what they do not understand.

4. You sleep soundly or a lot.

5. Be willing to take the bad with the good.

6. In an argument, the one who forgives wins.

7. If a person is not in want, he or she does not understand what it is like for those who are.

8. Don't expect people to do things they are not capable of doing.

Critical Thinking

Answers will vary. Sample answers are given.

1. According to the authors, most newspapers are biased toward sensational stories about Africa that focus on disaster.

2. Answers will vary.

Answer Key

Chapter 6

Section 1 Guided Reading

Answers may vary. Possible answers are given.
Accept all thoughtful and accurate answers.

1. spread to Ethiopia from Egyptian Coptic Church
2. isolated from Christianity and the rest of the world
3. became a unique form of Christianity
4. Arabs did not invade Ethiopia but conquered surrounding areas.
5. Muslim traders came to Ethiopia and brought Islam with them.
6. capital of Christian Ethiopia for about 300 years
7. no electricity or telephones
8. people live by farming, herding cattle, or fishing
9. present capital of Ethiopia
10. modern city with a traditional rural section
11. monastery

Section 1 Quiz

1. F; A place where priests live, work, and study is called a monastery.
2. T
3. F; Lalibela was the capital of Christian Ethiopia for about 300 years.
4. F; The capital of Ethiopia is Addis Ababa.
5. T
6. c   7. a   8. a   9. c   10. d

Section 2 Guided Reading

1. by making Swahili the national language
2. He created one political party for all elections in order to avoid parties being based on ethnic groups.
3. that it meant "freedom and work"; that only through hard work could the country end poverty
4. The word *ujamaa* means "togetherness" or "being a family." Ujamaa villages were part of

Nyerere's self-reliance plan. Many families were asked to move from their scattered family homesteads to villages where it was easier for the government to provide education and clean water.
5. He kept peace in Tanzania and greatly improved education.
6. Tanzania's new leaders ended it.
7. They said that farmers should put more effort into growing cash crops.
8. It became a multiparty system.
9. literacy
10. foreign debt
11. multiparty system

Section 2 Quiz

1. e   2. a   3. b   4. d   5. c
6. d   7. c   8. a   9. c   10. b

Section 3 Guided Reading

1. Most are indigenous Africans, including more than 40 different ethnic groups—each with its own culture and language. Most Kenyans are Christian or Muslim. A few people are of European or Asian descent.
2. They value land and family.
3. Example: the government pays for part of a child's education, but the people often work together to build and support schools.
4. women
5. carrying water, milking cows and goats, cleaning their homes before going to school
6. play soccer and dodgeball, make toy cars, dolls, and other toys; once in a while watch a movie
7. Many people are moving from the country to the city to find work.
8. men; The men in the cities often become homesick for their loved ones and homes; the women at home must do twice as much work.
9. by starting self-help groups; The women grow cash crops in addition to their own food; they use the cash for such group projects as building nursery schools, installing water pipes in the village, and making loans.

Answer Key

10. They often welcome each other, share rooms, and help each other.

11. Both the city man and the country man are part of him; he can be comfortable in both places; the city has not stopped him from being a Maasai.

12. harambee

Section 3 Quiz

1. e	2. c	3. a	4. b	5. d
6. c	7. b	8. c	9. d	10. d

Vocabulary Activity

Answers: Sentences will vary. Sample answers are given.

1. The students of Iyasus Moa built monasteries and schools throughout Ethiopia.

2. A lingua franca makes it possible for people who speak different first languages to talk to one another.

3. In order to help their economy, the leaders of Tanzania have created a huge foreign debt.

4. As part of harambee, the government paid for some of each child's education and the people helped build schools.

5. After the government started the multiparty system, there were people from more than ten parties running in the election.

Reteaching

Answers will vary. Sample answers are given.

1. The majority of Ethiopians are either Muslim or Christian.

2. As Muslim Arabs took over Ethiopia's coastal regions, Ethiopian Christians moved inland, became surrounded by Muslims, and had little contact with Christians elsewhere.

3. In rural areas, people do not have electricity, telephones, or cars; in the cities, there is a mix of modern and traditional ways of life.

4. Nyerere made Swahili the national language, established a one-party system, and asked farmers to move to ujamaa villages.

5. Tanzania's new leaders ended ujamaa and allowed a multiparty system.

6. Most Kenyans are indigenous Africans, are farmers, value the land, and value their families.

7. Men raise cash crops, women raise food crops and herd livestock, and the children help with the work.

8. As the population grows, many men are moving to the cities to find work, while the women stay in the villages to raise and support their children.

9. The women left behind in the villages grow cash crops, save the money as a group, and use the money to improve the villages and help one another.

10. Men from the same ethnic group share rooms and help one another.

Critical Thinking

1. A special feature of the music and dance of Africa is that it is polyrhythmic.

2. In most parts of Africa, music is much more a part of daily life than it is in the United States.

3. Choral singing is widespread in Africa.

4. The music of East Africa shows Arab and Islamic influences.

Chapter 7

Section 1 Guided Reading

Answers may vary. Possible answers are given. Accept all thoughtful and accurate answers.

1. Copper mining began in ancient times.

2. Congo has become one of the world's main sources of copper.

3. Congo also mines gold and diamonds.

4. third largest country in Africa

5. four major regions: Congo Basin (rain forest), Northern Uplands (savanna), Eastern Highlands (savanna, forests), Southern Uplands (grasslands, woods)

Answer Key

6. The power of the early kingdoms was based on knowledge of ironworking.

7. Belgians forced the harvest of wild rubber for Belgian profit.

8. Later Belgians mined copper and diamonds.

9. Mobutu was a military leader who established an authoritarian government and nationalized industries

10. after years of economic problems a rebellion began and a new government was established

11. authoritarian

12. nationalize

Section 1 Quiz

1. F; Congo has huge copper deposits in the southern province of Katanga.

2. T

3. F; Congo won its independence from Belgium in 1960.

4. F; In an authoritarian government, a single leader or small group of leaders has all the power.

5. T

6. c   7. a   8. d   9. b   10. a

Section 2 Guided Reading

1. 1,500 years ago

2. Afrikaners; Afrikaans

3. Britain won and declared South Africa an independent country in 1910.

4. Blacks could live in only 8 percent of the country; blacks could work in white areas for very low wages, but could not own land there.

5. the Afrikaner's political party, the National Party

6. It restricted where blacks could live; denied rights to citizenship and the vote; kept them in low-paying jobs and inferior schools; and barred them from white restaurants, schools, and hospitals.

7. They killed hundreds of men, women, and children, and threw thousands more in jail.

8. F. W. de Klerk; Nelson Mandela

9. Whites still controlled most of the biggest businesses and newspapers; whites had better-paying jobs and owned more property.

10. South African system in which racial groups were separate

11. to treat people unfairly based on race, religion, or gender

12. South African land where blacks were forced to live, in the driest and least fertile parts of the country

Section 2 Quiz

1. a   2. b   3. d   4. c   5. e
6. c   7. b   8. a   9. c   10. a

Vocabulary Activity

Answers will vary. Sample answers are given.

1. d; South African whites forced blacks to live in 10 homelands located throughout the country.

2. b; Mobutu Sese Seko was a strong leader in Congo who set up an authoritarian government.

3. e; Mobutu Sese Seko nationalized all of the industries in Congo that were owned by foreign companies.

4. a; The apartheid system of South Africa is no longer in use.

5. c; In South Africa under apartheid, it was legal to discriminate against people based on race.

Reteaching

1. mining copper, gold, diamonds, and other minerals

2. they thought their businesses would thrive with a strong ruler in control

3. setting up an authoritarian government, renaming the country Zaire, nationalizing industries, and borrowing money to build more industries

4. cutting government spending and throwing protestors into prison

Answer Key

5. a system of laws called apartheid, which made racial discrimination legal

6. denying them citizenship rights, keeping them in low-paying jobs and inferior schools, and barring them from public places reserved for whites

7. the protests, demonstrations, and trade bans began to have an effect and caused South Africa's President, F. W. de Klerk, to push through laws ending apartheid

8. blacks and whites live in different neighborhoods, whites still control most businesses and newspapers, and whites still have better-paying jobs and more property than blacks

Enrichment

Answers will vary. Sample answers are given.

1. Each family member had privacy, but family members were still close. The livestock were protected. The houses were easy to build and were made of materials that were nearby.

2. Yes, it would seem that they spent a great deal of time outdoors because their houses were small and did not have different rooms for different purposes.

Critical Thinking

1. Opinion
2. Fact
3. Fact
4. Opinion
5. Opinion

Teacher Notes   2

Activity Atlas
Discovery Activities About Africa   3

Activity Shop Lab
Desertification   6

Activity Shop Interdisciplinary
The Language of Music   7

Book Projects
Africa on Stage   8
Africa in Art   11
Africa 2000   14

Cooperative Learning Activities
Simulation: Magazine Article on an
    African River   17
Oral Report on an Ancient African
    Kingdom   21
Telling a Traditional African Story   25
Writing About the Cities of North Africa   29
Arts and Crafts of West Africa   33
Mural of East African Architecture   37
Musical Instruments of Central and
    Southern Africa   41

Grading Rubrics
Assessment of a Written Presentation   45
Assessment of an Oral Presentation   46
Assessment of a Visual Display   47
Assessment of a Model   48

Answer Key   49

Activities and Projects

Teacher Notes

To meet the needs of middle school students, **Prentice Hall World Explorer** includes activities designed for all learning styles. Every day, you encounter students who bring a wide range of skills and abilities to the classroom. You as teacher make choices about the kinds of activities that best complement your teaching plan. This booklet is designed to make it easy for you to incorporate hands-on activities into your classroom.

With support offered in this booklet, students can work independently or in cooperative groups to perform a variety of interesting and meaningful projects. For the Activity Atlas and Activity Shops, this booklet provides recording sheets, templates for graphs or charts, and helpful background information. For the Project Possibilities described in the student text, this booklet includes a section called Book Projects that offers ideas for breaking down and organizing each task.

In addition, this booklet includes cooperative learning activities for each chapter in the book. At least one of the cooperative activities is a simulation, in which students concentrate on a real-life issue. Each cooperative activity is four pages long and includes one or two student pages, one or two teacher pages, and a rubric page. The concept and skill objectives for each cooperative learning activity are clearly stated in the teacher page supporting each activity. You can customize your assignments, using particular projects to meet the needs of specific groups of students.

At the end of this booklet are four general grading rubrics for written and oral presentations, visual displays, and models. There is also an answer key for the student pages in this booklet.

Prentice Hall World Explorer offers a wide and exciting range of options to students. Use this booklet to help you take advantage of those options.

Discovery Activities About Africa

Explore Africa's Location and Size

Directions: Use this worksheet to record the relative locations and sizes of Africa and the United States.

1. What ocean lies between Africa and the United States?

_____

2. What role might the Equator play in the climates of nearby countries?

_____

3. How do you think the climates of the United States might differ from the climates of Africa? Why?

_____

4. How many times can you fit the map of the United States inside the map of Africa?

_____

Bonus!

• About how many miles apart are Casablanca, Morocco, and Washington, D.C.?

_____

• About how many miles apart are Washington, D.C., and San Francisco, California?

_____

• About how many miles apart are Casablanca and Cape Town, South Africa?

_____

Activities and Projects

Discovery Activities About Africa

Find Geo Cleo

Directions: Use this worksheet to complete the Geo Cleo activity in your textbook Activity Atlas. Fill in the name of the city that is described in each of Geo Cleo's radio messages.

1. "I'm in a region of tall grasses and few trees, or a savanna. I've landed in a city in Ethiopia near 10°N and 40°E." The city is named

   _____.

2. "Not too many places in Africa have Mediterranean vegetation. And I'm not even anywhere near the Mediterranean Sea! I am flying over a city on a very narrow coastal plain. The cliffs here are *really* steep." The city is named

   _____.

3. "Today, I flew above tropical rain forests growing right along the Equator. Going north, I saw these magnificent forests change into open grasslands, or savanna. I've just landed in a city in the savanna region north of where the Benue River meets the Niger River." The city is named

   _____.

   ### Bonus!

   - Write two messages that could have been sent by Geo Cleo. Each message should identify a city in Africa without naming it.

   _____
   _____
   _____
   _____
   _____
   _____
   _____
   _____
   _____
   _____

Discovery Activities About Africa

Analyze Temperatures Across the Continent

Directions: Use this worksheet to complete the Temperatures Across the Continent activity in your textbook Activity Atlas.

1. What are the average temperatures in the Sahara?

_____

2. What are the average temperatures in the Sahel?

_____

3. How do the temperatures in southern countries differ from those in countries located along the Equator?

_____

4. Why do you think the temperatures in extreme northern and southern parts of Africa are similar?

_____

Bonus!

- Compare the temperature map with the vegetation map in the Activity Atlas. How do you think temperature affects the vegetation found in the Sahara?

_____

_____

_____

_____

Activities and Projects

Desertification

Directions: Use this worksheet to answer questions and record results as you do the Activity Shop Lab in your textbook.

Procedure

1. In Step Two, the model represents wind blowing sand across good, grassy land. About how much sand gets caught in the grass?

   _____

2. In Step Three, the grass is thinner. How much sand is in the sod this time?

   _____

3. During Step Four, most of the grass is gone. How much sand is in the sod now? How does the sand affect the soil?

   _____

Observations

1. What happened to the sand as it blew across the grass?

   _____

2. What happened to the remaining grass and topsoil as the sand blew across the "overgrazed" sod?

   _____

Analysis and Conclusion

1. Why do you think it is important to people living in the Sahel to slow desertification?

   _____

The Language of Music

Directions: Use this worksheet to plan how you will build and use your drum as you do the Activity Shop Interdisciplinary in your textbook.

1. Research African Drums

a. Some types of African drums: _____

_____

_____

_____

b. My model drum: _____

c. Where drum is used: _____

2. Build Your Own Drum

a. Materials the drum is traditionally made from: _____

_____

b. Materials I could make my drum out of: _____

_____

c. How I will strike my drum: _____

3. Play Your Drum

a. How the drum is traditionally used: _____

_____

_____

_____

b. How I will use my drum: _____

_____

BOOK PROJECT

Africa on Stage

A. Choosing a Setting for Your Play

Which location in Africa will you choose? Which part of Africa did you find the most interesting? Is there a place that you would like to visit or even stay for a few years? You might look at a map of Africa to refresh your memory about the places you have studied. About which people did you learn the most? Where do they live?

Choose one or two locations to begin. Then narrow your choice to the one you think will work best. Use the chart below to record ideas for the location of your play.

African Locations

City or County	Region	Urban or Rural Area	Climate	Physical Features	Vegetation

Choose the location that you would most like to use for your play.

Africa on Stage

AFRICA

B. Creating Characters

Now that you have chosen a location for your play, it's time to think about who lives there. What are their lives like? Before you begin to write down your ideas, try finding more information about the area from library books and other resources. When you have a good sense about the people who live in this place, make notes about a few characters. Think of important details for each character.

You can use this chart to record your ideas. This will help you create your characters. Remember, the more details you think of, the better you will know each character.

Characters

Name and Age	Work	Hobbies	Home	Physical Features	Personality

Use the information on the chart when you begin to write.

Activities and Projects

BOOK PROJECT

Africa on Stage

C. Creating a Plot

You know the setting and characters for your play. What events could happen to these people? Are there problems they may have to solve? What things do they do during a normal day? How do the characters relate to each other?

Record ideas for plot events on the chart below. Think of three or four possible plots. In this way, you will have plenty of ideas when you begin to write your script.

Plot Events

Problem	Character(s) It Affects	Solution

Africa in Art

A. An Introduction to African Masks

Have you ever worn a mask? If you have, it was probably part of a costume for a special event or performance. Africans use masks in similar ways. They wear them for theater or dance performances, or for special events such as festivals or burials. Africans sometimes also wear masks while telling stories or teaching.

Often, the wearer of a mask starts a formal dance and then begins to improvise. Among the Yoruba of Nigeria and Benin, an Efe mask dancer arrives at midnight during a festival. The mask wearer dances while singing words that honor the community leaders. Then the Efe dancer begins telling jokes about events that have happened in the past year. Yoruba dancers for another festival begin with acrobatic stunts. Then they make fun of politicians, wrongdoers, and strangers, using dance and mime.

The person who makes a mask may carve it to look like a wild animal, a person, a dead ancestor, or even a disease. The carver must know whether the mask will be used in a dance. If it is, the mask must be lightweight and easy to move around in. If the mask will be used for decoration, it can be heavier. Africans make masks out of the materials that are available. They often use wood, cloth, or fiber for most of the mask. Once a mask is made, the mask-maker can decorate it using animal horns, porcupine quills, paint, shells, or beads.

Luba mask

Southern Igbo Ekpe mask

Teke (Bateke) mask

BOOK PROJECT

Africa in Art

B. Sources of Information About African Masks

In your library, you will probably find books about African countries, specific peoples of Africa, and African arts. Use the chart below to record information that you find. Be sure to record the sources so that you can easily find each one again if necessary.

Information and Sources

Source	Materials Used to Make Masks	How Masks Are Made	How Masks Are Used

Africa in Art

AFRICA

C. Creating a Mini-Museum Display

Think about the last time you went to a museum. What did you notice about the exhibits? Were they easy to understand? Did you enjoy looking at them? Now you have a chance to create your own display. What can you do to make it fun to look at and full of interesting information?

Materials

paper
cardboard
markers, crayons, paints
tape

photographs or photocopies of
    African masks
glue

Procedure

You might want to work in small groups on different displays. Each group can divide the jobs among its members. Be sure that each of you has an important job to do. Jobs can include drawing or painting pictures of masks, writing information, and putting the display together.

Use the chart below to record how you will share the work. In the spaces below each job you can write notes and comments to help you plan and finish the display.

When you are finished, share your work with the rest of the class.

Mini-Museum Display Jobs

Drawing or Painting	Writing	Making the Display

Activities and Projects

BOOK PROJECT

Africa 2000

A. Choosing Topics for Africa 2000

What topics would you like to include in the conference? Think of ideas that would be particularly interesting to other students. For example, you might have a presentation of music from different parts of Africa. Or you might decide to compare the economies of two or three African countries. If you need help thinking of ideas, review the text and read other books about Africa.

As you think of possible topics, write them in the chart below. Then add interesting information about the topic. Use the information on the chart to choose the topics that you think will work best for Africa 2000.

Africa 2000—Possible Topics

Topic	Information About the Topic

Africa 2000

B. Planning: **Conference Committees**

Working with others is a great way to get things done. A group can complete a job that would be too much for one person.

Once you have chosen the topics for the conference, divide the class into committees. Each committee will organize one part of the conference. Meet with your committee to plan how you will complete your jobs. Make sure that everyone has a job. Use the chart below to record the committee names, which students are on each one, and the jobs that need to be done.

Committees	Members' Names	What Needs to Be Done
Speakers		
Scheduling		
Publicity		
Food		
Press		
Other		

Activities and Projects

BOOK PROJECT

Africa 2000

C. Planning: Preparing for the Conference

When all the committees are ready, meet as a class to discuss final preparations for the conference. Work together to create a master chart that explains what still needs to be done. Post the chart where everyone can easily see it.

Use this chart to list important information about the conference. You can use the information on the chart to help create a master chart. The chart below will make a good checklist to be sure all important jobs are done.

Africa 2000

Time and Date	
Location	
Agenda Order of Topics Speakers' Names	
Food Dish Who Is Bringing It?	
Room Decorations and Preparation	
Cleanup	
Other	

AFRICA
Physical Geography

Simulation: Magazine Article on an African River

Imagine that you work for a magazine, such as *National Geographic*. The editors have asked you to work with a group to write an article about one of the four major rivers in Africa. Your group will choose a river, research information, and write an article. Your article should include a map and photographs.

Background

There are four major rivers on the continent of Africa. They are the Nile, the Congo, the Zambezi, and the Niger. African peoples have long used them as a source of food. River water has been used for drinking and agriculture. For centuries, people have used these rivers as highways for trade and communication. In more recent times, huge dams have been built to create electricity.

Procedure

1. **Choose and research a river.** Read all the steps in this project. Then meet with your team to choose one of the four rivers. Research information about the geography, history, people, trade, and agriculture along the course of the river. You can use reference books about Africa, an encyclopedia, and an atlas, or ask your teacher and librarian for help. Work together to decide how you will divide the work.

2. **Organize your research.** When you have gathered information, work as a group to organize your notes and research. Decide what facts, maps, and illustrations you want to include. Focus on how the river affects the land and people. If possible, find personal accounts or stories to include in your article. Try to find photos that will go well with the article. Organize the sections of your article in a clear and logical way.

3. **Write the article.** Divide the writing into sections that can be done by group members. Help each other with any problems that arise. Your article should include a title, photos or illustrations, and clear text that is fun to read and full of interesting facts. You might want to write headings for each section and captions for the illustrations.

4. **Edit and proofread your work.** Some group members can work as editors. Editors can check the work to see that it is well written. Then they can proofread for errors in spelling and punctuation.

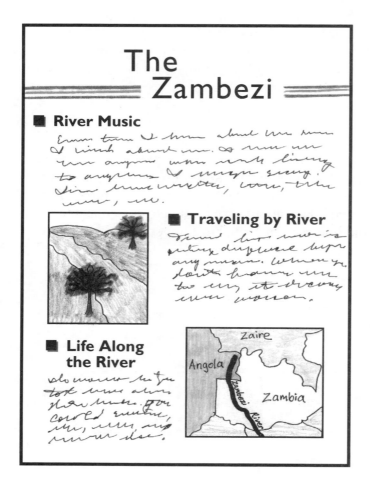

AFRICA
Physical Geography

Magazine Article on an African River

Content Objectives
- Students will gain a deeper understanding of the geography of Africa.
- Students will learn about different African rivers: how they affect trade, agriculture, power, food supply, and other important aspects of life.

Skill Objectives
- Using route maps
- Locating information
- Using the writing process
- Writing for a purpose—report

Advance Preparation
Gather resource books and maps on Africa. You might wish to photocopy maps of Africa. Students can illustrate these and use them as parts of their articles.

Suggested group size: six students

Suggested time: 40 minutes for research and organization; 40 minutes for writing and illustrating articles and marking routes; 40 minutes for presentation and discussion

Procedure
Divide the class into groups. Distribute student pages, and have students begin to plan their projects. You may wish to give a copy of the rubric for articles to each group.

Before students begin doing research, encourage them to find a variety of sources, including first-hand accounts. You might suggest that they brainstorm what they would like to learn, and pursue these topics.

As students work on their magazine articles, remind them to identify their audience and write accordingly. Stress the importance of using interesting topics, lively writing, and good illustrations.

When groups have finished their articles, have them share their work with other groups. Then the class can work together to create one magazine that includes all the river articles. When the final work is done, have students discuss the project. You might like to begin discussion with questions such as these:
- How have rivers affected people's lives in the area you chose?
- How might life be different if there weren't a river in the area you studied?
- How well do you think your group worked as a team?

Articles will be evaluated according to the following rubric.

Rubric for Magazine Articles

	Awesome	Admirable	Acceptable
Research	Students find very interesting facts, stories, and graphics about the river. They use a wide variety of sources.	Students find interesting information and some graphics about the river.	Students find some information about the river.
Writing	Articles are written in a clear and lively style. They are well organized and flow easily from section to section. The writing draws readers in and makes them want to read the article.	Articles are clearly written and informative. They are well organized.	Articles are informative and contain some interesting points, but could be better organized.
Presentation	Articles contain strong graphics, are neatly written or typed, and are easy to read.	Articles are neat and contain some graphics.	Articles are finished, but could be neater and easier to read.
Teamwork	Students share the research, writing, and presentation. All group members contribute equally.	Students work well together to create the magazine article.	Students work together, but do not share the work equally.

AFRICA
Shaped by Its History

Oral Report on an Ancient African Kingdom

Ancient kingdoms existed throughout the African continent centuries ago. The people of these kingdoms had a rich history and tradition. Work with a group to research one kingdom. Prepare an oral report about the people, land, and history of this place and share it with the class.

Background

Long before Europeans came to Africa, Africans formed kingdoms. They built cities, traded, established centers of learning, farmed, made tools and crafts, and protected themselves with armies. Kingdoms such as Ghana and Songhai were located on important trade routes. They contained thriving population centers where traders and merchants met and conducted business. Leaders and governments controlled and profited from the trade in their areas.

Procedure

1. **Choose and research an ancient kingdom.** Read all the steps in this project. Then meet with your group to choose one kingdom, such as Egypt, Nubia, Aksum, Mali, Ghana, Songhai, Zanzibar, or Zimbabwe. You might focus on a particular period of time or a specific leader, for example, Mansa Musa or Sundiata of Mali. Look for information on topics such as people, trade, learning, crafts, food resources, laws, government, religion, and buildings.

2. **Prepare your report.** When you have finished your research, work together to decide what you will use in the report. You might begin by determining categories that you think are important. Think about questions you have about life at the time and place. What interests you most?

3. **Write your report.** Work together to write the report. Decide how your group will present the information. Remember, this is going to be an oral report. Group members can choose which parts they would like to present. For example, your group might report on Songhai. One member might choose to describe the city of Gao during the time of Sonni Ali. Or, you could talk about the salt and gold trade between the Sahara and Ghana.

4. **Present your report.** Share what you have learned with the class. Be sure to speak slowly and clearly. Use a lively tone and look at your audience. You may want to read your report or just use notes. When you listen, pay careful attention. Try to imagine the people and place being described.

AFRICA
Shaped by Its History

Oral Report on an Ancient African Kingdom

Content Objectives
- Students will learn in detail about an ancient African kingdom.
- Students will have a stronger sense of the history of Africa.

Skill Objectives
- Writing for a purpose—report
- Locating information
- Organizing information

Advance Preparation
Gather the following materials:
- reference books on ancient African kingdoms
- paper, pens, and pencils

Suggested group size: four students

Suggested time: 40 minutes for research and organization; 40 minutes for writing and preparing oral reports; 40 minutes for speaking and discussion

Procedure
Divide the class into groups. Distribute student pages to each group. As students begin to plan their work, show them a copy of the rubric for oral reports.

Coach students about speaking to a group. Encourage them to look at their audience, to relax, and to speak slowly. Give them a chance to practice speaking and listening with partners.

After students have given their reports, encourage the class to discuss what they have learned. You can use these and other questions to stimulate discussion.
- How have your ideas about Africa changed?
- What was the most interesting thing you learned from the reports?
- Was working with a team easier or harder than working alone? Why?

Activities and Projects

AFRICA
Shaped by Its History

Reports will be evaluated according to the following rubric.

Rubric for Reports

	Awesome	Admirable	Acceptable
Research	Students locate detailed and fascinating information about the topic. They use many sources.	Students locate interesting facts about the topic.	Students find some information about the topic.
Writing	Reports are well organized, informative, and easy to understand. Each group member's work is part of a single unified report.	Reports are well organized. The writing is clear.	Reports are well written, but the individual sections do not go together very well.
Presentation	Students speak without reading, showing a relaxed command of the information. They make strong contact with the audience, are entertaining, and can be easily understood.	Students read well, are easy to under-stand, and make strong contact with the audience.	Students read their reports fairly well but do not strongly engage the audience.
Teamwork	All group members enthusiastically share in each stage of the report process.	Group members work together and share the work.	Some students do more work than others, but each group member con-tributes something.

Cultures of Africa

Telling a Traditional African Story

When someone tells a good story, almost everyone listens. In cultures without writing and books, stories were the main way to tell a people's history. Some storytellers can recite a tale or history for hours and hours. You can join this tradition by learning a story. In this activity, you will work with a group to learn and tell a story.

Background

In much of Africa, storytellers have been an important part of the community. Stories have been passed orally from one generation to the next. Storytellers keep the culture and traditions of a people alive. Folk tales, proverbs, and stories contain parts of a rich history. At the same time, many of them teach morals and life lessons.

Procedure

1. **Choose a story.** Read all the steps in this project. Then meet with your group to choose a story. Look in the library for books that contain African folk tales. Ask the librarian for help. When you find a story, be sure to identify the people it belongs to and where they live. Choose a story that you particularly like.

Activities and Projects

2. **Learn the story.** Work together to decide how you will learn and present the story. You might divide the story into sections and have each group member learn one part. Or you can memorize the entire story as a group, then recite the words in unison. This would work particularly well with stories in verse.

3. **Practice your story.** Good storytellers practice telling their stories again and again. Every time you tell the story, or your part of it, you will learn it better. You can do this with a partner, in small groups, or as a whole. Take time to go over the major points and details of each part. When you know a story really well, you don't have to say each part exactly the same way every time.

4. **Tell your story.** When you speak, try to communicate the feeling of the story. Use a dramatic voice. Try moving around as you speak. Make people and animal noises. Express yourself! Storytelling should be fun and entertaining.

Cultures of Africa

Telling a Traditional African Story

Content Objectives
- Students will learn a traditional African story.
- Students will gain a deeper understanding of how important stories are in African cultures.

Skill Objectives
- Drawing conclusions
- Locating information
- Organizing your time

Advance Preparation
Gather books that contain African folk tales.

Suggested group size: six students

Suggested time: 40 minutes for choosing and learning stories; 40 minutes for learning and practicing stories; 40 minutes for telling stories and discussion

Procedure
Divide the class into groups. Distribute student pages and have students begin to plan their project. You may wish to give a copy of the rubric for stories to each group.

Allow students plenty of time to practice telling their stories.

Encourage them to speak with feeling. Remind them that telling a story well comes with repeated practice. Explain that they don't have to memorize the story word for word if they know it well.

When students have told their stories, have a class discussion. You might like to use some of these questions to begin.
- What was your favorite story? Why?
- Who was your favorite character?
- Did any of the tales you heard or told remind you of other stories you know? What are they?
- How well did your group work together?

Cultures of Africa

Stories will be evaluated according to the following rubric.

Rubric for Stories

	Awesome	Admirable	Acceptable
Research	Students locate many stories and are able to choose one they particularly like.	Students find a variety of stories from which to choose.	Students choose a story from one or two possibilities.
Learning the Story	Students work hard to learn the story or their part of it. They spend a lot of time learning details and practicing speaking.	Students spend enough time to learn the story well.	Students learn the story but could be more focused in their practice time.
Storytelling	Students speak clearly and with feeling, communicating the essence and details of the story in a lively and entertaining way. They remember all the details of the tale. The audience is captivated by the telling.	Students speak clearly. They tell the story with feeling and remember most of the details of the story.	Students remember the important parts of the story. They speak clearly but could use more feeling and expression.
Teamwork	Group members work very well together, helping each other choose, learn, and tell the story. All members contribute equally to the project.	Group members each contribute to the story.	Group members complete the work, but some are far more involved and productive than others.

CHAPTER
4

Exploring North Africa

Writing About the Cities of North Africa

Major cities are often centers of government, culture, learning, and trade. The cities of North Africa are no exception. In this activity, you will work with a group to research information about one of the major cities of North Africa. Then you can decide how to present what you have learned.

Background

Within the countries of North Africa are many famous cities. Cities such as Cairo, Alexandria, Tripoli, Casablanca, Tunis, Algiers, and Rabat each have their own unique past and present. These places are historical landmarks that have played an important role in the life and lands of North Africa. As you locate them on a map, you will notice that they are almost all on the Mediterranean Sea. The exception is Cairo, which is on the Nile River. When you notice the vast deserts of North Africa, you can see why being close to water is extremely important.

Procedure

1. **Choose a city.** Read all the steps in this project. Begin by looking at a map of North Africa. Note the name of the country that contains each major city. Work with your group to choose one city.

2. **Research information about the city.** Divide up the jobs of finding information about the city you have chosen. You might decide to have partners or individuals locate different sources of information. You might also divide the work by topics such as people, geography, trade, culture, religion, education, music, art, entertainment, and history. Choose topics that interest you.

3. **Write about the city.** As a group, decide how you would like to present your information. You might consider creating an encyclopedia page. The page could include information, maps, photographs and illustrations, charts, or graphs. Or think of your own idea. When you have decided on the form, prepare it for the rest of the class. Work together to be sure that it is well organized, clearly written, and full of interesting facts, stories, and illustrations.

4. **Present what you have learned.** When you are ready, share your information with the class. Listen to what other groups have to say about the cities they have chosen. If possible, work as a class to combine your work into a single document about the cities of North Africa.

Exploring North Africa

Writing About Cities of North Africa

Content Objectives

- Students will learn about North African cities.
- Students will gain a deeper understanding of the people, land, and history of North Africa.

Skill Objectives

- Using the writing process
- Locating information
- Organizing information

Advance Preparation

Gather reference books that contain information about North African cities as well as atlases that include the area.

Suggested group size: four students

Suggested time: 40 minutes for choosing a city and gathering information; 40 minutes for organizing and writing; 40 minutes for finishing writing and sharing; 40 minutes for combining work into one form and discussing the project

Procedure

Divide the class into groups and distribute student pages and the rubric for the project. Encourage students to find as many sources of information as they can. Point out that using a variety of sources provides a broader base of information from which to draw. Point out that there are many possible ways in which they can present their information. Suggest that they brainstorm ideas for presentation before they begin work.

When each group has finished its work, have students think of ways to combine their projects into one whole. Explain that they should try to create a unified presentation about North African cities.

Have students discuss both the content and process of the project. These questions might help stimulate discussion.

- How have your impressions about North Africa and its cities changed?
- Would you like to visit any of these cities? Why?
- How are the cities you have studied and heard about similar to and different from each other? How do they compare with American cities?
- What was the best part about doing this project as a team?

Exploring North Africa

Reports will be evaluated according to the following rubric.

Rubric for City Reports

	Awesome	Admirable	Acceptable
Research	Students use a wide variety and great number of sources. They find information on many topics, including both first- and secondhand accounts.	Students work from a variety of sources and locate information about many topics.	Students work from a few good sources.
Writing	The writing is focused, clear, lively, and very well organized. It is easy to read and makes the reader want to learn more. The report presents a strong picture of the city.	The writing is well organized and easy to read. The report is full of interesting information and stories.	The writing is fairly clear but could be better organized.
Presentation	Students' work is presented very neatly and includes a great variety of graphics. Each part of the work is done with great care and attention to detail.	Students' work is presented well and includes some graphics.	Students' work is neat and readable but could include graphics.
Teamwork	Group members work as a team on each part of the project. Groups work together to complete the final part of the project.	Group members work well as a team.	Group members work as a team, but some members are less willing than others to do the work.

Exploring West Africa

Arts and Crafts of West Africa

Traditional West African artists and craftspeople use skills that are many centuries old. In this activity, you will work with a team to find examples of West African arts or crafts. Then you will use art materials to recreate or draw objects, such as decorated clay pots or woven baskets. You can decide how you would like to represent the objects you've seen.

Background

West African people create many traditional items, including clay pots, cloth, baskets, masks, and wood carvings. Most of these objects are used in everyday life. Many have been made in a similar way for centuries. In Ghana and Mali, people prepare food in clay pots. The pots are often decorated with traditional designs. Weavers make baskets that are used to carry a wide variety of items. In other places, wood carvers make masks and statues. The crafts of West Africa have been passed down from generation to generation. They preserve strong ties to the past.

Procedure

1. **Choose a craft.** Read all the steps in this project. Begin by finding books on the countries or arts of West Africa. Be sure that you have chosen one of the countries covered in this chapter. Then work as a group to find photographs of arts and crafts that you like. You may have to look at several books to find photos that work well. These might include pictures of kente cloth, pottery, baskets, ancient gold objects, or tools.

Candles

Kente cloth

2. **Choose objects.** Each group can choose four objects to copy. Try to find objects that stand out because of their design, color, or decoration. When you have chosen the objects, decide how you would like to work as a group. For example, you might each make one object. Or you might work with a partner. Learn for each object who made it, where it was made, and how it is used. You can include this information when you present your work to the class.

3. **Make, draw, or paint the objects.** Use art materials to create a copy or drawing of the objects you have chosen. You will probably be working from a photograph. Do the best you can to copy what you see. If you have experience with weaving or pottery, you might be able to help others create an accurate replica. Decide how you will display your work so that each object can be easily seen. Label the objects with important information.

4. **Show your work.** When your group has finished work, show the class what you have made. As you present each item, tell what you know about the materials from which it is made, how it is used, where it is from, and who made it.

Exploring West Africa

Arts and Crafts of West Africa

Content Objectives
- Students will learn about West African arts and crafts.
- Students will have a better knowledge of the people and traditions of West Africa.

Skill Objectives
- Locating information
- Organizing your time

Advance Preparation
Gather the following materials:
- reference books about countries, peoples, arts, and crafts of West Africa
- clay (If students have experience with ceramic clay, encourage them to use it. Otherwise, students can use modeling clay.)
- paper, paints, markers, pens, and pencils

Suggested group size: four students

Suggested time: 40 minutes for choosing a country and finding photographs of objects; 40 minutes for representing the objects; 40 minutes for sharing work and discussion

Procedure
Divide the class into groups. Hand out the student pages. If you wish, give students the rubric for this project as well.

Ask students whether they have examples of West African art in their homes. If they have permission, encourage them to share such pieces with the class.

Have students discuss what they learned about West African arts, crafts, and traditions. You might use the following questions to begin the discussion.
- What object did you see that you liked the most? Why?
- How are the arts and crafts of West Africa related to daily life?
- Would you like to make other objects from traditional West African culture? What are they?
- How would you evaluate your team's ability to work together?

Exploring West Africa

Arts and crafts objects will be evaluated according to the following rubric.

Rubric for Arts and Crafts Objects

	Awesome	Admirable	Acceptable
Research	Students find many sources and a great number of examples of arts and crafts. They gather detailed information about each of the objects they choose.	Students find a variety of sources and some information about each object.	Students find four good examples and learn a bit about them.
Craft	Students recreate clay pots, woven baskets, woven cloth, or other objects. They create a work that is accurate in size, shape, and detail.	Students make an accurate representation of an object, using paints, markers, or drawing materials.	Students do a fairly accurate representation of an object.
Presentation	Groups present four objects and are able to explain in detail about the country, people, materials, and uses for each. Each object is labeled and well displayed.	Groups present four objects and can explain a bit about some of them. The objects are well displayed.	Groups present four objects, but they could be displayed with more care. Students have little information to share.
Teamwork	Team members work together, sharing the research, creation, and presentation of each object. They share in decisions and support each other well.	Team members work well together, sharing most of the work equally.	Team members work together but have difficulty making decisions as a group.

CHAPTER 6

Exploring East Africa

Mural of East African Architecture

Buildings in East Africa come in many sizes and types. The variety of architecture is almost as great as the variety of landscapes. Each location influences the architecture found there. For example, along the eastern coast, you can find an Indian influence in some architecture. In the dense, remote forests of the interior, the climate and resources dictate how and what people can build. For this activity you will find examples of different kinds of buildings in East Africa. Then you will create a mural that pictures them and identifies where they are located.

Background

As in all parts of the world, the people of East Africa have built buildings for many purposes, including living, working, and conducting religious ceremonies. In traditional villages of Kenya and Tanzania, small mud and stick huts have been the common dwelling for centuries. In Lalibela, Ethiopia, there are churches that were built by Christians hundreds of years ago. If you visit large cities such as Dar es Salaam, you will see modern high-rise offices and apartments.

Procedure

1. **Find examples of architecture.** Read all the steps in this project. Look in books about the countries of East Africa. In each book you will find examples of different types of buildings. With other members of your group, choose a variety of buildings that you find interesting. Research information about each building, such as what it is made from, how it was built and by whom, when it was built, how it is used, and where it is located.

2. **Make illustrations.** Work together to decide how to illustrate each building. You are going to put them on a mural/map of East Africa. You might photocopy examples directly from books. Or you could make drawings or paintings from the illustrations you find. Each illustration should be on paper that can be glued onto the mural.

3. **Create the mural.** Some members of each group can work together to create the mural. If possible, make a map of East Africa that shows the country borders. You can do this by using an overhead projector. Or do a general outline of the area. Once you have made the mural, group members can attach their illustrations to it in the appropriate places.

4. **Write information.** Next to each illustration, write any information you have about the building. Write the facts that you would like to know if you were looking at the mural. When you have finished, display the mural where everyone can see it.

Exploring East Africa

Mural of East African Architecture

Content Objectives
- Students will learn about the great variety of architecture in East Africa.
- By studying architecture, students will gain a deeper understanding of how people live in different parts of East Africa.

Skill Objectives
- Locating information
- Organizing your time

Advance Preparation
Gather the following materials:
- reference books about East African countries and architecture
- overhead projector
- large sheets of paper, glue, pens, markers, and paints
- stapler or tape

Suggested group size: six students

Suggested time: 40 minutes for choosing examples of buildings and researching information about them; 40 minutes for making illustrations; 40 minutes for creating the mural

Procedure
If possible, provide students with a mural-sized map of East Africa. Students may be able to help you use an overhead projector to create the map.

Students making the mural may have to join several large sheets of paper with staples or tape.

When the mural is complete, encourage students to talk about East African architecture. These questions might be helpful.
- How would you compare the buildings in different locations of East Africa?
- What factors do you think influenced the different types of architecture you found?
- What was your favorite building? Why?
- How well did your group work together?

Exploring East Africa

Murals will be evaluated according to the following rubric.

Rubric for Architecture Mural

	Awesome	Admirable	Acceptable
Research	Students locate a great variety of photographs and illustrations of East African architecture. They use many reference sources.	Students locate several good examples of buildings in a few reference sources.	Students locate a few good examples, but use only one or two reference sources.
Writing/ Illustration	Students write clearly and relate information that is fun and interesting to read. Photos and illustrations are strong and easy to see.	Students write clearly and offer useful information. Illustrations are easy to see.	Students offer some information. Illustrations are fairly easy to look at.
Presentation	Murals are beautiful to look at and informative. Writing is neat. Photos and illustrations are clearly connected to locations on the map.	Murals are neat and clear. They are informative and fun to look at.	Murals contain illustrations of architecture and a general outline of East Africa. Writing could be neater and illustrations more clearly connected to locations on the map.
Teamwork	Group members work well as a team. They share equally the work of finding illustrations, deciding on their presentation, and completing the project.	Group members work well as a team. They share most of the work of the project.	Group members work together, but some students do more of the work than others.

Exploring Central and Southern Africa

Musical Instruments of Central and Southern Africa

Music, song, and dance play an important role in cultures throughout Africa. People across the continent have invented a great variety of instruments. These include percussion, wind, and string instruments made from parts of animals, wood, clay, gourds, shells, bamboo, and metal. In this activity, you will make cards that picture and identify musical instruments from Central and Southern Africa.

Background

Music is an important part of life in all of Africa. This is particularly true in cultures south of the Sahara. In traditional cultures, music has been strongly connected to work, play, religion, and ceremonies for centuries. In some areas, music has been used to communicate over long distances. Until recently, people have created instruments from the materials they could find locally. Forest dwellers make drums out of wood. Some people in deserts or treeless plains may have few or no instruments. In areas with plentiful game, some people may use the horns or hides of animals.

Mbira

Side-blown horn

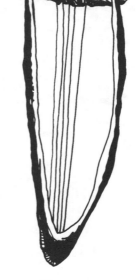

Harp

Procedure

1. **Research information about instruments.** Read all the steps in this project. Work with your group to divide the jobs that you think need to be done. Then begin by looking in books and encyclopedias for examples of musical instruments from the area. Copy photographs or illustrations that you find.

2. **Decide how to share what you know.** Choose as a group a way to present illustrations and information about each instrument. You might try making cards. These could contain a labeled illustration on one side and detailed information on the other. Or you might like to make a poster that shows examples of each type of instrument.

3. **Make illustrations and write information.** Some members of each group can photocopy or draw illustrations of each instrument. Other group members can write information about the instruments. Remember that your work must be a size that can be used in the form you have chosen.

4. **Present your work.** Combine the illustrations and writing. Be sure you do this in a way that can be easily seen and understood. Then display or share your work.

Exploring Central and Southern Africa

Musical Instruments of Central and Southern Africa

Content Objectives
- Students will learn about music and musical instruments of Central and Southern Africa.
- Students will have a better understanding of the importance of music in traditional African cultures.

Skill Objectives
- Drawing conclusions
- Locating and organizing information
- Organizing your time

Advance Preparation
Gather the following materials:
- reference books about Central and Southern African peoples, music, and instruments
- heavy paper for making cards, such as card stock or cardboard
- glue, pens, markers, and paints

Suggested group size: eight students

Suggested time: 40 minutes for finding musical instruments; 40 minutes for making illustrations and writing information; 40 minutes for presenting the work

Procedure
You may wish to help students find sources of information. Encourage them to look in reference books about the countries of Central and Southern Africa as well as in books about musical instruments.

If possible, provide sound recordings of traditional music from countries mentioned in Chapter 7. You might have students listen to recordings two times. First, students can simply listen to the music. Then they can listen again to identify the sounds of individual instruments.

When students have presented their work, have them discuss the project. Use these questions if you like.
- Do you think you could make any of the instruments you have seen? Which ones might you like to make or play?
- What have you noticed about the materials that were used to make the instruments?
- How important do you think music is in the cultures you learned about? Why do you think this?
- Do you think that working in a group made the project easier to complete?

Activities and Projects

Exploring Central and Southern Africa

Musical instrument illustrations will be evaluated according to the following rubric.

Rubric for Musical Instrument Illustrations

	Awesome	Admirable	Acceptable
Research	Students obtain information from many sources. They find several examples of instruments of each type and locate excellent photos and illustrations.	Students obtain information from several sources. They find good examples and information.	Students obtain information from a few sources. They find examples with only a limited amount of information.
Writing/ Illustration	Students include only important information that is easy to understand. Illustrations are clear and enable students to identify each instrument.	Students include important information. Illustrations enable students to identify the instruments.	Students include some information but leave out some important facts. Illustrations may be a bit sloppy.
Presentation	Students' work is neat, clear, and interesting to view. The end product gives a beautiful, informative, and readily understood explanation about each instrument.	Students' work is neat and clear. The end product offers a good description of each instrument.	Students' work is fairly neat. The end product explains different instruments but could be easier to look at and understand.
Teamwork	Groups work well together. They support each other, make decisions together, and work with equal enthusiasm on all parts of the project.	Groups work as a team, make decisions together, and share most of the work.	Groups work together on most of the project, but some members are not as involved in the work as others.

Assessment of a Written Presentation

Use this rubric to assess students' essays, written reports, and any other written materials such as captions for maps or diagrams.

	Awesome	Admirable	Acceptable	Unacceptable
Creativity	The presentation has a highly interesting topic that is conveyed in an extremely engaging manner. Students include several original ideas, including some that are unusual.	The presentation has an interesting topic that is conveyed in an engaging manner. Students include one or two original ideas.	The presentation has an appropriate topic that is conveyed with a few interesting details.	The topic of the presentation may be inappropriate, and/or students use only obvious examples to back up their main points.
Content	The presentation includes excellent information gathered from a variety of sources. All the elements, such as captions for illustrations and the title, are concise and informative.	The presentation includes good information gathered from three or four sources. The project's general conclusions are supported by the data presented.	The information in the presentation is relevant, but students may have used only two reference sources.	The information in the presentation may not be relevant to the topic, and/or students use only one reference source, resulting in a limited understanding of the subject.
Organization	The information is very well organized and conveyed in a logical order. Each main point is supported by interesting and appropriate details.	The information is conveyed in a logical order, and the report is easy to follow and understand.	The information is presented in a logical order, and the supporting details almost always follow the appropriate main points.	The information is not presented logically, and supporting details are either missing or misplaced.
Spelling, Grammar, and Neatness	The written material is very neat and attractively presented. Students use correct spelling and grammar.	The written material is attractive and neat. Students make very few spelling or grammatical errors.	The written material is legible. Students make a few spelling and grammatical errors.	The written material is mostly legible, but some sections are very hard to read. Students make more than three spelling and grammatical errors.

Activities and Projects

Assessment of an Oral Presentation

Use this rubric to assess students' oral reports and their public speaking skills.

	Awesome	Admirable	Acceptable	Unacceptable
Content	The presentation is highly persuasive and informative. Students emphasize important information about the topic and include many fascinating details in their presentation.	The presentation is persuasive and informative. Students include pertinent information about the topic and illustrate their points with three or four interesting details.	The presentation is informative. Students convey correct information about the topic and illustrate their points with one or two details.	The presentation is somewhat or not at all informative. Some of the information in it may be incorrect. Students make only broad statements about the topic, giving few or no details.
Preparation	Students gather information from several appropriate sources. They prepare note cards to guide them as they speak and create attractive visual aids to enhance the presentation.	Students gather information from three or four sources. They prepare notes to use while they speak and create informative visual aids for the presentation.	Students gather information from one or two sources. Instead of preparing notes, they write the report word for word, as it will be given.	Students use only one reference source to prepare for the presentation. They may be unable to complete their presentation because of lack of preparation.
Organization	The information is very well organized, logically ordered, and easy to follow. Students include interesting and appropriate examples to support their main points.	Students convey the information in a logical order, and the presentation is easy to follow and understand.	Students present the information in a logical order. Generally, the supporting details follow the main points.	The information is not presented logically, and supporting details are either missing or misplaced.
Speaking	Students are enthusiastic during the presentation. They enunciate clearly, project well, maintain eye contact with their audience, and speak in complete sentences.	Students are engaged during the presentation. They enunciate clearly, project well, and speak mostly in complete sentences.	Students present their material clearly and try to maintain eye contact.	Students come across as disinterested during the presentation. They may be hard to understand and speak in fragmented sentences.

Assessment of a Visual Display

Use this rubric to assess students' maps, diagrams, murals, graphs, illustrated stories or articles, and any other visual displays.

	Awesome	Admirable	Acceptable	Unacceptable
Content	The display conveys accurate information from several appropriate sources. Students include excellent renditions of all the necessary elements, such as a title and a legend for a map.	The display conveys accurate information from more than one source. Students include all the necessary elements, such as clearly labeled axes on a graph.	The display conveys accurate information from a reliable source. Important elements are present and convey most of the necessary information.	The display may contain inaccurate information. Important elements, such as the legend for a map, are missing.
Creativity	Students employ a highly innovative approach to creating the display. They combine several original ideas with existing materials to create a unique display.	Students combine one or two original ideas with existing materials to create an interesting display.	Students create an informative display that includes a few interesting ideas or details.	Rather than using their own ideas to make a unique display, students copy from an existing source.
Color and Form	Elements of the display are highly attractive and compatible with other elements. Whenever possible, students use colors to convey information instead of as mere decoration.	Elements of the display are attractive and work well together. Students use colors that are appropriate to the subject matter and often convey content as well as being decorative.	Elements of the display are the correct size and in the correct places. Students pay sufficient attention to conveying content with color.	Some elements of the display may be inappropriately sized. For example, a map legend may be larger than the map itself. Colors are used haphazardly.
Drawing and Labeling	Students are very careful and neat when they render their display; for example, they use straightedges to draw lines. All necessary parts of diagrams and maps are labeled clearly.	Students carefully draw elements of their displays so that the information in them is easy to understand. They include appropriate labels whenever necessary.	Students create a generally neat and readable display. They include some good labels, most of which are easy to read.	Several elements in the display are hurriedly drawn and sloppy. Students use too few labels, or the labels do not convey the correct information.

Activities and Projects

Assessment of a Model

Use this rubric to assess students' models, dioramas, and any other three-dimensional projects.

	Awesome	Admirable	Acceptable	Unacceptable
Research	Students conduct extensive research for their model, using several appropriate sources. They gather more material than they eventually use, resulting in a high level of precision.	Students gather information from three or four appropriate and varied sources. For example, they use the Internet or magazines as well as general encyclopedias.	Students gather information from one or two appropriate sources. They may rely very heavily on only one of the sources.	Students use only one reference source to prepare their model, resulting in a limited understanding of the subject.
Content	The model is an excellent representation of the scene or phenomenon being studied. Students exhibit a thorough understanding of how the model relates to the real world.	Students use the model to accurately depict a particular scene or phenomenon. Students can explain how the model works and answer questions about their work.	Students create a model that demonstrates a particular scene or phenomenon. They mostly understand how their model relates to the real world.	The model shows a scene or demonstrates a phenomenon, but it contains errors or incongruous elements, such as a human and a dinosaur in the same scene.
Quality of Construction	The model is very sturdy and well constructed. In dioramas, glue, tape, and other such materials are hidden, resulting in a highly realistic scene.	The model is sturdy. In dioramas, construction materials, such as glue and tape, are not evident, and the scene looks realistic.	Although the model may be sturdy, construction materials, such as glue and tape, are easy to see, detracting somewhat from the realism of the scene.	Even though some parts of the model may be sturdy, other parts have fallen apart. Elements of the model have been hurriedly taped together.
Presentation	The model is highly attractive and detailed, although none of the details are extraneous. In dioramas, students render elements of the scene very realistically.	The model is attractive and includes many interesting details. Students draw and color elements of dioramas so that they are easy to understand.	The model adequately presents a scene. Most of the elements of dioramas are easy to make out or understand.	The model fails to present a scene adequately. Students pay little attention to color or shape when they make the elements of a diorama.

Answer Key

Discovery Activities About Africa
ACTIVITY ATLAS

Explore Africa's Location and Size
1. the Atlantic Ocean
2. Being near the Equator would ensure a warm climate.
3. Answers may vary. Possible response: African climates might tend to be warmer because Africa is much farther south. The southernmost parts of the United States might have similar climates to parts of Africa.
4. between two and three times

Bonus!
- 4,600 miles
- about 2,400 miles
- about 6,300 miles

Find Geo Cleo
1. Addis Ababa, Ethiopia
2. Cape Town, South Africa
3. Abuja, Nigeria

Bonus!
- Answers will vary. Possible answer: "Today I flew west across the Kalahari Desert and turned slightly north. I landed in the inland capital of a country that borders the Atlantic Ocean."

Analyze Temperatures Across the Continent
1. 65–90°F
2. 90–97°F
3. The average temperature range is lower in southern countries than in those near the Equator.
4. The temperatures are similar because the areas are similar distances from the Equator.

Bonus!
- Most of the vegetation in the Sahara is desert scrub; the high temperatures and lack of rainfall make it difficult for plants to survive.

Desertification
ACTIVITY SHOP LAB

Procedure
1. Answers will vary.
2. More sand is in the sod than in Step Two.
3. Answers will vary. There is probably enough sand to cover most of the sod. The sand may cover the soil, and the wind may have eroded the soil.

Observations
1. The sand got caught in the grass.
2. The wind beat down the grass, and the sand piled up and covered the topsoil.

Analysis and Conclusion
1. Many people who live in the Sahel depend on the land for farming and grazing. If the land becomes a desert, it will be useless for farming and grazing.

The Language of Music
ACTIVITY SHOP INTERDISCIPLINARY

1. Research African Drums
a. Answers will vary. Students should name several different types of African drums.
b. Answers will vary. Students should name a type of drum.
c. Answers will vary. Students should name the country where the drum is used.

Answer Key

2. Build Your Own Drum

a. Answers will vary. Students should name the materials from which the drum is made.

b. Answers will vary. Students should name some materials that they could use to make a drum.

c. Answers will vary. Students should explain whether the drum is beaten with the hand or with a drumstick.

3. Play Your Drum

a. Answers will vary. Students should explain how the drum is used.

b. Answers will vary. Students should explain how they will demonstrate the use of their drum for the class.

Africa on Stage
BOOK PROJECT

A. Students should fill in the chart with information about the name, location, and setting for one or more places in Africa.

B. Students should fill in the chart with details about each character.

C. Answers will vary.

Africa in Art
BOOK PROJECT

B. Students should fill in the chart with details about different types of African masks and the source of information about each mask.

C. Displays will vary.

Africa 2000
BOOK PROJECT

A. Students should fill in the chart with possible topics for the Africa 2000 conference.

B. Students should fill in the chart with the names of committee members and a description of the jobs for each committee.

C. Students should fill in the chart with a checklist of the necessary tasks for putting on the conference, including the names of those who are responsible for each task.

CHAPTER 1 Africa: Physical Geography

Test A   2
Test B   5

CHAPTER 2 Africa: Shaped by Its History

Test A   8
Test B   11

CHAPTER 3 Cultures of Africa

Test A   14
Test B   17

CHAPTER 4 Exploring North Africa

Test A   20
Test B   23

CHAPTER 5 Exploring West Africa

Test A   26
Test B   29

CHAPTER 6 Exploring East Africa

Test A   32
Test B   35

CHAPTER 7 Exploring Central and
           Southern Africa

Test A   38
Test B   41

Final Exam

Test A   44
Test B   47

Answer Key   50

Tests

TEST A

CHAPTER
1

AFRICA
Physical Geography

A. Key Terms

Directions: Complete each sentence in Column I by writing the letter of the correct term from Column II in the blank. You will not use all the terms. *(10 points)*

Column I

_____ **1.** A large, raised area of mostly level land is called a(n) _____ .

_____ **2.** A larger river can be fed by a(n) _____ , which is a small river or stream that flows into it.

_____ **3.** Many plants can be grown in soil that is _____ .

_____ **4.** Sometimes farmers must _____ , or artificially water their crops.

_____ **5.** Many African countries want to _____ , or add variety to, their economies.

Column II

a. cash crop

b. cataract

c. diversify

d. economy

e. escarpment

f. fertile

g. irrigate

h. plateau

i. tributary

B. Key Concepts

Directions: Write the letter of the correct answer in each blank. *(45 points)*

_____ **6.** Because the land area of much of Africa is high, the continent is often called a
    a. coastal plain.   **c.** plateau.
    b. mountain.   **d.** river valley.

_____ **7.** The Nile, Congo, Zambezi, and Niger are the names of
    a. major mountains in Africa.   **c.** major coastal plains in Africa.
    b. major rivers in Africa.   **d.** major rift valleys in Africa.

_____ **8.** Why is it impossible for ships to sail from Africa's interior to the sea?
    a. Cataracts interrupt the rivers' flow.   **c.** Rift valleys interrupt the rivers' flow.
    b. Escarpments interrupt the rivers' flow.   **d.** Tributaries interrupt the rivers' flow.

_____ **9.** Africa's location near the Equator, its elevation, and its relationship to large bodies of water and landforms affect its
  a. language.
  c. archaeology.
  b. government.
  d. climate.

_____ **10.** What area of land supports tall grasses, thorny bushes, and scattered trees?
  a. coastal plain
  c. rain forest
  b. desert
  d. savanna

_____ **11.** How do many nomads make their living in the Sahara?
  a. They live in one place so they can care for their herds.
  c. They travel to find water and food for their herds.
  b. They live in the cities where they can sell their goods.
  d. They create large farms in the desert to grow food.

_____ **12.** Three fifths of Africa's farmland is used for
  a. harvesting trees.
  c. commercial farming.
  b. cash crops.
  d. subsistence farming.

_____ **13.** The major part of Africa's economy is
  a. trading.
  c. farming.
  b. mining.
  d. manufacturing.

_____ **14.** Why are African countries diversifying their economies?
  a. to protect the workers against economic hardships
  c. to produce only one major mineral each year
  b. to focus on one important cash crop
  d. to produce only goods that are made in factories

C. Critical Thinking

Directions: Answer the following questions on the back of this paper or on a separate sheet of paper. *(20 points)*

15. Identifying Central Issues   Explain how the Nile affects the lives of people in Africa. In your answer, briefly identify what the Nile is and where it is located.

16. Expressing Problems Clearly   Why do you think that Africa must balance crops, minerals, and industry to protect its economy in the modern world?

D. Skills: Interpreting Diagrams

Directions: Use the diagram below to answer the following questions. Write your answers in the blanks provided. *(25 points)*

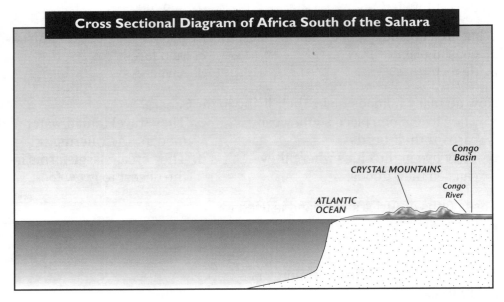

Cross Sectional Diagram of Africa South of the Sahara

Congo Basin

CRYSTAL MOUNTAINS

Congo River

ATLANTIC OCEAN

17. In general, how would you describe the subject of the diagram?

_____

_____

18. What major body of water is labeled on the diagram?

_____

_____

19. Name two landforms labeled on the diagram.

_____

_____

20. What is the name of the landform at the highest point on the diagram?

_____

_____

21. How can this diagram help you describe the physical geography of Africa?

_____

_____

Physical Geography

A. Key Terms

Directions: Match the definitions in Column I with the terms in Column II. Write the correct letter in each blank. You will not use all the terms. *(10 points)*

Column I

_____ **1.** a deep trench

_____ **2.** a large, raised area of mostly level land

_____ **3.** add variety to an economy

_____ **4.** a person who moves from place to place to make a living

_____ **5.** bits of rock and dirt on river bottoms

Column II

a. cash crop

b. diversify

c. elevation

d. nomad

e. oasis

f. plateau

g. rift

h. silt

i. subsistence farming

B. Key Concepts

Directions: Write the letter of the correct answer in each blank. *(45 points)*

_____ **6.** The four geographic regions of Africa defined in this book are
  a. North, South, East, and West.
  b. Northeast, South, Central and South, and East.
  c. North, West, East, and Central and Southern.
  d. South, East, North, and Central and Eastern.

_____ **7.** Africa is often called the "plateau continent" because the elevation of much of the land is
  a. high.
  b. low.
  c. uneven.
  d. flat.

_____ **8.** Because of the cataracts found in Africa's major rivers, it is impossible for ships to
  a. control the flooding of the Nile.
  b. sail all the way from the interior to the sea.
  c. sail to other lands.
  d. carry much cargo.

_____ 9. Because much of Africa is between the Tropic of Cancer and the Tropic of Capricorn, most of the country is located in a
   a. moderate climate region.
   b. subtropical climate region.
   c. tropical climate region.
   d. temperate climate region.

_____ 10. What are the three factors that influence the climate of Africa?
   a. location near the Arctic, amount of rain, and large plateaus
   b. location near the Equator, elevation, and how close a place is to bodies of water and landforms
   c. elevation, large desert areas, and the distance from the South Pole
   d. flat grasslands, temperature, and the amount of rain

_____ 11. The landform that extends across most of North Africa is
   a. the Sahara.
   b. the Namib Desert.
   c. the Nile River.
   d. Mount Kilimanjaro.

_____ 12. Africa's most important natural resources are
   a. electricity, trade, and timber.
   b. crops, minerals, and timber.
   c. manufacturing, trade, and crops.
   d. solar energy, trade, and timber.

_____ 13. Unlike farmers who raise cash crops, subsistence farmers raise crops to
   a. sell to Western countries.
   b. support entire villages.
   c. support their families.
   d. sell to other African countries.

_____ 14. How does producing a variety of crops, raw materials, and manufactured goods affect African countries?
   a. They can afford to buy costly equipment for mining.
   b. They can protect their economies in an unstable world market.
   c. They cannot protect themselves if a major cash crop fails.
   d. They cannot survive a serious drought.

C. Critical Thinking

Directions: Answer the following questions on the back of this paper or on a separate sheet of paper. *(20 points)*

15. **Making Comparisons**   Compare and contrast the deserts and tropical savannas of Africa. In your answer, describe the climate, vegetation, and daily life of the people living in each place.

16. **Drawing Conclusions**   Based on what you know about Africa's landforms, rivers, climate, vegetation, and economy, where do you think most people in Africa live? Explain your answer.

D. Skills: Interpreting Diagrams

Directions: Use the diagram below to answer the following questions. Write your answers in the blanks provided. *(25 points)*

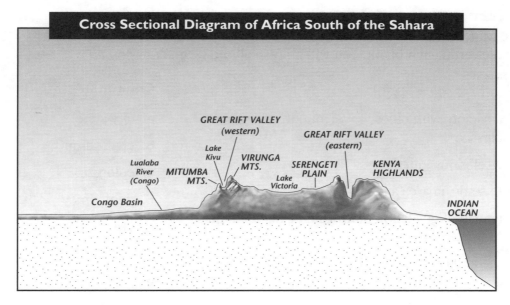

Cross Sectional Diagram of Africa South of the Sahara

17. What is shown on this diagram?

_____

_____

18. What are two landforms indicated on the diagram?

_____

_____

19. What major body of water is shown on the diagram?

_____

_____

20. Is the Great Rift Valley higher or lower in elevation than the surrounding land?

_____

_____

21. What are two facts about the geography of Africa that you can learn by studying this diagram?

_____

_____

TEST A

CHAPTER
2

AFRICA
Shaped by Its History

A. Key Terms

Directions: Match the definitions in Column I with the terms in Column II. Write the correct letter in each blank. You will not use all the terms. *(10 points)*

Column I

_____ **1.** a society with cities, government, and social classes

_____ **2.** a religious journey

_____ **3.** to settle an area and take over its government

_____ **4.** a form of government in which citizens help to make government decisions

_____ **5.** the ability to read and write

Column II

a. city-state

b. civilization

c. colonize

d. democracy

e. ethnic group

f. literacy

g. pilgrimage

h. surplus

B. Key Concepts

Directions: Write the letter of the correct answer in each blank. *(45 points)*

_____ **6.** The earliest humans in East Africa got their food by
  a. hunting and gathering.
  b. trading and hunting.
  c. domesticating and herding.
  d. farming and gathering.

_____ **7.** The earliest people in Egypt settled
  a. in the mountains.
  b. near the coast.
  c. along the banks of the Nile River.
  d. in the Sahara.

_____ **8.** The power of West African kingdoms was based on
  a. the herding of sheep and cows.
  b. the trade of gold for salt.
  c. the manufacture of clothing.
  d. the farming of oats and wheat.

_____ **9.** Which European country controlled the trade on East Africa's coast until well into the 1600s?
   a. England   **c.** France
   b. Spain   **d.** Portugal

_____ **10.** Why did Europeans build empires in Africa after the end of the African slave trade?
   a. for the natural resources found there   **c.** to unite the African people
   b. to stop the spread of Islam   **d.** because they were overcrowded in Europe

_____ **11.** In order to win independence from the colonial powers, African leaders encouraged the growth of
   a. religion.   **c.** nationalism.
   b. farming.   **d.** trade.

_____ **12.** How did World War II affect Africa?
   a. It inspired Africans to demand their independence.   **c.** It decreased the growth of cash crops.
   b. It increased trade between Africa and the United States.   **d.** It encouraged European countries to seize more African colonies.

_____ **13.** In order to depend less on one export, African countries are trying to
   a. decrease their exports.   **c.** increase their foreign debt.
   b. diversify their economies.   **d.** expand their farm communities.

_____ **14.** A serious environmental problem facing Africa today is a decrease in the
   a. crop harvests.   **c.** amount of fertile land.
   b. size of the desert.   **d.** number of trees that are planted.

C. Critical Thinking

Directions: Answer the following questions on the back of this paper or on a separate sheet of paper. *(20 points)*

15. Drawing Conclusions   How was the Nile River important to the history of Egypt?

16. Identifying Central Issues   How did Europe's relationship with Africa change after 1500?

Tests

D. Skill: Recognizing Bias

Directions: The selection in the box describes literacy in Africa. Read the selection. Then answer the following questions by writing your answers in the blanks provided. *(25 points)*

> In African countries, the number of people who know how to read is growing. The growth in the literacy rates occurred after the countries gained independence. In Tanzania, 15 percent of people could write when the country became independent. Now the literacy rate is about 70 percent. These figures show that people need freedom so they can learn to read and write.

17. What is one opinion stated as a fact in this selection?

_____

_____

18. What statements in the selection are facts?

_____

_____

19. Are any facts in the selection used to support opinions?

_____

_____

20. What is the bias in this selection?

_____

_____

21. Write the last sentence of an unbiased paragraph about literacy in Africa.

_____

_____

AFRICA
Shaped by Its History

A. Key Terms

Directions: Complete each sentence in Column I by writing the letter of the correct term from Column II in each blank. You will not use all the terms. *(10 points)*

Column I

_____ 1. To adapt plants and tame animals for human use is to ____ them.

_____ 2. Many Muslims make a religious journey, or a ____ , to Mecca.

_____ 3. Throughout Africa's history, European countries sought to ____ the continent, or settle the land and take over the government.

_____ 4. In order to protest colonial rule, Africans would sometimes ____ , or refuse to use, a product or service.

_____ 5. A feeling of pride in one's country is called ____ .

Column II

a. boycott

b. colonize

c. domesticate

d. ethnic group

e. literacy

f. migrate

g. nationalism

h. pilgrimage

B. Key Concepts

Directions: Write the letter of the correct answer in each blank. *(45 points)*

_____ 6. What is a civilization that arose on the Nile River about 5,000 years ago?
   a. South Africa   **c.** Egypt
   b. Nigeria   **d.** Senegal

_____ 7. When Bantu-speaking peoples settled in Central and Southern Africa they introduced
   a. farming, herding, and iron tools.   **c.** farming, mining, and forestry.
   b. manufacturing, forestry, and farming.   **d.** trade, mining, and forestry.

_____ 8. The kingdoms in West Africa were powerful because of
   a. the farming of wheat and corn.   **c.** the manufacturing of cloth and tools.
   b. the trading of gold for salt.   **d.** the herding of cows and sheep.

_____ **9.** Islam was spread from Mali into many other parts of Africa by
    a. British soldiers.
    b. Muslim traders.
    c. Arab farmers.
    d. Portuguese sailors.

_____ **10.** One important effect of trade on the culture of coastal East Africa was the development of
    a. Buddhism.
    b. Christianity.
    c. farming.
    d. Swahili.

_____ **11.** When the Portuguese realized how wealthy the East African city-states were, they wanted to
    a. establish schools in the area.
    b. seize the riches of the area.
    c. introduce English to the area.
    d. teach farmers new methods to grow crops.

_____ **12.** By the 1600s, Portuguese traders were trading
    a. gold for African salt.
    b. guns for enslaved Africans.
    c. clothing for African crops.
    d. salt for African guns.

_____ **13.** How did World War II affect European colonial powers like Great Britain?
    a. It weakened them economically.
    b. It strengthened them economically.
    c. It expanded their colonial holdings in Africa.
    d. It encouraged them to seek new colonies.

_____ **14.** In order to meet the challenges faced by African countries, African governments are working to increase the
    a. rate of land erosion.
    b. literacy rate.
    c. sale of only one food export.
    d. rate of foreign debt.

C. Critical Thinking

Directions: Answer the following questions on the back of this paper or on a separate sheet of paper. *(20 points)*

15. Recognizing Cause and Effect How do you think Pan-Africanism helped African countries gain their independence?

16. Identifying Central Issues What are two economic problems facing many African countries today, and how are the leaders trying to solve these problems?

D. Skill: Recognizing Bias

Directions: The selection in the box describes life in East Africa. Read the selection. Then answer the following questions by writing your answers in the blanks provided. *(25 points)*

> Africa can be divided into four regions: (1) North, (2) West, (3) East, and (4) Central and Southern. The best place to live in Africa is East Africa. East Africa has beautiful mountains—the most beautiful in the world—and plateaus. The grasslands are nicer than the grasslands in any other part of Africa. Some countries in East Africa lie on the coast. Anyone who likes mountains, oceans, or grasslands would love to live in East Africa.

17. What is one opinion stated as a fact in this selection?

_____

_____

18. What phrase in the passage makes a biased comparison between East Africa and the other areas in Africa?

_____

_____

19. What kind of information could the writer add that would make the passage less biased?

_____

_____

20. How would you describe the tone of the selection?

_____

_____

21. Revise the second sentence in the passage so it is not biased.

_____

_____

TEST A

Cultures of Africa

A. Key Terms

Directions: Complete each sentence in Column I by writing the letter of the correct term from Column II in the blank. You will not use all the terms. *(10 points)*

Column I

_____ 1. The movement of customs and ideas from one place to another is called _____ .

_____ 2. A(n) _____ is a group of lineages that share one ancestor .

_____ 3. A West African storyteller is called a _____ .

_____ 4. The people of West Africa value the bond of _____ , or family relationship.

_____ 5. When the British ruled East Africa, people would work on a _____ , a large farm where cash crops are grown.

Column II

a. clan

b. cultural diffusion

c. griot

d. kinship

e. lineage

f. plantation

B. Key Concepts

Directions: Write the letter of the correct answer in each blank. *(45 points)*

_____ 6. Why is Islam so important in North Africa?
   a. People must practice Islam in order to trade here.
   b. It divides the people who live in rural and urban areas.
   c. It forms a common bond of culture among the people.
   d. Only the wealthiest people practice Islam.

_____ 7. The mixing of cultures in North Africa occurred because of
   a. geographic isolation and trade.
   b. trade and conquest.
   c. language and trade.
   d. disease and conquest.

_____ 8. The countries that form North Africa are
   a. Kenya, Algeria, Ethiopia, Mali, and Egypt.
   b. Egypt, Libya, Tunisia, Algeria, and Morocco.
   c. Ethiopia, Nigeria, Mali, Algeria, and Egypt.
   d. Niger, Congo, Mali, Nigeria, and Algeria.

_____ **9.** Why does West Africa have a wide variety of cultures?
    a. There are many ethnic groups living here.
    b. There are five main languages in the area.
    c. There is only one religion uniting all the people.
    d. There is only one way of making a living.

_____ **10.** One important change affecting family life in West Africa is that people are moving
    a. from one village to another.
    b. within their clan.
    c. from cities to villages.
    d. from villages to cities.

_____ **11.** Why does East Africa have great cultural diversity?
    a. It is along the Indian Ocean.
    b. It is on the Atlantic Ocean.
    c. It is on the Mediterranean Sea.
    d. It has many rivers running through it.

_____ **12.** The Swahili language is important in East Africa because it is used
    a. only in schools.
    b. for business and communication.
    c. by educated people in the cities.
    d. in the home.

_____ **13.** South Africa influenced nearby countries by inspiring people
    a. to struggle for majority rule.
    b. to establish monarchies.
    c. not to take part in their governments.
    d. to form political parties abroad.

_____ **14.** What is one way in which the country of South Africa has affected the region of Southern Africa economically?
    a. by borrowing money from every country in the region
    b. by mining minerals from nearby countries
    c. by buying most of its manufactured goods from other countries
    d. by using workers from all over the area in its mines

C. Critical Thinking

Directions: Answer the following questions on the back of this paper or on a separate sheet of paper. *(20 points)*

15. Making Comparisons Compare the relationship among ethnic groups in North Africa to that among groups in West Africa.

16. Recognizing Cause and Effect How has location affected the development of East African and North African cultures?

Tests

D. Skill: Assessing Your Understanding

Directions: Read the following passage. Then answer the questions. Write your answers in the blanks provided. (*25 points*)

There are several reasons why ancient Egyptian civilization developed close to the Nile River. The soil near the banks of the Nile was fertile, so farmers grew most of their crops here. The regular flooding of the river left deposits that kept the soil rich year after year. During the time of flooding, when farmers couldn't plant and take care of crops, many of them worked as builders. The Nile also provided a way to travel. Egyptians built boats with huge sails that they used to sail from city to city.

17. What is this passage about?

_____

_____

18. How does this passage relate to what you already know about Egypt?

_____

_____

19. What most interested you in this passage?

_____

_____

20. What does this passage tell you about the importance of the Nile River in the history of Egypt?

_____

_____

21. How could the information in this passage help you in your future schoolwork?

_____

_____

Cultures of Africa

A. Key Terms

Directions: Match the definitions in Column I with the terms in Column II. Write the correct letter in each blank. You will not use all the terms. *(10 points)*

Column I

_____ 1. groups of people who trace their roots to an early ancestor

_____ 2. family that includes parents and children

_____ 3. the spread of customs and ideas

_____ 4. the term applied to people who share similar beliefs and customs

_____ 5. a person who moves from place to place to work

Column II

a. clan

b. cultural diffusion

c. culture

d. lineage

e. migrant worker

f. nuclear family

g. plantation

B. Key Concepts

Directions: Write the letter of the correct answer in each blank. *(45 points)*

_____ 6. The different peoples of North Africa are unified by
    a. the French language and Islam.
    b. a common heritage and Confucianism.
    c. Islam and the Arabic language.
    d. a family relationship and Buddhism.

_____ 7. How did the mixing of cultures take place in North Africa?
    a. through trade and manufacturing
    b. through religion and multiparty government
    c. through trade and conquest
    d. through language and conquest

_____ 8. Because West Africa has hundreds of different ethnic groups, it has
    a. one central government.
    b. a variety of cultures.
    c. two common languages.
    d. two religions.

_____ **9.** How has urbanization affected life in West Africa?
  a. People are moving from cities to villages.
  b. Schools are being built in cities.
  c. People are moving from villages to cities.
  d. Highways are being built linking one village to another.

_____ **10.** One important method of preserving West African traditions is
  a. through sign language.
  b. by speaking a common language.
  c. by living on plantations.
  d. storytelling by griots.

_____ **11.** East Africa's cultural diversity results from its
  a. government.
  b. location.
  c. trade.
  d. politics.

_____ **12.** What culture do Africans who have African and Arab ancestry belong to?
  a. Berber
  b. Swahili
  c. Tuareg
  d. Maasai

_____ **13.** The economic needs of the country of South Africa have affected the whole region of Southern Africa because they create a great demand for
  a. labor.
  b. manufactured goods.
  c. imported food.
  d. water.

_____ **14.** What was one important result of the formation of the National Union of Mineworkers in South Africa?
  a. The workers' union was illegal.
  b. The workers led a movement for equal rights.
  c. The workers gained great economic power.
  d. The workers' interest in education led to school reform.

C. Critical Thinking

Directions: Answer the following questions on the back of this paper or on a separate sheet of paper. *(20 points)*

15. Recognizing Cause and Effect   What effect does Islam have on the culture of North Africa?

16. Identifying Central Issues   Explain this statement "South Africa is just one country in Southern Africa, but it has had the greatest impact on the region."

D. Skills: Assessing Your Understanding

Directions: Read the following passage. Then answer the questions. Write your answers in the blanks provided. *(25 points)*

> Ancient Egypt is one of the world's oldest civilizations. Its early history is divided into three periods: the Old Kingdom, the Middle Kingdom, and the New Kingdom. In between each period, there was a time of weak and unstable governments. During the Old Kingdom, the pyramids were built. During the Middle Kingdom, the capital was moved to Thebes. During the New Kingdom, Thebes and another city, Memphis, became important cultural and commercial centers in the world.

17. What is the main point of this passage?

_____

_____

18. How does this passage relate to what you already know about Egypt?

_____

_____

19. What topic in the reading do you want to learn more about?

_____

_____

20. What does this passage tell you about ancient Egyptian history?

_____

_____

21. How could you use the information in this passage in a school report?

_____

_____

Tests

TEST A

CHAPTER
4

Exploring North Africa

A. Key Terms

Directions: Match the definitions in Column I with the terms in Column II. Write the correct letter in each blank. You will not use all the terms. *(10 points)*

Column I

_____ 1. a platform cut into the mountainside

_____ 2. rural Egyptian farmers

_____ 3. an old section of a city in Algeria

_____ 4. an open-air market

_____ 5. the capital of Egypt

Column II

a. Arab

b. bazaar

c. Berber

d. Cairo

e. Ramadan

f. terrace

g. fellaheen

h. casbah

B. Key Concepts

Directions: Write the letter of the correct answer in each blank. *(45 points)*

_____ 6. The official religion of Egypt is
   a. Judaism.   **c.** Islam.
   b. Christianity.   **d.** Buddhism.

_____ 7. Most fellaheen
   a. do not own land.   **c.** do not follow Islamic practices.
   b. live in Cairo.   **d.** make a living by fishing.

_____ 8. Egyptian Muslims bring their religion into their daily life by
   a. obeying the words of Buddha.   **c.** following the teachings of the Quran.
   b. traveling to Cairo.   **d.** eating only during Ramadan.

_____ 9. Many Egyptian people move to the cities from rural areas in order to
    a. live in large homes.   **c.** practice their religion.
    b. expand their farms.   **d.** find jobs and a better education.

_____ 10. One way that Islam affects everyday life in Egypt is by requiring that men and women
    a. live in separate compounds.   **c.** pray once a day.
    b. dress modestly.   **d.** do not eat meat.

_____ 11. Unlike the Berbers, the Arabs who conquered North Africa were
    a. navigators.   **c.** sailors.
    b. nomads.   **d.** artisans.

_____ 12. The Berber village governments are based on
    a. the military.   **c.** the family.
    b. a dictatorship.   **d.** a monarchy.

_____ 13. Most people living in Berber villages are
    a. teachers and craftpersons.   **c.** traders and gatherers.
    b. farmers and herders.   **d.** sailors and farmers.

_____ 14. What unites many of the Berbers and Arabs who live in Algeria's cities?
    a. They speak Spanish and are nomads.   **c.** They speak Arabic and practice Islam.
    b. They all practice Christianity.   **d.** They work in separate neighborhoods.

C. Critical Thinking

Directions: Answer the following questions on the back of this paper or on a separate sheet of paper. *(20 points)*

15. **Drawing Conclusions**   Why do you think the Berbers eventually learned to live peacefully with their Arab conquerors? In your answer, consider the importance of religion and customs to both peoples.

16. **Making Comparisons**   Compare how people live in Egyptian and Algerian cities and towns.

Tests

D. Skill: Using Regional Maps

Directions: Use the map below to answer the following questions. Write your answers in the blanks provided. *(25 points)*

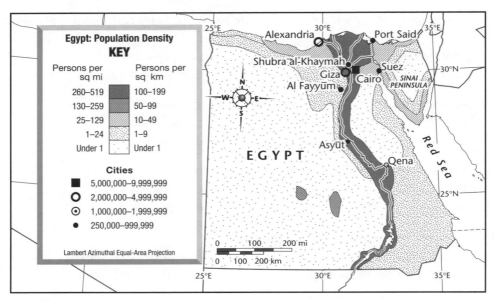

17. What region is shown on the map?

_____

_____

18. What basic information does the map provide about the region?

_____

_____

19. Name a city with a population density between 2,000,000 and 4,999,999.

_____

_____

20. What areas of the country have the largest population?

_____

_____

21. How might a population distribution map be helpful in learning about the way of life of the people of a particular region?

_____

_____

Exploring North Africa

A. Key Terms

Directions: Complete each sentence in Column I by writing the letter of the correct term from Column II in the blank. You will not use all the terms. *(10 points)*

Column I

_____ 1. The rural farmers of Egypt are called _____ .

_____ 2. The old section of an Algerian city is the _____ .

_____ 3. In Cairo, people often shop in an open-air market called a(n) _____ .

_____ 4. Egypt's capital and largest city is _____ .

_____ 5. In order to grow crops in a steep place, a Berber farmer creates a(n) _____ , which is a platform cut into the mountainside.

Column II

a. Arab

b. bazaar

c. Berber

d. Cairo

e. Ramadan

f. fellaheen

g. casbah

h. terrace

B. Key Concepts

Directions: Write the letter of the correct answer in each blank. *(45 points)*

_____ 6. The Quran is sacred to Muslims because they believe
   a. it is the word of God.
   b. it is an exciting book to read.
   c. it tells the story of Muhammad's life.
   d. it contains the story of Islam.

_____ 7. How do Egyptian Muslims bring their religion into their daily lives?
   a. by praying once a day in a church
   b. by not reading the Sharia
   c. by praying and fasting
   d. by keeping Islamic law separate from Egyptian law

_____ 8. Islamic law requires that all men and women
   a. eat during the day.
   b. pray once a day.
   c. face away from Mecca during prayer.
   d. dress modestly in public.

Tests

_____ **9.** Why do people move to Cairo from rural areas?
    a. to find jobs and a better education
    c. to avoid traffic jams and housing shortages
    b. to live in places that are not crowded
    d. to build large farms for their families

_____ **10.** One of the main sources of Sharia is
    a. the Bible.
    c. Egyptian songs.
    b. the Quran.
    d. village life.

_____ **11.** The Berbers and the Arabs are the two main ethnic groups of
    a. Egypt.
    c. Cairo.
    b. Algeria.
    d. Saudi Arabia.

_____ **12.** What was one key difference between the early Berbers and Arabs?
    a. The Arabs were farmers and the Berbers were nomads.
    c. The Berbers were farmers, and the Arabs were nomads.
    b. The Arabs were craftpersons, and the Berbers were nomads.
    d. The Arabs were sailors, and the Berbers were nomads.

_____ **13.** The Berber village governments are based on
    a. a dictatorship.
    c. a monarchy.
    b. the military.
    d. the family.

_____ **14.** After the Arabs conquered North Africa, the Berbers learned to
    a. accept Islam.
    c. destroy their own village governments.
    b. fight their conquerors.
    d. give up farming.

C. Critical Thinking

Directions: Answer the following questions on the back of this paper or on a separate sheet of paper. *(20 points)*

15. Recognizing Cause and Effect What effects does the practice of Islam have on daily life in Egypt? In your answer, discuss at least three effects.

16. Making Comparisons How are Arab and Berber traditions similar and different?

D. Skill: Using Regional Maps

Directions: Use the map below to answer the following questions. Write your
answers in the blanks provided. *(25 points)*

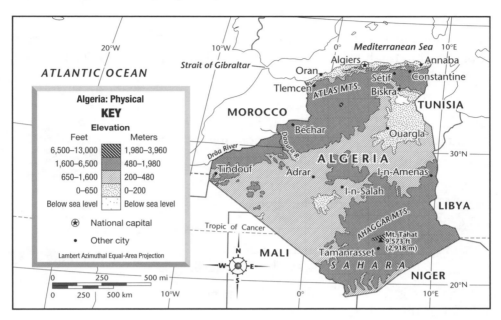

17. What country is shown on this map?

_____

_____

18. What basic information can this map give you?

_____

_____

19. What is the elevation of Adrar?

_____

_____

20. What is the capital of Algeria and what is its elevation?

_____

_____

21. What countries border Algeria?

_____

_____

Tests

Name _____ Class _____ Date _____

TEST A

CHAPTER
5

Exploring West Africa

A. Key Terms

Directions: Complete each sentence in Column I by writing the letter of the correct term from Column II in the blank. You will not use all the terms. *(10 points)*

Column I

_____ 1. By taking a count of all the people living in a country, or a(n) _____, the government finds out how many citizens actually live here.

_____ 2. Throughout history, many countries have fought for their _____, or political independence.

_____ 3. Grazing large herds of animals in one place can _____, or slowly wear away, the soil there.

_____ 4. When there is a long period with little or no rain, or a(n) _____, many crops die.

_____ 5. Because many ethnic groups live in West Africa, it is a(n) _____ region.

Column II

a. census

b. coup

c. desertification

d. drought

e. erode

f. multiethnic

g. sovereignty

B. Key Concepts

Directions: Write the letter of the correct answer in each blank. *(45 points)*

_____ 6. The main ethnic groups in Nigeria are
   a. Igbo, English, and Berber.
   b. Yoruba, Igbo, and Hausa-Fulani.
   c. Spanish, Fulani, and Hausa.
   d. French, Abuja, and Igbo.

_____ 7. For hundreds of years, the Hausa-Fulani have been known as great
   a. artisans.
   b. traders.
   c. farmers.
   d. miners.

_____ 8. How do most Yoruba who live in Nigeria make their living?
   a. by herding
   b. by manufacturing
   c. by farming
   d. by trading

_____ **9.** What was Great Britain's main goal when it ruled the Gold Coast?
- **a.** encouraging the growth of traditional religions
- **b.** controlling the country's economy
- **c.** expanding the growth of food crops
- **d.** encouraging the country's independence

_____ **10.** What was one important change that Kwame Nkrumah made after becoming president of Ghana?
- **a.** increasing world prices for the country's chief export, cocoa
- **b.** paying back the country's loans
- **c.** renaming the country
- **d.** solving the country's economic problems

_____ **11.** President Jerry Rawlings reformed Ghana's politics and economy by
- **a.** encouraging European traditions and values.
- **b.** building a dam on the Volta River.
- **c.** spending millions of dollars to build a conference center.
- **d.** stressing the traditional African value of hard work.

_____ **12.** Why is the Sahel so important to Mali?
- **a.** A small part of the country lies in this zone.
- **b.** A great percentage of the country lies in this zone.
- **c.** A large number of the citizens live beyond this zone.
- **d.** Many large factories are located here.

_____ **13.** What environmental change is threatening the way of life of the people of Mali?
- **a.** The desert is spreading south.
- **b.** The forests are spreading north.
- **c.** The savanna is getting too little rainfall.
- **d.** The Sahel is getting too much rainfall.

_____ **14.** Most people in Mali make their living by
- **a.** manufacturing, trading, and weaving.
- **b.** mining, forestry, and farming.
- **c.** trading, farming, and herding.
- **d.** manufacturing, mining, and herding.

C. Critical Thinking

Directions: Answer the following questions on the back of this paper or on a separate sheet of paper. *(20 points)*

15. Recognizing Cause and Effect   What effect is desertification having in Mali and other countries of the Sahel? In your answer, include a brief description of what desertification is.

16. Making Comparisons   How would you compare the contributions of Kwame Nkrumah and Jerry Rawlings to Ghana's economic development?

Tests

D. Skill: Using Distribution Maps

Directions: Use the distribution map below to answer the following questions. Write your answers in the blanks provided. *(25 points)*

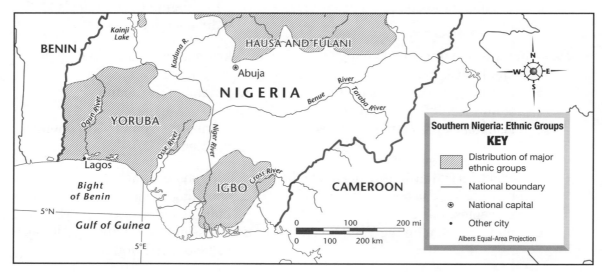

17. What does this map show the distribution of?

_____

_____

18. How is the distribution shown on this map?

_____

_____

19. What ethnic groups are shown?

_____

_____

20. What geographic features lie between the areas lived in by the Yoruba and Igbo ethnic groups?

_____

_____

21. What geographic features lie between the areas lived in by the Yoruba and the Hausa and Fulani ethnic groups?

_____

_____

Exploring West Africa

A. Key Terms

Directions: Match the definitions in Column I with the terms in Column II. Write the correct letter in each blank. You will not use all the terms. *(10 points)*

Column I

_____ 1. a long period of little or no rain

_____ 2. including many ethnic groups living within a country's borders

_____ 3. political independence

_____ 4. a takeover of a government

_____ 5. a count of all the people living in a country

Column II

a. census

b. coup

c. desertification

d. drought

e. ethnic group

f. multiethnic

g. sovereignty

B. Key Concepts

Directions: Write the letter of the correct answer in each blank. *(45 points)*

_____ 6. The three main ethnic groups in Nigeria are
    a. Yoruba, Fulani, and Hausa.
    b. Igbo, Yoruba, and Hausa-Fulani.
    c. Hausa-Fulani, Muslim, and Tuareg.
    d. Tuareg, Fulani, and Hausa.

_____ 7. How do most Yoruba support themselves?
    a. by mining
    b. by manufacturing
    c. by trading
    d. by farming

_____ 8. Why are the results of the census so important to the people of Nigeria?
    a. The three smallest ethnic groups will not vote in the election.
    b. The three largest ethnic groups will elect the president.
    c. The smallest ethnic group will receive extra government benefits.
    d. The largest ethnic group will have the most power in government.

_____ **9.** Why did Great Britain make the Gold Coast a colony?
   a. to improve the living conditions of the people
   b. to control the country's economy
   c. to establish a monarchy
   d. to encourage the people to become independent

_____ **10.** Kwame Nkrumah was thrown out of office because the people blamed him for the
   a. country's economic problems.
   b. growth of West African traditions.
   c. conflicts between ethnic groups.
   d. desertification of the Sahel.

_____ **11.** What is one way that Jerry Rawlings reformed Ghana's politics and economy?
   a. by asking people to give up their traditional religions
   b. by encouraging farmers to stop growing cocoa
   c. by stressing a renewal of traditional values
   d. by building a dam on the Volta River

_____ **12.** How is the Sahara a threat to the people of Mali?
   a. It is shrinking and will destroy the nomadic way of life.
   b. It is spreading south and will destroy the Sahel.
   c. It is attracting settlers who used to live in the Sahel.
   d. It is spreading to the east and will destroy the rain forest.

_____ **13.** The people in Mali who are most affected by desertification are the
   a. Tuareg.
   b. Igbo.
   c. Akan.
   d. Yoruba.

_____ **14.** One possible cause of desertification is
   a. mining.
   b. overgrazing.
   c. overplanting.
   d. planting.

C. Critical Thinking

Directions: Answer the following questions on the back of this paper or on a separate sheet of paper. *(20 points)*

15. Identifying Central Issues   What are three ways in which Ghana has changed since its independence?

16. Expressing Problems Clearly   How is desertification affecting the way of life for people in parts of Mali? In your answer, explain what desertification is.

D. Skill: Using Distribution Maps

Directions: Use the distribution map below to answer the following questions. Write your answers in the blanks provided. *(25 points)*

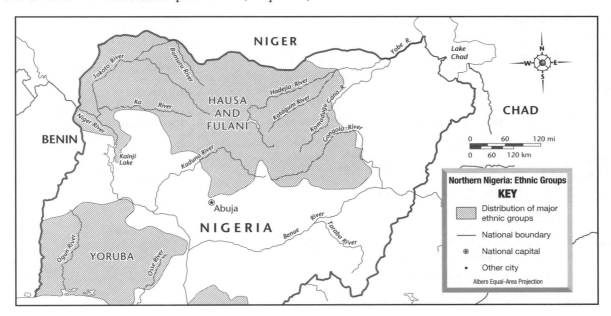

17. What does this map show the distribution of?

_____

_____

18. What does the shading mean on this map?

_____

_____

19. What two ethnic groups are labeled?

_____

_____

20. What ethnic group is in the majority in this part of Nigeria?

_____

_____

21. How do rivers appear to affect the distribution of ethnic groups?

_____

_____

Tests

TEST A

CHAPTER
6

Exploring East Africa

A. Key Terms
Directions: Match the definitions in Column I with the terms in Column II. Write the correct letter in each blank. You will not use all the terms. *(10 points)*

Column I

_____ 1. a place where priests and nuns live, work, and study

_____ 2. money owed to foreign countries

_____ 3. A language that many people speak as a second language is a _____ .

_____ 4. a national campaign in Kenya that encouraged the people there to work together to improve their country

_____ 5. A country that has more than two political parties has a _____ .

Column II

a. foreign debt

b. harambee

c. lingua franca

d. multiparty system

e. monastery

f. shamba

B. Key Concepts
Directions: Write the letter of the correct answer in each blank. *(45 points)*

_____ 6. The religions practiced by most Ethiopians today are
   a. traditional African religions and Christianity.
   b. Coptic Christianity and Islam.
   c. Judaism and Christianity.
   d. Buddhism and Islam.

_____ 7. Why did the Ethiopian Christian Church develop in a unique way?
   a. Ethiopian Christians were isolated from other Christians.
   b. Ethiopian Christians wanted to develop their own religion.
   c. Ethiopians encouraged Christians to convert to Judaism.
   d. Many Ethiopian Christians could not read English.

_____ 8. The rural town of Lalibela is famous as a(n)
   a. manufacturing center.
   b. political center.
   c. educational center.
   d. religious center.

_____ **9.** Why did President Nyerere adopt a new national language for Tanzania?
   a. so the people would keep their traditions
   b. so the government wouldn't be controlled by one ethnic group
   c. so the government wouldn't be controlled by the military
   d. so the people would vote in every election

_____ **10.** President Nyerere believed that a one-party system would help to
   a. continue a dictatorship.
   b. avoid ethnic hatred.
   c. begin a civil war.
   d. overthrow the monarchy.

_____ **11.** One important change made by Tanzania's new leaders was
   a. ending the foreign debt.
   b. adopting a new national language.
   c. ending ujamaa.
   d. raising fewer cash crops.

_____ **12.** Why do many Kenyan women remain in the countryside?
   a. They don't have to work as hard in the villages.
   b. They don't have to take care of children in their villages.
   c. There are few jobs in the cities.
   d. It's easier to support their families by farming.

_____ **13.** In Kenyan villages, the women solve community problems by
   a. asking the local government for help.
   b. asking their extended families for help.
   c. forming self-help groups.
   d. attending schools.

_____ **14.** Because of Kenya's geography, most of the people there are
   a. miners.
   b. farmers.
   c. artisans.
   d. manufacturers.

C. Critical Thinking

Directions: Answer the following questions on the back of this paper or on a separate sheet of paper. *(20 points)*

15. Identifying Central Issues   What are two major changes leaders in Tanzania made after President Nyerere left office?

16. Making Comparisons   Explain the similarities and differences in the ways people live in Nairobi and in Addis Ababa.

D. Skill: Using Isolines

Directions: Use your knowledge about isolines and the map below to answer the following questions. Write your answers in the blanks provided. *(25 points)*

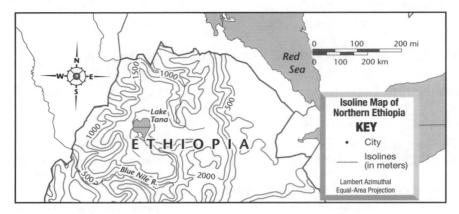

17. What is the difference in elevation, or interval, between each pair of isolines?

_____

_____

18. What is the lowest elevation shown on this map?

_____

_____

19. How does the land in the eastern part of this area differ from the land in the western part?

_____

_____

20. How can you tell whether an incline is steep or gradual by looking on this map?

_____

_____

21. If you were traveling to Lake Tana, why would you avoid traveling from the South?

_____

_____

Exploring East Africa

A. Key Terms

Directions: Complete each sentence in Column I by writing the letter of the correct term from Column II in the blank. You will not use all the terms. *(10 points)*

Column I

_____ 1. A monk is a priest who lives, works, and studies in a(n) _____ .

_____ 2. The president of Kenya began a campaign called _____ , which encouraged all citizens to work together to improve their country.

_____ 3. Many governments have elections using a _____ system.

_____ 4. Often a poor nation will have a large _____ , which is money owed to a foreign country.

_____ 5. People who speak different first languages can communicate in a common language called _____ .

Column II

a. foreign debt

b. harambee

c. lingua franca

d. monastery

e. shamba

f. multiparty system

g. urban

B. Key Concepts

Directions: Write the letter of the correct answer in each blank. *(45 points)*

_____ 6. The religions practiced by most Ethiopians today are
   a. Buddhism and Christianity.
   b. Judaism and Buddhism.
   c. Coptic Christianity and Islam.
   d. Judaism and Islam.

_____ 7. As Arabs took control of North and East Africa, some Ethiopians
   a. adopted Islam.
   b. adopted Christianity.
   c. resisted the Arabs.
   d. took control of West Africa.

_____ 8. Why did the Christian Church in Ethiopia develop differently than it did in other countries?
   a. Few Ethiopians became Christians.
   b. Most Ethiopians practiced traditional African religions.
   c. Ethiopian Christians had little contact with other Christians.
   d. Ethiopian Christians maintained close ties with other Christians.

_____ **9.** What was one way President Nyerere kept peace among different ethnic groups in Tanzania?

    a. by encouraging ethnic groups to speak their own language

    b. by adopting a national language that reflected only Arab culture

    c. by encouraging people to speak only English

    d. by adopting a national language that mixed African and Arab cultures

_____ **10.** President Nyerere's ujamaa program failed because many people

    a. didn't have enough water.

    b. wanted to work their own land.

    c. refused to work on family homesteads.

    d. produced too many crops.

_____ **11.** One important political change made by Tanzania's new leaders was

    a. forming a dictatorship.

    b. forming a monarchy.

    c. starting a one-party system.

    d. starting a multiparty system.

_____ **12.** Because of Kenya's geography and climate, the land there is suitable for

    a. manufacturing.

    b. mining.

    c. farming.

    d. forestry.

_____ **13.** What is one example of how harambee affects life in Kenya?

    a. People place little value on their family relationships.

    b. People work together in villages to build schools.

    c. People leave Kenya to live in other countries.

    d. People refuse to help other villagers farm their land.

_____ **14.** Why do so many Kenyan women remain in the villages?

    a. to farm the land

    b. to attend colleges

    c. to work in factories

    d. to work in tourist hotels

C. Critical Thinking

Directions: Answer the following questions on the back of this paper or on a separate sheet of paper. *(20 points)*

15. Recognizing Cause and Effect How did Ethiopia's location affect its early development? In your answer, consider the country's economy and its religion.

16. Drawing Conclusions In Kenya, many people are moving from the country to the city. How does the principle of harambee affect the people who move as well as the people who stay? In your answer, tell what harambee is and give at least two examples of it.

D. Skill: Using Isolines

Directions: Use your knowledge about isolines and the map below to answer the following questions. Write your answers in the blanks provided. *(25 points)*

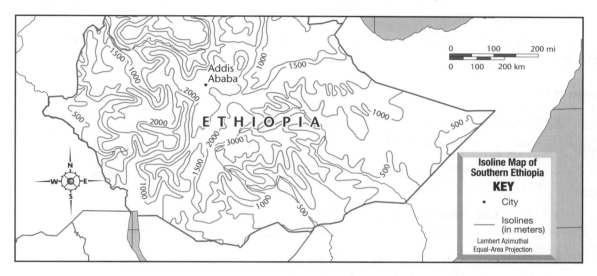

17. What is the difference in elevation, or interval, between each pair of isolines?

_____

_____

18. What is the highest elevation shown on this map?

_____

_____

19. What is the elevation of Addis Ababa?

_____

_____

20. How can you tell whether an incline is steep or gradual by looking at this map?

_____

_____

21. If you were traveling to Addis Ababa, from which direction would you come?

_____

_____

TEST A

Exploring Central and Southern Africa

A. Key Terms

Directions: Complete each sentence in Column I by writing the letter of the correct term from Column II in the blank. You will not use all the terms. *(10 points)*

Column I

_____ 1. To take a foreign-owned company and put it under government control is to ____ it.

_____ 2. A single leader or small group of leaders have all the power in a(n) ____ government.

_____ 3. The South African system in which racial groups were kept separate is called ____ .

_____ 4. When people treat a person unfairly because of his or her race, religion, or gender, they ____ against that person.

_____ 5. An area of land on which South African blacks were forced to live is a(n)____ .

Column II

a. apartheid

b. authoritarian

c. discriminate

d. homeland

e. Mandela

f. nationalize

g. Katanga

B. Key Concepts

Directions: Write the letter of the correct answer in each blank. *(45 points)*

_____ 6. Some of Congo's most important natural resources include
    a. water, natural gas, and sugar.
    b. copper, forests, and wildlife.
    c. sugar, wheat, and cocoa.
    d. forests, fruits, and vegetables.

_____ 7. The Belgian rulers of the Congo were mainly interested in the country's
    a. resources.
    b. history.
    c. language.
    d. culture.

_____ 8. What is one change Mobutu made after assuming control of Congo?
    a. He built many schools.
    b. He called for a general election.
    c. He nationalized foreign-owned industries.
    d. He established a monarchy.

_____ 9. What happened after Congo's economy collapsed?
   a. The government raised taxes.
   b. The government spent less money on schools.
   c. The government spent more money on health services.
   d. The government gave food to the poor people of the country.

_____ 10. Since independence, what has happened to the living conditions of most of the people in Congo?
   a. They have improved slightly.
   b. They have remained the same.
   c. They have declined.
   d. They have improved a great deal.

_____ 11. After South Africa became independent, the white-led government passed laws that
   a. permitted black people to own good land.
   b. kept land and wealth in white hands.
   c. improved the living conditions of black citizens.
   d. punished the British, French, and German settlers.

_____ 12. How did the apartheid laws affect South Africans?
   a. Everyone paid higher taxes.
   b. White and black workers were united.
   c. Racial discrimination became legal.
   d. All South Africans could vote.

_____ 13. Who did South Africans elect as their new president after the end of apartheid?
   a. Mobutu Sese Seko
   b. Nelson Mandela
   c. F. W. de Klerk
   d. Nomfundo Mhlana

_____ 14. The new South African government passed laws that ended
   a. black ownership of some land.
   b. economic problems facing the country.
   c. higher taxes in many poor villages.
   d. legal discrimination on the basis of race.

C. Critical Thinking

Directions: Answer the following questions on the back of this paper or on a separate sheet of paper. *(20 points)*

15. **Identifying Central Issues**   How would you describe life in Congo since independence? In your answer, discuss the social, political, and economic situations.

16. **Drawing Conclusions**   Why do you think the Africans living in the Congo Free State and South Africa fought for their independence from their white-led governments?

Tests

D. Skill: Organizing Your Time

Directions: Imagine that you have two weeks to write a three-page paper about life in South Africa today. Then answer the following questions about the plan you would make before you start the assignment. Write your answers in the blanks provided. *(25 points)*

17. What goal would you write at the top of the page?

_____

_____

18. What would be the first step in your plan?

_____

_____

19. What would be the next three steps in your plan?

_____

_____

20. How much time would each step take?

_____

_____

21. After completing your plan, what is your final step in organizing your time?

_____

_____

Exploring Central and Southern Africa

A. Key Terms

Directions: Match the definitions in Column I with the terms in Column II. Write the correct letter in each blank. You will not use all the terms. *(10 points)*

Column I

_____ **1.** to take under government control industries owned by foreign countries

_____ **2.** a kind of government in which a single leader or small group of leaders have all the power

_____ **3.** a South African system that legalized unfair treatment of blacks

_____ **4.** to treat people unfairly based on race, religion, or gender

_____ **5.** an area of South Africa where blacks were forced to live

Column II

a. apartheid

b. authoritarian

c. F. W. de Klerk

d. discriminate

e. homeland

f. Mobutu

g. nationalize

B. Key Concepts

Directions: Write the letter of the correct answer in each blank. *(45 points)*

_____ **6.** Most of Congo's wealth is produced by
   a. farming.
   b. forestry.
   c. mining.
   d. manufacturing.

_____ **7.** Belgium ruled the Congo in order to control the country's
   a. manufacturing.
   b. copper and diamonds.
   c. forestry and water.
   d. crops and wildlife.

_____ **8.** Why did foreign companies help Mobutu Sese Seko take control of Congo?
   a. to protect their businesses
   b. to provide medical care for the people
   c. to educate the children
   d. to improve the transportation system

Tests

_____ **9.** What did Mobutu do after he assumed power in Congo?
    a. improved the educational system
    b. held a general election
    c. nationalized foreign-owned industries
    d. established a multiparty political system

_____ **10.** Congo's economy collapsed in the late 1970s because the price of copper
    a. went up and down.
    b. increased.
    c. stayed the same.
    d. dropped sharply.

_____ **11.** Why did the British battle the Afrikaners for control of the Transvaal?
    a. because diamonds and gold were discovered there
    b. because the government collapsed
    c. because black Africans asked the British for help
    d. because copper was discovered there

_____ **12.** The apartheid laws passed by the National Party made
    a. racial discrimination legal.
    b. state elections necessary.
    c. a one-party system permanent.
    d. a dictatorship possible.

_____ **13.** How did blacks in South Africa live under the apartheid system?
    a. They attended the same schools as whites.
    b. They made economic advancements.
    c. They had almost no rights at all.
    d. They moved to cities and villages throughout the country.

_____ **14.** How did the election of Nelson Mandela change life in South Africa?
    a. All black citizens had to carry identification cards.
    b. White people were no longer able to own land.
    c. Legal discrimination on the basis of race ended.
    d. All farms became nationalized.

C. Critical Thinking

Directions: Answer the following questions on the back of this paper or on a separate sheet of paper. *(20 points)*

15. Identifying Central Issues Comment briefly on the following statement: "Resources dominate the history of Congo." Refer to at least two facts from the chapter in your answer.

16. Recognizing Cause and Effect How did South Africa's apartheid laws affect the lives of black people there?

D. Skill: Organizing Your Time

Directions: Imagine that you have three weeks to write a five-page paper about the history of Congo. Then answer the following questions about the plan you would make before you start the assignment. Write your answers in the blanks provided. *(25 points)*

17. When would you start the assignment?

_____

_____

18. What would be the first step in your plan and how much time would it take?

_____

_____

19. What would be the second step in your plan and how much time would it take?

_____

_____

20. What would be the third step and how much time would it take?

_____

_____

21. How much time would you have left to complete the last step?

_____

_____

Tests

Africa

A. Key Terms

Directions: Complete each sentence in Column I by writing the letter of the correct term from Column II in the blank. You will not use all the terms. *(10 points)*

Column I

_____ **1.** A person who moves around to various places to make a living is called a(n) _____ .

_____ **2.** The holy book of the religion of Islam is called the _____ .

_____ **3.** A(n) _____ is a section of rocky rapids or a waterfall.

_____ **4.** Throughout Africa's history, countries fought for their _____ , or political independence from colonial rulers.

_____ **5.** After Kenya gained independence, the new president began a campaign called _____ , which encouraged people to work together.

Column II

a. coup

b. drought

c. escarpment

d. cataract

e. harambee

f. nomad

g. oasis

h. Quran

i. sovereignty

B. Key Concepts

Directions: Write the letter of the correct answer in each blank. *(45 points)*

_____ **6.** Why is Africa often called the "plateau continent"?
   a. The elevation of much of the land area is high.
   b. The elevation of much of the land area is low.
   c. The land covering much of the continent rises near the sea.
   d. The land covering much of the continent is very hilly.

_____ **7.** What was one important effect of World War II on the people of Africa?
   a. It decreased their economic dependence on farming.
   b. It increased their dependence on their European rulers.
   c. It inspired them to win their freedom.
   d. It encouraged them to decrease their foreign debt.

_____ **8.** Most of Africa's major lakes are located in or near
   a. the Great Rift Valley.
   b. Egypt.
   c. the grasslands of West Africa.
   d. South Africa.

_____ **9.** What is the major part of Africa's economy?
   a. mining   **c.** manufacturing
   b. forestry   **d.** farming

_____ **10.** What is one important difference between the peoples of North Africa and West Africa?
   a. North Africans have not been influenced by cultures of other countries.
   c. West Africans are members of one major ethnic group.
   b. West Africans are not united by a single religion or common language.
   d. North Africans are not united by a single religion.

_____ **11.** Egyptian Muslims have brought Islam into their daily lives by
   a. encouraging immodest dress.
   c. praying and fasting.
   b. keeping their country's laws separate from the Sharia.
   d. closing many mosques.

_____ **12.** How does desertification threaten the people of Mali?
   a. by ruining the forests in the savanna
   c. by destroying the fertile land of the Sahel
   b. by making manufacturing in the cities impossible
   d. by causing flooding of the major rivers

_____ **13.** The major religions of Ethiopia are
   a. Christianity and Judaism.
   c. Islam and Judaism.
   b. Buddhism and Christianity.
   d. Christianity and Islam.

_____ **14.** In South Africa, the system that legalized racial discrimination was called
   a. Swahili.
   c. ujamaa.
   b. apartheid.
   d. souq.

C. Critical Thinking

Directions: Answer the following questions on the back of this paper or on a separate sheet of paper. *(20 points)*

15. Making Comparisons   Explain the similarities and differences between the ways of life in Cairo, Egypt, and an Egyptian village or between those in Nairobi, Kenya, and a Kenyan village.

16. Identifying Central Issues   Briefly describe one economic, one social, and one environmental issue facing African countries today. In your description, tell how African countries are trying to meet these challenges.

Tests

D. Skill: Using Distribution Maps

Directions: Use the distribution map below to answer the following questions. Write your answers in the blanks provided. *(25 points)*

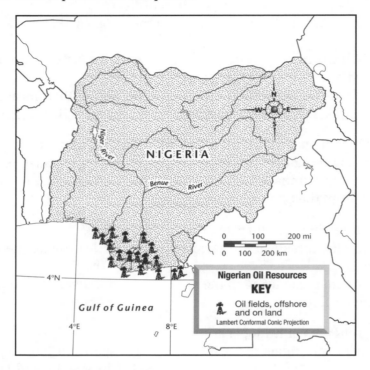

17. In general, what does this map show?

_____

_____

18. How is this resource indicated on the map key?

_____

_____

19. In general, what part of Nigeria has the most petroleum resources?

_____

_____

20. Are there more oil fields on land or offshore? How can you tell?

_____

_____

21. How could you use this map in writing a report about Nigeria?

_____

_____

Africa

A. Key Terms

Directions: Match the definitions in Column I with the terms in Column II. Write the correct letter in each blank. You will not use all the terms. *(10 points)*

Column I

_____ 1. the holy book of the religion of Islam

_____ 2. able to support many plants

_____ 3. traditional open-air market

_____ 4. kind of government controlled by one person or one small group

_____ 5. the change of productive land into land that is too dry or damaged to support life

Column II

a. authoritarian

b. bazaar

c. coup

d. desertification

e. drought

f. fertile

g. pilgrimage

h. plateau

i. Quran

B. Key Concepts

Directions: Write the letter of the correct answer in each blank. *(45 points)*

_____ 6. Africa is called the "plateau continent" because the elevation of the land is generally
    a. low.
    b. high.
    c. hilly.
    d. mountainous.

_____ 7. Most of North Africa is covered by
    a. the Kalahari Desert.
    b. a tropical rain forest.
    c. the Sahara.
    d. savanna.

_____ 8. In the 1400s, the Portuguese began exploring the coast of West Africa in order to
    a. build cities along the Nile River.
    b. establish farms in the area.
    c. buy African slaves.
    d. trade directly for gold and ivory.

Tests

_____ **9.** As Muslim traders traveled to different parts of Africa, they spread their
   a. religion.
   b. monarchy.
   c. weapons.
   d. politics.

_____ **10.** What two factors contributed to the mixing of cultures in North Africa?
   a. farming and forestry
   b. government and education
   c. trade and conquest
   d. religion and history

_____ **11.** Most Muslims in Egypt agree that the laws of the country should be based on
   a. Buddhist teachings.
   b. Islamic law.
   c. Confucian sayings.
   d. Christian practices.

_____ **12.** Why was Nkrumah overthrown by a military coup in Ghana?
   a. Many people blamed him for the country's economic problems.
   b. Citizens didn't like the monarchy he started.
   c. People didn't want a return to traditional African values.
   d. Farmers were producing too many crops to sell to other countries.

_____ **13.** Why did the Ethiopian Christian Church develop its own unique form of Christianity?
   a. It fought continually with the Muslim Arabs.
   b. It had little contact with Christians in other countries.
   c. It wasn't founded until the middle of the 1900s.
   d. It was influenced by the Muslim Arabs.

_____ **14.** What was the name of the system that made racial discrimination legal in South Africa?
   a. apartheid
   b. harambee
   c. ujamaa
   d. desertification

C. Critical Thinking

Directions: Answer the following questions on the back of this paper or on a separate sheet of paper. *(20 points)*

15. Identifying Central Issues   What is meant by the phrase "the scramble for Africa" when referring to the 1700s and 1800s? In your answer, explain why Great Britain wanted control of the Gold Coast and South Africa.

16. Distinguishing Fact From Opinion   Read the following statements. Then identify each as either a fact or an opinion. Give a reason for your choice.
   a. In 1990, South Africa's president, F. W. de Klerk, introduced laws that tore down the apartheid system.
   b. On the surface, things do not appear much different. But you know they are—you can feel it. The laws have changed, and that is a big deal.

D. Skill: Organizing Your Time

Directions: Imagine that you have one week to write a two-page paper about the climate and vegetation in North Africa. Then answer the following questions about the plan you would make before you start the assignment. Write your answers in the blanks provided. *(25 points)*

17. What goal would you write at the top of the page?

_____

_____

18. When would you start working on the assignment?

_____

_____

19. What would be the first step in your plan? How long would it take?

_____

_____

20. What would be the next three steps in your plan? How long would they take?

_____

_____

21. After completing the plan, what would be your final step to organize your time?

_____

_____

Answer Key

Chapter 1

Test A

1. h	**2.** i	**3.** f	**4.** g	**5.** c
6. c	**7.** b	**8.** a	**9.** d	**10.** d
11. c	**12.** d	**13.** c	**14.** a	

15. Answers will vary. A possible answer: The Nile is a river that flows north from its two sources, the White Nile and the Blue Nile, into the Mediterranean Sea. It's the world's longest river, and it carries water from the mountains of Africa's plateaus to the sea. It's also useful for traveling. The land surrounding the Nile is fertile farmland. The Aswan High Dam created Lake Nasser, which waters desert crops and provides electricity.

16. Answers will vary. A possible answer: Most of Africa's workers are farmers, and three fifths of the farmland is used by subsistence farmers, who raise crops to support their families. As a result, the economy is sensitive to influences such as rainfall and the world price of cash crops. To protect itself economically, Africa must diversify by producing a variety of raw materials, cash crops, and manufactured goods that the rest of the world needs.

17. It's a cross section of Africa, south of the Sahara.

18. the Atlantic Ocean

19. Crystal Mountains, Congo Basin,

20. Crystal Mountains

21. By indicating the elevation, it shows how sharply the coastal plain drops off to the shoreline.

Test B

1. g	**2.** f	**3.** b	**4.** d	**5.** h
6. c	**7.** a	**8.** b	**9.** c	**10.** b
11. a	**12.** b	**13.** c	**14.** b	

15. Answers may vary. A possible answer: Deserts have a hot, dry climate. It may not rain for years at a time. Very few things can grow there. The people who live in the desert are usually nomads and herders. They herd their livestock from one area to another in order to

get enough food and water. In the savanna, there is also a dry season. During this time, trees lose their leaves and rivers dry up. However, there is a wet season also, when plants can grow. Tall grasses, thorny bushes, and some trees grow in the savanna. In the dry season, people trade, build houses, and visit friends. In the wet season, farmers plant their crops.

16. Answers may vary. A possible answer: I think most people live on the banks of rivers such as the Nile. Most people in Africa make their living from farming, and the Nile deposits fertile soil along its banks. Also, the river provides a constant source of water and transportation.

17. It's a cross section of part of Africa.

18. Answers may vary. Possible answers include: Congo Basin, Mitumba Mountains, Great Rift Valley, Virunga Mountains, Serengeti Plain, Kenya Highlands.

19. the Indian Ocean

20. lower

21. Answers may vary. A possible answer: You can learn that a great plateau makes up much of Africa. You can learn about some of Africa's mountains and valleys.

Chapter 2

Test A

1. b	**2.** g	**3.** c	**4.** d	**5.** f
6. a	**7.** c	**8.** b	**9.** d	**10.** a
11. c	**12.** a	**13.** b	**14.** c	

15. Answers may vary. A possible answer: The Nile River was very important because it was the place where the Egyptian and Nubian civilizations arose. People settled there because they could farm the land along the banks of the river. This land had been made fertile by the layer of silt left behind during the annual Nile flood.

16. Answers may vary. A possible answer: The relationship had begun as trade between equals. However, the Europeans wanted to control the African trade themselves and settle the continent. The slave trade forced the

Answer Key

migration of millions of Africans from their homes. After it ended, European countries colonized the continent to capture its resources and to establish empires there.

17. Answers will vary. Possible response: People need freedom before they can learn to read and write.

18. Fifteen percent of people in Tanzania were literate when independence was gained. Today about 70 percent of people are literate.

19. Answers will vary. Possible response: The growth in literacy rates occurred after countries gained independence.

20. The bias is that people must be free in order to read and write.

21. Answers will vary. Sample response: As countries have gained their independence, more people are learning to read and write.

Test B

1. c	2. h	3. b	4. a	5. g
6. c	7. a	8. b	9. b	10. d
11. b	12. b	13. a	14. b	

15. Answers may vary. A possible answer: The movement probably encouraged countries to seek their independence because it stressed unity and cooperation among all Africans. The Pan-African leaders tried to unify all Africans, whether they lived in Africa or not. Their slogan,"Africa for Africans," encouraged people on the continent to free themselves from their European rulers.

16. Answers may vary. A possible answer: Because most African countries depend economically on exporting one or two products, they are sensitive to the rise and fall of world prices. To solve this problem, African countries are trying to diversify their economies. A second problem is how to feed their growing populations. To grow more food, governments are helping farmers develop hybrid plants.

17. Answers will vary. Possible response: The best place to live in Africa is East Africa.

18. Answers will vary. Possible response: The grasslands are nicer than the grasslands in any other part of Africa.

19. Answers will vary. Possible response: The writer could add information about other areas in Africa.

20. Answers will vary. Possible response: The tone is superior. Students may say the writer is bragging.

21. Answers will vary. Possible response: East Africa is a good place for people to live.

Chapter 3

Test A

1. b	2. a	3. c	4. d	5. f
6. c	7. b	8. b	9. a	10. d
11. a	12. b	13. a	14. d	

15. Answers will vary. A possible answer: In North Africa the different groups are united by Islam and the Arabic language. On the other hand, in West Africa the hundreds of different ethnic groups practice different religions and speak different languages. The groups are not as united.

16. Answers may vary. A possible answer: Because North Africa is located on the Mediterranean Sea, it has always been a center of trade. As a result of this trade link and the conquest of other empires, a mixing of cultures in North Africa occurred. Similarly, East Africa's cultural diversity has resulted from its location along the Indian Ocean. When Arab traders settled in the coastal villages of East Africa, their culture mixed with African cultures and resulted in Swahili.

17. life along the Nile River in ancient Egypt

18. Answers will vary. A possible answer: It tells about life in a North African country I read about in the chapter.

19. Answers may vary. A possible answer: I was interested in the idea that farmers worked on the pyramids during the yearly flood.

20. Egyptian civilization was founded along the banks of the Nile.

21. Answers may vary. A possible answer: I could use this information in a report about ancient Egypt.

Tests

Answer Key

Test B

1. a   **2.** f   **3.** b   **4.** c   **5.** e

6. c   **7.** c   **8.** b   **9.** c   **10.** d

11. b   **12.** b   **13.** a   **14.** b

15. Answers may vary. A possible answer: In North Africa, people are united across ethnic lines by their common belief in the Muslim religion. Islamic law affects every aspect of daily life.

16. Answers may vary. A possible answer: South Africa has had great political influence. The struggle of black South Africans for political rights inspired similar movements in nearby countries, especially in Namibia and Zimbabwe. South Africa has also had economic influence. Because it produces so many of the manufactured goods, minerals, and agricultural products of the continent, South Africa has had a tremendous need for labor. As a result, workers come to South Africa from other countries in the region.

17. to describe different periods of ancient Egyptian history

18. Answers will vary. Possible answer: I already knew about the pyramids. This selection tells me during what period they were built.

19. Answers may vary. Possible answer: I'd like to know more about Thebes and Memphis.

20. There are three periods of ancient Egyptian history, with periods of instability between them.

21. Answers may vary. A possible answer: I could use this information in a report about the pyramids.

Chapter 4

Test A

1. f   **2.** g   **3.** h   **4.** b   **5.** d

6. c   **7.** a   **8.** c   **9.** d   **10.** b

11. b   **12.** c   **13.** b   **14.** c

15. Answers will vary. A possible answer: When most Berbers accepted Islam, the Arabs' religion, peace came to the region. Also, the traditions of both people are similar. They both live in extended families. To accommodate differences between the two traditions, the Berbers were willing to compromise. For example, they adapted to Arab rule by keeping their own village governments along with the Arab central government in Algeria.

16. Answers will vary. A possible answer: The lifestyles in Egyptian and Algerian cities and towns are very similar. The cities in both countries are crowded, since about half of all Egyptians and Algerians live in these urban centers. In both countries, the cities blend the modern with the traditional; in Egypt there are bazaars, and in Algeria there are mosques and open-air markets. Most of the Egyptians in the rural areas are farmers who live in villages along the Nile River or the Suez Canal. In Algeria, the Berbers and Arabs who live in rural areas are farmers and nomads. Many of these villagers in both countries have retained a way of life that has remained unchanged since ancient times.

17. Egypt

18. It tells where people live.

19. Possible answers: Alexandria and Giza.

20. Many people live along the Nile River and the Suez Canal. That is where the major cities are.

21. Answers may vary. A possible answer: This map shows that although Egypt is a fairly large country, most of its population lives in the highly dense area around the waterways. For this reason, people in Egypt might have some problems with crowding.

Test B

1. f   **2.** g   **3.** b   **4.** d   **5.** h

6. a   **7.** c   **8.** d   **9.** a   **10.** b

11. b   **12.** c   **13.** d   **14.** a

15. Answers will vary. A possible answer: Since the teachings of the Quran affect Egyptian law as well as the behavior of individual Muslims, Islam has many effects on daily life in Egypt. One effect is that men and women both dress modestly in public. Another effect is that five times a day, people face toward Mecca and

Answer Key

pray. A third effect is that people try to follow the Quran's teachings about honesty, honor, and giving to others.

16. Answers may vary. A possible answer: Traditionally, both Arabs and Berbers live in extended families. However, Arabs are traditionally nomads while Berbers are traditionally farmers. Also, Berbers ruled themselves with family-based village governments while Arabs had larger governments.

17. Algeria

18. This map shows Algeria's elevation, the locations of cities, and the location of the capital. It also shows major landforms and political boundaries.

19. 650–1,600 feet

20. Algiers, which has an elevation of 0–650 feet

21. Libya, Mali, Niger, Morocco, and Tunisia

Chapter 5

Test A

1. a	2. g	3. e	4. d	5. f
6. b	7. b	8. c	9. b	10. c
11. d	12. b	13. a	14. c	

15. Answers may vary. A possible answer: Desertification takes place when fertile lands are changed into lands that are too dry or damaged to support life. As the Sahara spreads south, countries of the Sahel, including Mali, are threatened by desertification. If the land becomes infertile, people will be unable to farm or graze their livestock there, as they have for hundreds of years.

16. Answers may vary. A possible answer: Under Nkrumah, Ghana developed serious economic problems. He borrowed millions of dollars to build expensive projects, such as a dam and a superhighway. However, when the world prices for cocoa fell, Ghana could not repay its loans. Under Rawlings, however, Ghana's economy grew. As a result of this growth, the country has built better roads and irrigation systems.

17. ethnic groups in southern Nigeria

18. Different shadings are used to show the different ethnic groups.

19. The Yoruba, the Igbo, and the Hausa and Fulani are shown.

20. the Niger and the Kaduna rivers

21. the Niger River

Test B

1. d	2. f	3. g	4. b	5. a
6. b	7. d	8. d	9. b	10. a
11. c	12. b	13. a	14. b	

15. Answers may vary. A possible answer: 1. Ghana has brought in more modern technology. 2. Nkrumah hurt the economy of the country by spending too much money. 3. Rawlings improved the economy by stressing traditional values of hard work and sacrifice. He built roads and irrigation systems.

16. Answers may vary. A possible answer: Desertification is the change of fertile land into land that is too dry or damaged to support life. For hundreds of years, the Tuareg have lived in the Sahel, which is now being threatened by desertification. The Tuareg are nomads who make their living by herding livestock from place to place. Desertification has threatened their food and water supplies, and many of their livestock have died during droughts. If the Sahel can't support the Tuareg and their herds, these people may have to settle permanently near towns or cities.

17. ethnic groups in northern Nigeria

18. Shading is used to show the distribution of different ethnic groups.

19. the Yoruba and the Hausa and Fulani

20. The Hausa and Fulani are the majority group.

21. Both groups live near many rivers.

Chapter 6

Test A

| 1. e | 2. a | 3. c | 4. b | 5. d |

Answer Key

6. b **7.** a **8.** d **9.** b **10.** b
11. c **12.** d **13.** c **14.** b

15. Answers may vary. A possible answer: The new leaders ended ujamaa and decided that farms should produce more cash crops. They also changed the election system and allowed new political parties to form. As a result, Tanzania now has a multiparty system of government.

16. Answers will vary. A possible answer: Similarities: Addis Ababa is the capital of Ethiopia, and Nairobi is the capital of Kenya. Both are modern cities with all the amenities of city life. Differences: Addis Ababa has a traditional, rural side with some residents living in houses made of stone and mud. Only a small percentage of Ethiopia's people live in rurual areas. However, the population of Nairobi continues to grow as more people arrive there from villages looking for work.

17. 500 meters

18. 500 meters

19. The land in the eastern part is lower and more level than the land in the western part, which is higher.

20. The closer the isolines are, the steeper the incline is.

21. Traveling from the South would require going through rugged hills and crossing the Blue Nile River.

Test B

1. d **2.** b **3.** f **4.** a **5.** c
6. c **7.** a **8.** c **9.** d **10.** b
11. d **12.** c **13.** b **14.** a

15. Answers will vary. A possible answer: Ancient Ethiopia bordered the Red Sea, and the main source of the Nile River was in its highlands. As a result, the country was a center of trade. People also learned about each other's religions by trading goods along the Nile River and the Red Sea, and Coptic Christianity slowly spread from Egypt to Ethiopia.

16. Answers will vary. A possible answer: Harambee is a Swahili word meaning "to pull together." Independent Kenya's first president

had a campaign called harambee. One example of harambee is that when men move to the city, members of their ethnic group will share rooms with them and help them out. Another example of harambee is that the women who have stayed at home have formed self-help groups to help each other earn money and solve problems.

17. 500 meters

18. 3000 meters

19. 2000 meters

20. The closer the isolines are, the steeper the incline is.

21. Answers will vary. A possible answer: I would travel from the Northeast, where there are fewer steep hills.

Chapter 7

Test A

1. f **2.** b **3.** a **4.** c **5.** d
6. b **7.** a **8.** c **9.** b **10.** c
11. b **12.** c **13.** b **14.** d

15. Answers may vary. A possible answer: Economically, socially, and politically, life has been very difficult for people in Congo since independence. Mobutu's economic plans failed, and the economy collapsed. Mobutu responded to the economic problems by cutting his government's social spending, which hurt the poor people most. Since he had all the political power, he was able to imprison anyone who protested against his policies.

16. Answers will vary. A possible answer: Under their Belgian rulers, the Africans in the Congo Free State suffered and starved. The Belgians were interested only in mining the country's vast mineral resources. In South Africa, the white-led government enforced apartheid, which made discrimination legal, and granted black South Africans almost no rights.

17. Write a three-page paper about life in South Africa today.

18. researching and taking notes on life in South Africa today

Answer Key

19. review notes; write first draft of report; review the final copy

20. Answers may vary. A possible answer: Step 1: four days, Step 2: one day, Step 3: two days, Step 4: one day

21. transferring the information to a calendar, writing down which step of the chart I will work on each day.

Test B

1. g	**2.** b	**3.** a	**4.** d	**5.** e
6. c	**7.** b	**8.** a	**9.** c	**10.** d
11. a	**12.** a	**13.** c	**14.** c	

15. Answers will vary. A possible answer: The power of the early rulers of Congo depended on their knowledge of ironworking. The first Europeans who came to the area were looking for gold. Later, the Belgians were interested in controlling the Congo's resources, especially its copper and diamonds.

16. Answers may vary. A possible answer: The apartheid laws divided South Africans into categories based on race that left blacks with almost no rights at all. Black South Africans lived in poverty in poor rural areas. They were denied citizenship rights, including the right to vote, and were kept in low-paying jobs. They weren't allowed to enter white restaurants, schools, or hospitals.

17. today

18. research the history of Congo; This would take five days. [Time may vary.]

19. review notes; This would take one day. [Time may vary.]

20. write draft of assignment; This would take four days. [Time may vary.]

21. I would have four days to review and revise my final paper. [Time may vary.]

Final Exam A

1. f	**2.** h	**3.** d	**4.** i	**5.** e
6. a	**7.** c	**8.** a	**9.** d	**10.** b
11. c	**12.** c	**13.** d	**14.** b	

15. Answers will vary. Possible answer (1): Cairo is the largest city in Africa. While parts of the city look like a modern Western city, there are also traditional bazaars. Since many people move there from rural areas to find jobs and a better education, the city is crowded with traffic jams and housing shortages. Some people live on rowboats on the Nile. In Egyptian villages, traditions have changed little in 4,000 years. The farmers there live in homes built of mud bricks or stones and still use ancient farming techniques. In both the city and the villages, Islam is an important part of daily life. Possible answer (2): In Nairobi, the capital of Kenya, the population is always increasing. People arrive daily looking for work. Many of the newcomers walk to their jobs from the outskirts of the city, where they live. Men from the same ethnic group often live together and help each other. Women and children often stay behind in Kenyan villages when the men leave to seek work in the cities. In villages, the women grow cash crops in addition to the food they grow to feed their own families. They work together in self-help groups to solve common problems. In both the city and the villages, people practice harambee.

16. Answers may vary. A possible answer: Since about 75 percent of African countries have economies that depend on the export of one or two products, they are extremely sensitive to the rise and fall of world prices. To solve this problem, they are diversifying their economies. An important social issue is education. African children often work on family farms or sell products in the markets instead of attending school. Now countries are building more schools and working to increase the literacy rate. An environmental problem is soil erosion. When forests are cut down, the soil is washed away. To solve this problem, farmers in some countries now plant certain crops, such as yams, in long rows. Between the rows they plant trees to hold the soil in place.

17. petroleum resources in Nigeria

18. an oil derrick

19. The area along the southern coast has the most oil fields.

Tests

Answer Key

20. You can tell that there are more oil fields on land because there are more icons on land.

21. Answers may vary. A possible answer: I could use this map in writing a report about the resources of Nigeria.

Final Exam B

1. i   **2.** f   **3.** b   **4.** a   **5.** d

6. b   **7.** c   **8.** d   **9.** a   **10.** c

11. b   **12.** a   **13.** b   **14.** a

15. Answers may vary. A possible answer: The "scramble for Africa" refers to the efforts by European countries to colonize Africa because of the vast mineral resources and opportunities to establish empires here. Great Britain made the Gold Coast into a colony because it wanted to control the economy of the country, particularly the cocoa, timber, and gold. Great Britain fought the Afrikaners for control of South Africa for the same reason—they wanted to control the land and wealth. For example, when diamonds and gold were discovered in the Transvaal, the British pushed the Afrikaners off their land.

16. Statement *a* is a fact because it can be proved to be true. Statement *b* is an opinion because it reflects a personal point of view.

17. Write a two-page paper about the climate and vegetation of North Africa in one week.

18. today

19. Research the climate and vegetation of North Africa in a library. I would take two days. [Times may vary.]

20. review notes (one day); write first draft of report (two days); review the final copy (one day) [Times may vary.]

21. to get a calendar and write down which step of the flowchart I will work on each day

Chapter 1 Africa: Physical Geography

Letter Home
Carta para la familia   3
Section 1 Guided Reading and Quiz
   Lectura dirigida y Examen   4
Section 2 Guided Reading and Quiz
   Lectura dirigida y Examen   6
Section 3 Guided Reading and Quiz
   Lectura dirigida y Examen   8
Chapter Summary
Resumen del capítulo   10
Vocabulary Activity
Actividad de vocabulario   11

Chapter 2 Africa: Shaped by Its History

Letter Home
Carta para la familia   12
Section 1 Guided Reading and Quiz
   Lectura dirigida y Examen   13
Section 2 Guided Reading and Quiz
   Lectura dirigida y Examen   15
Section 3 Guided Reading and Quiz
   Lectura dirigida y Examen   17
Section 4 Guided Reading and Quiz
   Lectura dirigida y Examen   19
Section 5 Guided Reading and Quiz
   Lectura dirigida y Examen   21
Chapter Summary
Resumen del capítulo   23
Vocabulary Activity
Actividad de vocabulario   24

Chapter 3 Cultures of Africa

Letter Home
Carta para la familia   25
Section 1 Guided Reading and Quiz
   Lectura dirigida y Examen   26
Section 2 Guided Reading and Quiz
   Lectura dirigida y Examen   28
Section 3 Guided Reading and Quiz
   Lectura dirigida y Examen   30
Section 4 Guided Reading and Quiz
   Lectura dirigida y Examen   32
Chapter Summary
Resumen del capítulo   34
Vocabulary Activity
Actividad de vocabulario   35

Chapter 4 Exploring North Africa

Letter Home
Carta para la familia   36
Section 1 Guided Reading and Quiz
   Lectura dirigida y Examen   37
Section 2 Guided Reading and Quiz
   Lectura dirigida y Examen   39
Chapter Summary
Resumen del capítulo   41
Vocabulary Activity
Actividad de vocabulario   42

Chapter 5 Exploring West Africa

Letter Home
Carta para la familia   43
Section 1 Guided Reading and Quiz
   Lectura dirigida y Examen   44
Section 2 Guided Reading and Quiz
   Lectura dirigida y Examen   46
Section 3 Guided Reading and Quiz
   Lectura dirigida y Examen   48
Chapter Summary
Resumen del capítulo   50
Vocabulary Activity
Actividad de vocabulario   51

Chapter 6 Exploring East Africa

Letter Home
Carta para la familia   52
Section 1 Guided Reading and Quiz
   Lectura dirigida y Examen   53
Section 2 Guided Reading and Quiz
   Lectura dirigida y Examen   55
Section 3 Guided Reading and Quiz
   Lectura dirigida y Examen   57
Chapter Summary
Resumen del capítulo   59
Vocabulary Activity
Actividad de vocabulario   60

Spanish Support

CHAPTER 7 **Exploring Central and Southern Africa**

Letter Home
Carta para la familia   61
Section 1   Guided Reading and Quiz
    Lectura dirigida y Examen   62
Section 2   Guided Reading and Quiz
    Lectura dirigida y Examen   64
Chapter Summary
Resumen del capítulo   66
Vocabulary Activity
Actividad de vocabulario   67

Glossary *Glosario*   68

Answer Key *Respuestas*   74

ÁFRICA
Geografía física

CAPÍTULO
1

La Línea Abierta de Ciencias Sociales

Querida familia:

Durante las próximas semanas, en nuestra clase de ciencias sociales estudiaremos al África. Estudiaremos la geografía, la historia y las culturas del continente. Algunos de los temas que veremos son: las cuatro regiones de África, la importancia de la ubicación de cada región, la gran diversidad cultural del continente y la forma como está cambiando la vida para muchos de sus habitantes.

En el Capítulo 1, estudiaremos las principales características físicas del África, incluyendo el Gran Valle del Rift, el Sahara, el Sahel, los cuatro ríos principales y las grandes elevaciones en el interior del continente. También veremos cómo la latitud, la elevación y la distancia que hay a las grandes extensiones de agua y a los accidentes geográficos afectan el clima de África. Cuando pasee por su vecindario, anime a su hijo o hija a hablar sobre el clima: ¿Es lluvioso o no, está haciendo calor o frío? ¿Cómo afecta el clima su estilo de vida? ¿Es el clima bueno para el cultivo de alimentos? ¿Cómo cree él o ella que se compara el clima de su región con los climas de África?

Estudiar un atlas mundial puede ser un buen inicio para hablar sobre el tema. Usted puede comparar la latitud de su comunidad con la de otras regiones de África y predecir cómo la diferencia de latitud puede afectar el clima. También puede ayudar a su hijo o hija a buscar artículos con fotografías de África. Las fotografías y los artículos son de mucha utilidad para pegarlos en nuestro tablero de actividades de la clase.

Esté a la espera de nuevas noticias sobre los estudios de África de nuestra clase. Cada vez que comencemos un nuevo capítulo, usted recibirá una carta de la la línea abierta de ciencias sociales. Espero que tanto usted como su hijo o hija disfruten al compartir nuestros estudios de África.

Atentamente,

Spanish Support

LECTURA DIRIGIDA Y REPASO

La tierra y el agua

A. Durante la lectura

Instrucciones: A medida que vayas leyendo la Sección 1, escribe tus respuestas a las siguientes preguntas en los espacios en blanco.

I. ¿Por qué se conoce a África como "el continente de la gran meseta"?

_____

2. ¿Cerca de qué accidente geográfico están localizados la mayoría de los lagos principales de África?

_____

3. ¿Cuáles son los nombres de los cuatro ríos principales de África?

_____

4. ¿Por qué es imposible para los barcos navegar desde el interior del continente africano hasta el mar?

_____

B. Repaso de los términos clave

Instrucciones: Para completar cada oración, escribe el término correspondiente en el espacio en blanco.

5. zona plana y extensa que se eleva por encima del terreno a su alrededor _____ .

6. la altura de la tierra sobre el nivel del mar _____ .

7. risco largo y empinado _____ .

8. hendidura profunda en la tierra _____ .

9. salto rocoso de un río _____ .

10. trozos de roca y lodo en el fondo de los ríos _____ .

11. que puede producir muchas plantas _____ .

12. arroyo o río pequeño que desemboca en un río más grande _____ .

CAPÍTULO 1
ÁFRICA
Geografía física

La tierra y el agua

A. Términos y conceptos clave

Instrucciones: Lee las oraciones a continuación. Si una oración es verdadera, escribe V en el espacio en blanco. Si es falsa, escribe F. En otra hoja de papel, vuelve a escribir las oraciones falsas para convertirlas en verdaderas.

_____ **1.** Una zona elevada, extensa y plana se llama meseta.

_____ **2.** A través de África, la elevación, o la altura bajo el nivel del mar, es relativamente baja.

_____ **3.** Cuando la tierra es fértil, muy pocas plantas crecen allí.

_____ **4.** Un arroyo o río pequeño que desemboca en un río más grande es un tributario.

_____ **5.** En muchas partes de África, la franja costera termina en un acantilado o risco empinado.

B. Ideas principales

Instrucciones: En cada espacio en blanco, escribe la letra que mejor conteste la pregunta.

_____ **6.** África se conoce comúnmente como "el continente de la gran meseta" porque el terreno por lo general es
  a. plano. **c.** elevado.
  b. húmedo. **d.** seco.

_____ **7.** ¿Cuál es uno de los principales accidentes geográficos del este de África?
  a. el Kilimanjaro **c.** la represa de Aswan
  b. el Sahara **d.** el Río Congo

_____ **8.** Los barcos no pueden navegar desde el interior de África hasta el mar
  a. debido a las cataratas de los ríos.
  b. debido a las inundaciones mensuales de los ríos.
  c. porque hay muchas grietas en los ríos.
  d. debido a la poca profundidad de los ríos.

_____ **9.** ¿Cuáles son tres de los ríos más importantes de África?
  a. el Ghana, el Zambeze y el Níger **c.** el Nilo, el Congo y el Níger
  b. el Kilimanjaro, el Congo y el Nilo **d.** el Guinea, el Zambeze y el Sahara

_____ **10.** ¿Por qué se pudieron cultivar las tierras que rodean al Río Nilo?
  a. Debido a las inundaciones frecuentes que depositaban ricos sedimentos.
  b. Debido a las lluvias fuertes que suplían el agua necesaria para los cultivos.
  c. Debido a que los comerciantes establecieron centros de comercio en la zona.
  d. Debido a que los agricultores podían comprar muchos tipos de semillas de los comerciantes.

Spanish Support

LECTURA DIRIGIDA Y REPASO

El clima y la vegetación

A. Durante la lectura

Instrucciones: A medida que vayas leyendo la Sección 2, completa la siguiente tabla con la información del clima y la vegetación en África. Bajo cada idea principal, escribe dos ideas que la apoyen.

Idea principal A
Hay tres factores principales que afectan el clima de África.

I. _____
_____

2. _____
_____

3. _____
_____

Idea principal B
Hay tres tipos principales de regiones en África según su vegetación.

4. _____
_____

5. _____
_____

6. _____
_____

B. Repaso de los términos clave

Instrucciones: Para completar cada oración, escribe el término correspondiente en el espacio en blanco.

7. En los terrenos muy áridos, los agricultores tienen que _____ sus cultivos con frecuencia.

8. Algunas veces en medio del desierto, los viajeros pueden hallar _____ con agua y alguna vegetación.

9. Las personas que se mudan de un lugar a otro para sobrevivir se llaman _____ .

Nombre _____ Clase _____ Fecha _____

CAPÍTULO 1
ÁFRICA
Geografía física

El clima y la vegetación

A. Términos y conceptos clave

Instrucciones: Empareja las definiciones de la Columna I con los términos de la Columna II. Escribe la letra correspondiente en cada espacio en blanco.

Columna I

_____ 1. En los países donde casi no llueve, los agricultores tienen que regar artificialmente, o _____ , sus cultivos.

_____ 2. Un lugar en medio de una región árida con lluvias cortas y suaves, y agua potable subterránea se conoce como _____ .

_____ 3. Una persona que se muda a varios lugares para sobrevivir es _____ .

_____ 4. El lugar donde el extremo sur del Sahara se junta con la sabana se llama _____ .

_____ 5. A veces deja de llover por varios años seguidos en ciertas zonas del _____ en África del Sur.

Columna II

a. Sahel

b. un nómada

c. irrigar

d. un oasis

e. Desierto de Namib

B. Ideas principales

Instrucciones: En cada espacio en blanco, escribe la letra que mejor conteste la pregunta.

_____ 6. La distancia de una región a la línea ecuatorial, su elevación, y su cercanía a grandes extensiones de agua y accidentes geográficos influyen en
    a. su clima.
    b. su terreno.
    c. sus recursos minerales
    d. su industria.

_____ 7. En África, ¿cómo hacen los agricultores de las regiones áridas para prepararse para la posible falta de lluvias?
    a. Cultivan un solo producto.
    b. Cultivan diferentes productos.
    c. No irrigan sus cultivos.
    d. Compran las cosechas.

_____ 8. En África Central, gran parte del bosque húmedo ha sido destruido, porque se
    a. han cortado los árboles.
    b. han sembrado muchos árboles.
    c. ha usado el terreno para la agricultura industrial.
    d. ha irrigado el terreno para mantener la humedad de los árboles.

_____ 9. Al norte y al sur del bosque húmedo, África está cubierta por
    a. desiertos.
    b. montañas.
    c. sabanas.
    d. el Sahel.

_____ 10. La mayoría de los nómadas que viven en el Sahara son
    a. artesanos.
    b. comerciantes.
    c. fabricantes.
    d. pastores.

Spanish Support

LECTURA DIRIGIDA Y REPASO

Los recursos naturales

A. Durante la lectura

Instrucciones: A medida que vayas leyendo la Sección 3, completa la tabla a continuación con información de la agricultura y la minería en África. Luego, para completar cada oración, escribe el término correspondiente en el espacio en blanco.

Productos de África

Agricultura
1.
Minería
2.

3. La mayoría de los trabajadores africanos son _____ .

4. Los países africanos están tratando de diversificar su _____ con el desarrollo de nuevos cultivos, nuevas materias primas y productos manufacturados.

5. En la mayoría de África, las compañías _____ explotan las minas y se llevan las ganancias.

6. África tiene pocas _____ para producir productos de sus propias materias primas.

B. Repaso de los términos clave

Instrucciones: En los espacios en blanco a continuación, escribe las definiciones para los siguientes términos clave.

7. agricultura de subsistencia

_____

_____

8. cultivo para la exportación

_____

_____

CAPÍTULO 1
ÁFRICA
Geografía física

Los recursos naturales

A. Términos y conceptos clave

Instrucciones: Empareja las definiciones de la Columna I con los términos de la Columna II. Escribe la letra correspondiente en cada espacio en blanco.

Columna I

_____ 1. un sistema en el que los agricultores cultivan cosechas para sostener a sus familias

_____ 2. un cultivo, como el té, el café o el cacao, que los agricultores cosechan para vender

_____ 3. añadir variedad a la economía

_____ 4. una materia, como el petróleo, el oro o los diamantes, que se halla en la tierra

_____ 5. todas las cosas que la gente hace para ganarse la vida en un lugar en particular

Columna II

a. economía

b. agricultura de subsistencia

c. recursos minerales

d. diversificar

e. cultivo para la exportación

B. Ideas principales

Instrucciones: En cada espacio en blanco, escribe la letra que mejor conteste la pregunta.

_____ 6. ¿Cómo se usan tres quintas partes de la tierra cultivable de África?
    a. para cultivos para la venta   **c.** para grandes plantaciones
    b. para agricultura de subsistencia   **d.** para sembrar árboles de madera fina

_____ 7. La mayor parte de la economía de África depende
    a. de la manufactura.   **c.** del comercio.
    b. de la cosecha de árboles.   **d.** de la agricultura.

_____ 8. ¿En qué parte de África crecen los árboles de madera fina?
    a. sólo en África Oriental   **c.** sólo en África Central y África del Sur
    b. sólo cerca al Nilo   **d.** en las cuatro regiones de África

_____ 9. ¿Qué sucede en algunas regiones de África cuando se pierden las cosechas para la venta?
    a. Hay más trabajos en manufactura.
    b. Hay suficientes importaciones para que la gente sobreviva.
    c. Hay escasez de alimentos.
    d. Hay suficiente agricultura de subsistencia para producir alimento para todos.

_____ 10. Para protegerse a sí mismos en un mundo con una economía incierta, muchos países africanos están tratando de
    a. importar todos los productos manufacturados que usan.
    b. diversificar sus economías.
    c. hacer préstamos de dinero entre sí.
    d. producir sólo un cultivo importante para la venta.

Spanish Support

RESUMEN DEL CAPÍTULO

CAPÍTULO
1

ÁFRICA
Geografía física

Preguntas guía:

- ¿Cuáles son las principales características físicas de África?
- ¿Qué factores afectan la manera de supervivencia de los africanos?

Podemos dividir a África en cuatro regiones: África del Norte, África Occidental, África Oriental, y África Central y África del Sur. Cada región tiene climas y accidentes geográficos distintos. África del Norte se caracteriza por tener montañas rocosas y grandes desiertos. África Occidental consta en su mayoría de llanuras aptas para la agricultura. África Oriental tiene llanuras, cerros, montañas y mesetas. África Central y África del Sur son, en su mayoría, planas o con grandes llanuras y algunos bosques densos, montañas y pantanos.

La mayor parte del terreno africano es elevado. La montaña más alta es el Kilimanjaro en África Oriental, que mide 19,340 pies de altura (5,895 m). El interior del continente forma una extensa meseta. A lo largo de la mayoría de las costas de África hay una angosta llanura, que en varios lugares es pantanosa o árida. En África Oriental hay un gigantesco valle que se extiende por 4,000 millas (6,400 km). Se formó hace millones de años y se conoce con el nombre del Gran Valle del Rift. Los cuatro ríos principales de África son el Nilo, el Congo, el Zambeze y el Níger. Todos fluyen desde las montañas hacia el mar.

La mayor parte de África está ubicada entre el Trópico de Cáncer y el Trópico de Capricornio. Como consecuencia, muchas partes de África son tropicales y calidas. Sin embargo, hay otros factores que afectan su clima, como la elevación y la distancia a las grandes extensiones de agua y a los accidentes geográficos. Es más frío a mayores elevaciones. Cerca de la línea ecuatorial es denso, con bosques cálidos donde llueve la mayor parte del tiempo. Al norte y sur de la línea ecuatorial hay llanuras. Esas llanuras tienen estaciones secas y húmedas. Más allá de las llanuras hay desiertos, como el Sahara al norte y los desiertos de Namib y Kalahari al sur.

La mayoría de los trabajadores africanos son agricultores. Tres quintas partes de ellos practican la agricultura de subsistencia con cultivos de granos, frutas y hortalizas. Otros tienen cultivos para la venta de té, café y cacao, o cosechan árboles de madera fina. En África Occidental y África del Norte hay grandes yacimientos de petróleo. En otros lugares, los habitantes explotan minas de cobre, plata, uranio y diamantes para la exportación. Las economías de África dependen mucho de las condiciones climáticas y en particular de las lluvias y los precios de las cosechas. En los últimos años, muchos países han tratado de diversificar sus economías con nuevos cultivos, materias primas y productos manufacturados.

ÁFRICA
Geografía física

CAPÍTULO
1

Instrucciones: Empareja las definiciones de la Columna I con los términos clave de la Columna II. Escribe la letra correspondiente en cada espacio en blanco. Si es necesario, observa los términos en el glosario del libro texto.

Columna I

_____ **1.** persona que se muda de un lugar a otro constantemente para sobrevivir

_____ **2.** lugar fértil en el desierto donde hay agua y vegetación

_____ **3.** salto rocoso de un río o cascada

_____ **4.** altura del terreno sobre el nivel del mar

_____ **5.** arroyo o río pequeño que desemboca en un río principal

_____ **6.** zona plana y extensa que se eleva por encima del terreno a su alrededor

_____ **7.** trozos de roca y lodo depositado por los ríos

_____ **8.** cosecha que se cultiva para ser vendida

_____ **9.** suelo rico en el que pueden crecer muchas plantas

_____ **10.** zanja profunda en la tierra

_____ **11.** risco alto y empinado

_____ **12.** regar artificialmente las cosechas

_____ **13.** todas las cosas que la gente hace para sobrevivir en un lugar en particular

_____ **14.** cultivo de cosechas para sostener a una familia

_____ **15.** añadir variedad

_____ **16.** región en la que crecen pastos altos

Columna II

a. catarata

b. cultivo para la exportación

c. diversificar

d. economía

e. elevación

f. acantilado

g. fértil

h. irrigar

i. nómada

j. oasis

k. meseta

l. grieta

m. sabana

n. sedimento

o. agricultura de subsistencia

p. tributario

Spanish Support

CARTA PARA LA FAMILIA

ÁFRICA
Forjada por su historia

La Línea Abierta de Ciencias Sociales

Querida familia:

Durante los próximos días, en nuestra clase de ciencias sociales enfocaremos nuestros estudios en la historia de África. Aprenderemos sobre los primeros habitantes, el surgimiento de civilizaciones y reinos, la llegada de los europeos y la lucha de independencia, así como otros temas importantes del África contemporánea.

Para ayudar a que su hijo o hija comprenda mejor cómo eran los primeros habitantes africanos y las primeras civilizaciones, busque museos que tengan exhibiciones sobre las antiguas culturas africanas. Si no hay ninguna exhibición disponible, puede buscar artículos de revistas sobre temas relacionados con los primeros pobladores de África, el antiguo Egipto, Mali, Songhai, Aksum, Zimbabue o Ghana, por ejemplo; también puede que les interese artículos sobre los primeros métodos de agricultura africana y las primeras herramientas.

También vamos a estudiar la influencia europea en África y el comercio de esclavos africanos. Vamos a ver cómo los europeos formaron colonias y les quitaron el poder a los africanos para que ellos mismos gobernaran. Pregunte a su hijo o hija cómo se sentiría si de repente llegaran personas de otro país, se apoderaran del gobierno e impusieran sus leyes, costumbres y creencias. Hablar de cuál sería su reacción puede ser el comienzo de una conversación sobre la lucha por la libertad de muchos países africanos.

Esté al tanto de información que nos puede servir en la exploración de África. En las próximas semanas, vamos a estudiar las culturas de cada región y luego la de algunos países en detalle. Espero que tanto usted como su hijo o hija disfruten de aprender más sobre este continente tan diverso.

Atentamente,

CAPÍTULO 2
ÁFRICA
Forjada por su
historia

Los primeros habitantes de África

A. Durante la lectura

Instrucciones: A medida que vayas leyendo la Sección 1, completa la siguiente tabla con la información de los primeros habitantes de África.

Los primeros habitantes de África

¿Cómo conseguían sus alimentos?	1.
¿Qué les permitió establecerse en un lugar?	2.
¿Qué civilizaciones surgieron a lo largo del Nilo?	3.
¿Qué fueron las migraciones bantú?	4.
¿Cuáles fueron algunos de los efectos de esas migraciones?	5.

B. Repaso de los términos clave

Instrucciones: Escribe el término clave correspondiente para cada una de las siguientes definiciones.

6. una persona que recolecta alimentos silvestres y caza animales para sobrevivir
   _____

7. adaptar plantas silvestres y animales salvajes para nuestro uso _____

8. más de lo que se necesita _____

9. una sociedad con ciudades, un gobierno, clases sociales, arte y arquitectura _____

10. mudarse de un lugar a otro _____

11. un grupo de personas que comparten creencias y costumbres _____

Spanish Support

EXAMEN DE LA SECCIÓN

Los primeros habitantes de África

A. Términos y conceptos clave

Instrucciones: Lee las oraciones a continuación. Si una oración es verdadera, escribe V en el espacio en blanco. Si es falsa, escribe F. En otra hoja de papel, vuelve a escribir las oraciones falsas para convertirlas en verdaderas.

_____ **1.** Una persona que sobrevive de recolectar frutas, nueces y raíces silvestres se conoce como un cazador-recolector.

_____ **2.** Cuando las primeras comunidades producían excedentes de alimentos, tenían menos alimento del necesario.

_____ **3.** Con el tiempo, muchos grupos de agricultores de la Edad de Piedra se convirtieron en civilizaciones, las cuales se caracterizan por ser sociedades sin ciudades, sin gobernantes y sin clases sociales.

_____ **4.** Grupos de personas que hablaban el idioma bantú decidieron migrar, o permanecer, en África Occidental.

_____ **5.** Las personas que comparten distintos idiomas, religiones y costumbres forman grupos étnicos.

B. Ideas principales

Instrucciones: En cada espacio en blanco, escribe la letra que mejor conteste la pregunta.

_____ **6.** ¿Cómo hicieron los primeros habitantes de África Oriental para obtener alimentos?
    a. de la agricultura y la minería   **c.** de la caza y recolección
    b. de la cría de animales   **d.** del comercio

_____ **7.** Cuando los primeros habitantes empezaron a domesticar plantas y animales, estuvieron en condiciones de
    a. establecer comercio con otros países.
    b. establecerse en un solo lugar.
    c. conquistar a sus vecinos.
    d. desplazarse de un lugar a otro en busca de alimento.

_____ **8.** En el antiguo Egipto, los egipcios crearon jeroglíficos, que eran
    a. herramientas de hierro.   **c.** escritura pictográfica.
    b. estatuas.   **d.** embarcaciones.

_____ **9.** Cuando los habitantes de África Occidental aprendieron a trabajar el hierro, su población
    a. conquistó otras poblaciones.   **c.** empezó un período de paz.
    b. aumentó.   **d.** disminuyó.

_____ **10.** A través de los años, las personas que hablaban bantú se mudaron de su tierra natal y se establecieron en
    a. África del Norte.   **c.** África Oriental y África Occidental.
    b. África Occidental.   **d.** África Central y África del Sur.

CAPÍTULO 2
ÁFRICA
Forjada por su
historia

Los reinos y los imperios

A. Durante la lectura

Instrucciones: A medida que vayas leyendo la Sección 2, completa las siguientes preguntas en los espacios en blanco.

1. ¿Qué religión llegó hasta Aksum a través de las rutas de comercio?

_____

2. ¿Qué artículos se intercambiaban entre los reinos de África Occidental y África del Norte?

_____

3. ¿Qué efecto tuvieron los comerciantes en la cultura de África Occidental?

_____

4. ¿Qué ayudó a que las ciudades-estado de África se desarrollaran?

_____

5. ¿A lo largo de qué océano se expandió la red de comercio que empezó en África Oriental?

_____

B. Repaso de los términos clave

Instrucciones: Para completar cada oración, escribe el término correspondiente en el espacio en blanco.

6. El _____ es el libro sagrado de la religión islámica.

7. Uno de los cinco pilares del islamismo para los musulmanes es hacer una _____ a la Meca.

8. El idioma africano que mezcla palabras en árabe y africano se llama _____ .

9. Kilwa, Mombasa, y Malindi eran poderosas _____ de África Oriental.

Spanish Support

EXAMEN DE LA SECCIÓN

Los reinos y los imperios

A. Términos y conceptos clave

Instrucciones: Lee las oraciones a continuación. Si una oración es verdadera, escribe V en el espacio en blanco. Si es falsa, escribe F. En otra hoja de papel, vuelve a escribir las oraciones falsas para convertirlas en verdaderas.

_____ **I.** La Meca es el libro sagrado de la religión islámica.

_____ **2.** Aksum era un importante centro de comercio en África Oriental.

_____ **3.** Mansa Musa, el rey de Mali, hizo un peregrinaje, o viaje religioso, en 1324.

_____ **4.** El idioma bantú, desarrollado en África Oriental, es una mezcla de palabras árabes y africanas.

_____ **5.** Una ciudad que no tiene gobierno, pero que controla la mayoría de sus alrededores es una ciudad-estado.

B. Ideas principales

Instrucciones: En cada espacio en blanco, escribe la letra que mejor conteste la pregunta.

_____ **6.** La importancia de los primeros reinos de África Occidental fue por
    a. la manufactura de tela.
    b. el comercio de sal y algodón.
    c. la conquista de Aksum.
    d. el gobierno del rey de Mali.

_____ **7.** El comercio a través de África Occidental fue controlado en un principio por
    a. Mali.
    b. Ghana.
    c. Egipto.
    d. Etiopía.

_____ **8.** ¿Cómo se esparció el islamismo a muchas partes de África?
    a. por los comerciantes chinos
    b. por los misioneros cristianos
    c. por los faraones egipcios
    d. por los comerciantes musulmanes

_____ **9.** ¿Por qué Songhai se convirtió en el reino más poderoso de África Occidental?
    a. porque comerció con la India y la China
    b. porque controló ciudades y rutas importantes de comercio
    c. porque produjo bronce
    d. porque estableció poblaciones agrícolas a lo largo del Nilo

_____ **10.** En general, ¿qué ayudó al desarrollo de las ciudades-estado de África Oriental y África Occidental?
    a. la agricultura
    b. la manufactura
    c. el manejo de bosques
    d. el comercio

Nombre _____ Clase _____ Fecha _____

CAPÍTULO 2
ÁFRICA
Forjada por su historia

La conquista de África

A. Durante la lectura

Instrucciones: A medida que vayas leyendo la Sección 3, completa la siguiente tabla con información acerca del comercio europeo con África y su colonización.

Idea principal A
Tres factores principales aumentaron el contacto de los europeos con África.

1. Los inventos: _____

2. El comercio: _____

3. El comercio de esclavos: _____

_____

Idea principal B
Los principales efectos del contacto de los europeos con África fueron los siguientes.

4. La esclavitud: _____

5. Los recursos: _____

6. El gobierno: _____

7. La tierra: _____

8. La población: _____

_____

B. Repaso de los términos clave

Instrucciones: En el espacio en blanco a continuación, escribe la definición del siguiente término clave.

9. colonizar _____

EXAMEN DE LA SECCIÓN

La conquista de África

A. Términos y conceptos clave

Instrucciones: Empareja las definiciones de la Columna I con los términos de la Columna II. Escribe la letra correspondiente en cada espacio en blanco.

Columna I

_____ **1.** Un museo de La Casa de los Esclavos se encuentra en la isla de _____ .

_____ **2.** Para poder navegar en el mar, los navegantes del siglo XV usaron instrumentos nuevos como el _____ .

_____ **3.** Los horrores de las travesías de los esclavos son descritos en un libro escrito por _____ .

_____ **4.** Los exploradores holandeses establecieron un puesto de comercio en _____ , el extremo sur de África.

_____ **5.** Los países europeos querían _____ a África, es decir, querían establecerse allí.

Columna II

a. astrolabio

b. Cabo de la Buena Esperanza

c. colonizar

d. Gorée

e. Olaudah Equiano

B. Ideas principales

Instrucciones: En cada espacio en blanco, escribe la letra que mejor conteste la pregunta.

_____ **6.** El contacto entre africanos y europeos se dio en el siglo XV, principalmente con
    a. el comercio de esclavos.
    b. el comercio de productos.
    c. la conquista.
    d. las europeas que se establecier on en África.

_____ **7.** ¿Por qué los barcos portugueses iban a la costa este de África?
    a. para apoderarse de la riqueza de las ciudades-estado
    b. para establecer comunidades agrícolas
    c. para mejorar el nivel de vida de sus habitantes
    d. para apoyar a los gobernantes

_____ **8.** A finales del siglo XVII, los comerciantes portugueses intercambiaban
    a. marfil por yuca y ñame.
    b. armas por esclavos africanos.
    c. esclavos africanos por diamantes.
    d. cobre y bronce por africanos.

_____ **9.** ¿Qué enunciado describe mejor las consecuencias del comercio de esclavos en África?
    a. Hizo posible establecer un comercio equitativo entre los países africanos y europeos.
    b. Fortaleció el poder de los gobernantes locales.
    c. Fue una manera importante de esparcir la cultura africana al continente americano.
    d. Resultó en la pérdida de muchos trabajadores fuertes y saludables.

_____ **10.** ¿Cuál fue un resultado importante del desenfreno europeo por obtener territorio africano?
    a. Mejoró la vida de muchos africanos.
    b. Estableció nuevos límites políticos.
    c. Permitió el cultivo de muchos productos nuevos.
    d. Abrió campo para que los países africanos lograran la paz entre ellos.

CAPÍTULO 2
ÁFRICA
Forjada por su historia

La independencia y sus dificultades

A. Durante la lectura

Instrucciones: A medida que vayas leyendo la Sección 4, completa los espacios en blanco de las siguientes preguntas. Si es necesario, usa una hoja de papel adicional.

1. ¿Qué efecto tuvieron las fronteras establecidas por los europeos en los grupos étnicos de África?
_____

2. ¿Qué pensaban los líderes africanos que era necesario hacer para acabar con el gobierno colonial?
_____

3. ¿Qué es el panafricanismo y cuando empezó?
_____

4. ¿Cuál fue el efecto de la Segunda Guerra Mundial en los africanos que participaron en ella?
_____

5. ¿Cómo obtuvieron los Argelianos su independencia de Francia?
_____

6. ¿Por qué fue difícil para algunos de los nuevos países independientes de África gobernarse a sí mismos?
_____
_____

B. Repaso de los términos clave

Instrucciones: Para completar cada oración, escribe el término correspondiente en el espacio en blanco.

7. El sentimiento de orgullo por la tierra natal se llama _____ .

8. El movimiento que infundió la unión y cooperación africana se llama _____ .

9. Cuando los africanos de la Costa de Oro querían protestar contra los ingleses, organizaban _____ de ciertos productos y servicios.

10. Algunos países africanos han tenido una larga historia de _____ , en la que el gobierno es controlado por sus habitantes.

Spanish Support

Nombre _____ Clase _____ Fecha _____

La independencia y sus dificultades

A. Términos y conceptos clave

Instrucciones: Empareja las definiciones de la Columna I con los términos de la Columna II. Escribe la letra correspondiente en cada espacio en blanco.

Columna I

_____ **1.** el sentimiento de orgullo por la tierra natal

_____ **2.** un movimiento político que hace énfasis en la unidad de los africanos

_____ **3.** países que lucharon contra los ejércitos de Alemania, Italia y Japón en la Segunda Guerra Mundial

_____ **4.** una protesta organizada en la que las personas se rehusan a comprar o a usar ciertos productos o servicios

_____ **5.** una forma de gobierno en la que los ciudadanos ayudan en la toma de decisiones de los gobernantes

Columna II

a. los aliados

b. boicot

c. democracia

d. nacionalismo

e. panafricanismo

B. Ideas principales

Instrucciones: En cada espacio en blanco, escribe la letra que mejor conteste la pregunta.

_____ **6.** ¿Cuál era el lema del movimiento panafricano?
    a. Un continente, un idioma.
    b. África para los africanos.
    c. Alimentos para Zimbabue.
    d. No a los gobiernos independientes.

_____ **7.** ¿Cómo influyó la Segunda Guerra Mundial en el movimiento de independencia de África?
    a. Inspiró a los africanos a continuar siendo gobernados por los europeos.
    b. Debilitó a los países africanos.
    c. Animó a otros países a hablar en favor del colonialismo.
    d. Debilitó el poder de los colonizadores.

_____ **8.** Después de su independencia, la colonia de la Costa de Oro cambió su nombre por:
    a. Nigeria.
    b. Egipto.
    c. Ghana.
    d. Somalia.

_____ **9.** La manera en que Ghana y Argelia lograron su independencia demuestra que
    a. algunas colonias africanas lograron su independencia de manera pacífica.
    b. las colonias africanas no querían enfrentarse a los ejércitos europeos.
    c. el control de las colonias puede terminar de manera fácil.
    d. el control de las colonias puede no terminar de manera pacífica.

_____ **10.** Uno de los retos que enfrentaron muchos de los nuevos países africanos fue el de crear
    a. gobiernos estables.
    b. un nuevo sistema monetario.
    c. nuevos idiomas nacionales.
    d. nuevas rutas de comercio.

Nombre _____ Clase _____ Fecha _____

CAPÍTULO 2
ÁFRICA
Forjada por su
historia

África hoy en día

A. Durante la lectura

Instrucciones: A medida que vayas leyendo la Sección 5, completa la siguiente tabla con información sobre los distintos aspectos de África contemporánea.

Hechos y acciones

Economía	1.
Acción que se ha tomado	2.
Educación	3.
Acción que se ha tomado	4.
Medio ambiente	5.
Acción que se ha tomado	6.

B. Repaso de los términos clave

Instrucciones: En el espacio en blanco a continuación, escribe la definición de los siguientes términos clave.

7. cultivo de cosechas para sostener a una familia _____

8. cosechas que se cultivan a gran escala para la venta _____

9. una planta que es una combinación de dos o más tipos de una misma planta _____

10. la habilidad de leer y escribir _____

11. el promedio de años que se espera que una persona viva _____

Spanish Support

EXAMEN DE LA SECCIÓN

África hoy en día

A. Términos y conceptos clave

Instrucciones: Lee las oraciones a continuación. Si una oración es verdadera, escribe V en el espacio en blanco. Si es falsa, escribe F. En otra hoja de papel, vuelve a escribir las oraciones falsas para convertirlas en verdaderas.

_____ **1.** La producción a pequeña escala de productos como café, cacao y plátano se llama agricultura industrial.

_____ **2.** La habilidad de leer y escribir, o alfabetismo, varía en África de país a país.

_____ **3.** Los agricultores obtienen una planta híbrida cuando combinan dos o más tipos de distintas clases de plantas.

_____ **4.** Los países africanos trabajan fuertemente para sobreponerse a los problemas de salud y aumentar el promedio de vida, o el promedio de años que se espera que una persona viva.

_____ **5.** Con el desarrollo de la pesca, el procesamiento de pescados para exportación y la minería, el país de Senegal diversificó su economía.

B. Ideas principales

Instrucciones: En cada espacio en blanco, escribe la letra que mejor conteste la pregunta.

_____ **6.** La mayoría de las economías africanas están basadas en
    a. la agricultura y la cría de animales.   **c.** el manejo de bosques y la manufactura.
    b. la agricultura y la minería.   **d.** la manufactura y la agricultura.

_____ **7.** Cerca de tres cuartas partes de los trabajadores en África son
    a. comerciantes.   **c.** agricultores.
    b. fabricantes.   **d.** mercaderes.

_____ **8.** ¿Qué hacen hoy en día los países africanos para depender menos de la venta de productos de exportación?
    a. Importan más productos.
    b. Diversifican sus economías.
    c. Toman préstamos de grandes sumas de dinero de otros países.
    d. Venden menos productos de exportación.

_____ **9.** ¿Cuál es una de las metas más importantes en la educación de los países africanos hoy en día?
    a. enviar menos alumnos a las escuelas de los pueblos
    b. enviar a todos los alumnos a escuelas extranjeras
    c. mejorar el nivel de alfabetismo
    d. desanimar a los alumnos a estudiar sus propias culturas

_____ **10.** Uno de los problemas del medio ambiente más serios que enfrenta África hoy en día es
    a. la disminución de la erosión.   **c.** el aumento de la erosión.
    b. la pérdida de desiertos.   **d.** el aumento de bosques.

ÁFRICA
Forjada por su historia

CAPÍTULO
2

Pregunta guía:
- ¿Cómo han cambiado las culturas de África?

Es posible que los primeros seres humanos hayan vivido en África, y que hayan sobrevivido de la caza y la recolección de alimentos. A través de miles de años, los africanos aprendieron a criar animales y a labrar la tierra. La agricultura les permitió establecerse permanentemente en un solo lugar. Con el tiempo, algunos de esos grupos evolucionaron y formaron civilizaciones (sociedades con ciudades, gobernantes, escritura, arte y clases sociales). Hace más de 6,000 años surgieron civilizaciones en Egipto y Nubia. Hace cerca de 2,500 años, los habitantes de África Occidental aprendieron a calentar y moldear el hierro para elaborar armas y herramientas. Durante cientos de años, crecieron reinos en África Oriental y África Occidental. Entre esos se encuentran Aksum y Kilwa en el este; Ghana, Mali y Songhai en el oeste; y Zimbabue en el sur. En el año 1300, el islam ya se había convertido en una religión importante en Mali y otros reinos.

Los europeos establecieron un comercio de esclavos en África hacia el año 1500. Más de doce millones de africanos fueron esclavizados y llevados a América del Norte, de donde nunca regresaron. Los trabajadores más jóvenes y fuertes fueron arrebatados de su tierra natal. El resultado fue desastroso tanto para los esclavos como para su tierra natal.

El comercio de esclavos terminó en el siglo XIX. Los europeos comenzaron a invadir los recursos de África. Con mejores armas, los europeos dominaron la fiera resistencia africana. A finales del siglo XIX, los europeos habían establecido colonias en muchas partes de África. Usaron a África como fuente de materia prima y como lugar para vender sus propios productos. Durante su estadía, no construyeron fábricas en África y hasta hoy en día hay muy poca industria. Los africanos perdieron el poder de elegir a sus propios gobernantes. Los europeos se adueñaron de sus mejores tierras, crearon nuevas fronteras y obligaron a los africanos a trabajar para ellos.

Mientras los europeos colonizaban a África, muchos africanos seguían en su lucha por lograr la independencia. El panafricanismo fue un movimiento que empezó en la década de 1920, y que buscaba la unidad de todos los africanos. En las décadas posteriores a la Segunda Guerra Mundial, algunos países, como Inglaterra, comenzaron a dejar sus colonias africanas. La mayoría de los países africanos tuvieron muchos problemas después de su independencia, dada la poca experiencia a nivel de gobierno de aquellos que quedaron en el poder. Surgieron conflictos entre los grupos étnicos, y las condiciones económicas empeoraron en muchos casos.

Hoy en día, muchos países africanos trabajan fuertemente para conservar sus tradiciones, a la vez que se adaptan al mundo moderno. Tienen que enfrentar aspectos como el de fortalecer la economía, alimentar y educar a una población cada vez mayor y preservar el medio ambiente.

Spanish Support

ACTIVIDAD DE VOCABULARIO

CAPÍTULO 2

ÁFRICA
Forjada por su historia

Instrucciones: A continuación hay una lista de términos del Capítulo 2. Escribe una oración o una frase en otra hoja de papel que describa el significado de cada término. Si es necesario, mira el Capítulo 2 para que veas cómo se usan los términos.

1. boicot
2. ciudades-estado
3. civilización
4. colonizar
5. agricultura industrial
6. democracia
7. domesticar
8. grupos étnicos
9. cazadores-recolectores
10. híbridas
11. promedio de vida
12. alfabetismo
13. migrar
14. nacionalismo
15. panafricanismo
16. peregrinación
17. Corán
18. excedente
19. swahili

CAPÍTULO
3

Las culturas de África

La Línea Abierta de Ciencias Sociales

Querida familia:

Ahora vamos a explorar las culturas de África en nuestra clase de ciencias sociales. Estudiaremos las cuatro regiones geográficas principales que son: África del Norte, África Oriental, África Occidental, y África Central y África del Sur. Vamos a ver cómo la ubicación de África del Norte a lo largo del Mar Mediterráneo ha atraido el comercio y el intercambio de ideas culturales en la región. Vamos a estudiar la diversidad de culturas e idiomas de África Oriental y África Occidental y la manera en que Suráfrica ha influenciado la vida en la región central y sur del continente. Si usted tiene algún conocimiento previo de la forma de vida de los africanos o conoce a alguien que lo tenga, puede aportar mucho a nuestro estudio si comparte esa información con su hijo o hija.

Cuando lea el periódico, o escuche o vea las noticias, esté atento a informes sobre las culturas africanas. Dichos informes pueden incluir temas laborales, de política, música, arte, salud, o cambios en los estilos de vida de los africanos. Usted podría hablar de sus hallazgos con su hijo o hija. Si tiene acceso al Internet, juntos podrían explorar información sobre las culturas africanas con su computadora. A medida que hallen información acerca de la vida en África, anime a su hijo o hija a que la comparen con la vida en su comunidad.

Durante las próximas semanas, le enviaremos más información sobre las culturas en las distintas regiones de África. Espero que se divierta mientras comparte nuestra muy interesante exploración de África con su hijo o hija.

Atentamente,

Spanish Support

LECTURA DIRIGIDA Y REPASO

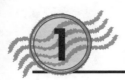

Las culturas de África del Norte

A. Durante la lectura

Instrucciones: A medida que vayas leyendo la Sección 1, completa la siguiente tabla con información sobre las culturas de África.

Aspectos de las culturas de África del Norte

La religión	1.
Las leyes del islamismo	2.
Los grupos étnicos	3.
Los cambios culturales	4.
Las influencias mediterráneas	5.

B. Repaso de los términos clave

Instrucciones: Completa los espacios en blanco de las siguientes oraciones con el término clave correspondiente de la Sección 1.

6. La _____ de una región incluye su alimento, vestuario, viviendas, ocupaciones, idioma, visión del mundo y religión.

7. Las leyes del islamismo se basan en _____ .

8. Los berebers son _____ que vive en África del Norte.

9. El movimiento de costumbres e ideas se llama _____ .

CAPÍTULO 3
**Las culturas
de África**

Las culturas de África del Norte

A. Términos y conceptos clave

Instrucciones: Completa los espacios en blanco de la Columna I con los términos de la Columna II. Escribe la letra correspondiente en cada espacio en blanco.

Columna I

_____ 1. Las culturas de África del Norte han sido influenciadas por su ubicación a lo largo de _____ .

_____ 2. La forma de vida de un grupo de personas que comparte creencias y costumbres similares es _____ .

_____ 3. _____ es la religión que une a los habitantes de África del Norte.

_____ 4. Los tuareg viajan a través del _____ con sus rebaños de camellos, cabras y otros tipos de ganado.

_____ 5. Al viajar, las personas esparcen sus costumbres e ideas de un lugar a otro a través de _____ .

Columna II

a. la difusión cultural

b. la cultura

c. el Mar Mediterráneo

d. el islamismo

e. Sahara

B. Ideas principales

Instrucciones: En cada espacio en blanco, escribe la letra que mejor conteste la pregunta.

_____ 6. Todos los aspectos de la vida cotidiana en África del Norte, como los negocios, el gobierno y la vida en familia, son gobernados por
    a. las leyes nacionales.
    b. las leyes del islamismo.
    c. las enseñanzas budistas.
    d. las leyes del Antiguo Testamento.

_____ 7. Los distintos grupos de África del Norte están unidos por
    a. el gobierno y el islamismo.
    b. el islamismo y el idioma francés.
    c. el idioma árabe y el islamismo.
    d. el budismo y el islamismo.

_____ 8. ¿Cuáles son los grupos étnicos más grandes de África del Norte?
    a. los yoruba y los árabes
    b. los árabes y los etíopes
    c. los bereberes y los árabes
    d. los bereberes y los tuareg

_____ 9. ¿Cómo ocurrió la mezcla de culturas en África del Norte?
    a. a través de conquistas y de la religión
    b. a través de decretos de gobierno y del comercio
    c. a través del comercio y la conquista
    d. a través de la religión y el comercio

_____ 10. ¿Cuál es una de las más recientes influencias en África del Norte?
    a. las antiguas tradiciones africanas
    b. la cultura occidental
    c. la difusión cultural
    d. las ideas orientales

Spanish Support

LECTURA DIRIGIDA Y REPASO

Las culturas de África Occidental

A. Durante la lectura

Instrucciones: A medida que vayas leyendo la Sección 2, completa la siguiente tabla con información de la cultura de África Occidental. Debajo de cada idea principal escribe dos oraciones que la apoyen.

Idea principal A
Las culturas de África Occidental son muy variadas.
1. _____
2. _____

Idea principal B
Los lazos familiares tienen mucha importancia en las culturas de África Occidental.
3. _____
4. _____

B. Repaso de los términos clave

Instrucciones: Para cada definición a continuación, escribe el término correspondiente en el espacio en blanco.

5. una gran variedad de culturas _____

6. una relación de familia _____

7. una familia que consta de padres e hijos _____

8. una familia que incluye otros parientes, además de los padres y los hijos _____

9. un grupo de familias con un antepasado en común _____

10. un grupo de linajes que comprueba la filiación de sus descendientes a un antepasado común

   _____

11. un narrador africano de cuentos que transmite su tradición oralmente _____

CAPÍTULO 3
Las culturas de África

Las culturas de África Occidental

A. Términos y conceptos clave

Instrucciones: Empareja las definiciones de la Columna I con los términos de la Columna II. Escribe la letra correspondiente en cada espacio en blanco.

Columna I

_____ 1. tener una gran variedad de culturas

_____ 2. familia que consta de padres e hijos

_____ 3. familia que incluye a otros parientes, además de los padres y los hijos

_____ 4. un grupo de familias con un antepasado en común

_____ 5. varios grupos de familias cuyas raíces llegan a un antepasado lejano

Columna II

a. clan

b. diversidad cultural

c. familia extensa

d. linaje

e. familia nuclear

B. Ideas principales

Instrucciones: En cada espacio en blanco, escribe la letra que mejor conteste la pregunta.

_____ 6. África Occidental tiene una gran variedad de culturas, porque tiene
    a. un clima estable.
    b. muchos grupos étnicos.
    c. variedad de vegetación.
    d. una sola religión.

_____ 7. ¿Cuál oración es verdadera acerca de los grupos étnicos de África Occidental?
    a. No tienen relaciones comerciales entre sí.
    b. Todos son agricultores.
    c. Hablan distintos idiomas.
    d. Viven en aldeas separadas.

_____ 8. ¿De qué manera significativa el parentesco afecta la vida en África Occidental?
    a. Hay una conciencia muy grande de comunidad.
    b. Hay mucha envidia entre los distintos clanes.
    c. No hay familias extensas en muchas aldeas.
    d. Las relaciones familiares no son muy importantes.

_____ 9. La tendencia de los aldeanos de mudarse a las ciudades en África Occidental se llama
    a. peregrinación.
    b. ruralismo.
    c. urbanización.
    d. colonización.

_____ 10. Al contar cuentos tradicionales, el griot ayuda a conservar
    a. las técnicas de la agricultura.
    b. el linaje.
    c. los idiomas africanos.
    d. las tradiciones de África Occidental.

Spanish Support

Las culturas de África Oriental

A. Durante la lectura

Instrucciones: A medida que vayas leyendo la Sección 3, contesta las siguientes preguntas en los espacios en blanco.

1. ¿Cuál es la causa principal de la diversidad cultural de África Oriental? ¿Por qué lo es?

_____

2. ¿Quiénes son los swahili? ¿Dónde viven ellos?

_____

3. ¿Cuál es la importancia de los swahili en África Oriental?

_____

4. ¿Por qué Kenia y Tanzania formentan el uso del idioma swahili?

_____

5. ¿Qué religiones tienen muchos seguidores en África Oriental?

_____

6. ¿Qué concepto tenían los africanos sobre la tierra antes de la llegada de los europeos?

_____

7. ¿Quién introdujo el concepto de terrenos de propiedad privada al África?

_____

8. ¿Qué sucedió con las viejas plantaciones en muchos de los países africanos después de que obtuvieron su independencia?

_____

9. ¿Cuál es el sentimiento de la mayoría de los habitantes de África Oriental con respeto al lugar donde crecieron?

_____

10. Si les preguntas dónde está su hogar, ¿qué respondería la mayoría de los habitantes de África Oriental?

_____

B. Repaso de los términos clave

Instrucciones: Para completar la oración, escribe el término correspondiente en el espacio en blanco.

11. Los ingleses organizaron _____ en África Oriental en los lugares donde cultivaban cosechas para la venta.

CAPÍTULO 3
**Las culturas
de África**

Las culturas de África Oriental

A. Términos y conceptos clave

Instrucciones: Empareja las definiciones de la Columna I con los términos de la Columna II.
Escribe la letra correspondiente en cada espacio en blanco.

Columna I

_____ 1. cultura africana que es una mezcla de antepasados africanos y árabes

_____ 2. granja grande donde se cultivan cosechas para la venta

_____ 3. país de África Oriental

_____ 4. ex presidente de Tanzania

_____ 5. la capital de Tanzania

Columna II

a. Dar es Salaam

b. Julius Nyerere

c. Kenia

d. plantación

e. swahili

B. Ideas principales

Instrucciones: En cada espacio en blanco, escribe la letra que mejor conteste la pregunta.

_____ 6. ¿Por qué se hablan tantos idiomas en África Oriental?
   a. porque todos asisten a la escuela
   b. porque la mayoría de las personas tiene que comerciar con otros países
   c. porque muchos grupos étnicos viven allí
   d. porque la región fue conquistada en un principio por distintos países europeos

_____ 7. África Oriental es diversa culturalmente a causa de
   a. su ubicación.   **c.** su geografía.
   b. su clima.   **d.** su sistema de transporte.

_____ 8. Dos religiones importantes con muchos miembros en África Oriental son
   a. el islamismo y el budismo.   **c.** el cristianismo y el budismo.
   b. el cristianismo y el confucianismo. **d.** el islamismo y el cristianismo.

_____ 9. Cuando los europeos se establecieron en África Oriental, introdujeron el concepto de
   a. el derecho a cultivar terrenos.   **c.** la agricultura de subsistencia.
   b. la propiedad privada de la tierra. **d.** el pastoreo de ganado.

_____ 10. Para muchos habitantes de África Oriental, su hogar en la aldea rural
   a. no tiene importancia para ellos.
   b. son olvidados cuando se mudan a las ciudades.
   c. son considerados como sus verdaderos hogares.
   d. son vendidos para comprar apartamentos en las ciudades.

Spanish Support

Las culturas de África Central y África del Sur

A. Durante la lectura

Instrucciones: A medida que vayas leyendo la Sección 4, completa la siguiente tabla con información detallada sobre las culturas de África Central y África del Sur.

	Para sobrevivir	Cambios en las tradiciones
África del Sur	1.	2.
África Central	3.	4.

B. Repaso de los términos clave

Instrucciones: En el espacio en blanco, escribe la definición de cada término.

5. nacionalismo

_____

6. trabajador migratorio

_____

CAPÍTULO 3
Las culturas
de África

Las culturas de África Central y África del Sur

4

A. Términos y conceptos clave

Instrucciones: Lee las oraciones a continuación. Si una oración es verdadera, escribe V en el espacio en blanco. Si es falsa, escribe F. Vuelve a escribir las oraciones falsas para convertirlas en verdaderas.

_____ **1.** Un partido político importante de Suráfrica es el Partido Africano.

_____ **2.** El país de Suráfrica ha tenido poca influencia en la región.

_____ **3.** Los buti, que viven en los bosques húmedos del Congo, tienen una cultura de más de 3,000 años de antigüedad.

_____ **4.** Las personas que se quedan en un solo lugar para trabajar se conocen como trabajadores migratorios.

_____ **5.** El país del Congo, en África del Sur, tiene pocos grupos étnicos.

B. Ideas principales

Instrucciones: En cada espacio en blanco, escribe la letra que mejor conteste la pregunta.

_____ **6.** ¿Qué efecto tuvo la lucha por los derechos políticos en la identidad de los surafricanos negros?
   a. Se comenzaron a sentir como gobernantes coloniales.
   b. Se comenzaron a sentir como miembros de su país.
   c. Se comenzaron a ver ligados a los americanos.
   d. Se comenzaron a ver a sí mismos como los líderes políticos de África.

_____ **7.** ¿Cómo afectó la lucha por la autonomía gubernamental en Suráfrica a otros países africanos?
   a. Los animó a seguir siendo colonias de los países europeos.
   b. Inspiró movimientos similares en países cercanos.
   c. Los animó a volverse parte de suráfrica.
   d. Los animó a establecer monarquías en sus países.

_____ **8.** Con el propósito de conseguir más trabajadores para las minas, las compañías surafricanas
   a. sólo empleaban trabajadores surafricanos.
   b. empleaban trabajadores de toda África del Sur.
   c. empleaban trabajadores de África del Norte.
   d. empleaban trabajadores de las aldeas de África del Norte.

Spanish Support

RESUMEN DEL CAPÍTULO

CAPÍTULO
3

Las culturas de África

Preguntas guía:

- ¿Cómo han cambiado las culturas de África?
- ¿Qué factores han afectado la forma de sobrevivencia de los africanos?

Cada una de las cuatro regiones de África tiene sus propias culturas. Dentro de cada región existen muchas formas de vida: tradicional y moderna, urbana y rural, rica y pobre.

Los habitantes de África del Norte están unidos por el islamismo y el idioma árabe. Más del 95 por ciento de los habitantes son musulmanes. Los musulmanes creen que existe un solo Dios y que Muhammed fue el mensajero de Dios. El Corán es el libro sagrado del islamismo, que habla acerca de Dios y sirve de guía para la vida de sus creyentes. El Corán condena el robo, el asesinato, los juegos de azar y las bebidas alcohólicas. Las leyes del islamismo se basan en el Corán y forman parte de todos los aspectos de la vida de los musulmanes.

En contraste con África del Norte, África Occidental no tiene un elemento cultural que la unifique. La región comprende 17 países, cientos de grupos étnicos y muchos de sus habitantes hablan varios idiomas. La mayoría de los habitantes de África Occidental son agricultores en las zonas rurales. Muchos de los que viven en la región del Sahel se dedican al pastoreo de animales, mientras que los habitantes de la costa atlántica se dedican a la pesca. El parentesco representa un fuerte vínculo entre las culturas de África Occidental. La cultura de África Occidental ha influido en la cultura de los Estados Unidos, porque muchos de los esclavos que trajeron eran de esa región.

Como África Oriental está ubicada a lo largo del Océano Índico, ha sido afectada por otras culturas africanas, asiáticas y árabes. Es una región de muchos grupos étnicos y muchos idiomas. Un elemento unificador en África Oriental ha sido el idioma swahili, el idioma oficial de Kenia y Tanzania. El swahili es el segundo idioma de millones de habitantes de África Oriental. En África Oriental, tanto el islamismo como el cristianismo tienen muchos seguidores. Los habitantes de África Oriental se sienten muy ligados a la tierra en que nacieron. La mayoría de ellos consideran su hogar la aldea de su familia o clan.

Al negarle derechos a los surafricanos negros, Suráfrica los obligó a luchar por sus libertades básicas. Esa lucha produjo un fuerte instinto de nacionalismo, que inspiró a otros países en la región. Suráfrica es el país más rico e industrializado de África. Trabajadores migratorios se desplazan de todas las regiones a su alrededor para trabajar allí. Esos trabajadores se convirtieron en una fuerza poderosa para lograr cambios políticos en la región.

Hay zonas de África Central donde las personas aún viven en pequeños campamentos forestales. Otros habitantes de la región viven en congestionadas zonas pobres para poder trabajar en zonas urbanas. En la región hay muchas religiones, incluyendo el cristianismo, creencias africanas tradicionales y el islamismo.

Las culturas de África

Instrucciones: Empareja las definiciones de la Columna I con los términos de la Columna II. Escribe la letra correspondiente en cada espacio en blanco. Si es necesario, puede mirar los términos en el glosario de tu libro texto.

Columna I

_____ 1. un grupo de familias con un antepasado común

_____ 2. una familia que incluye padres e hijos

_____ 3. sentimiento de orgullo por la tierra natal o país

_____ 4. un grupo de linajes que comprueban la filiación de sus descendientes a un antepasado en común

_____ 5. una granja grande donde se cosechan cultivos para la venta

_____ 6. el movimiento de costumbres e ideas de una cultura a otra

_____ 7. una relación de familia

_____ 8. una gran variedad de culturas

_____ 9. una familia que incluye otros parientes, además de los padres y los hijos

_____ 10. un narrador africano de cuentos que transmite su tradición oralmente

_____ 11. la forma de vida de personas que comparten costumbres y creencias similares

_____ 12. una persona que se muda de un lugar a otro en busca de trabajo

Columna II

a. clan

b. difusión cultural

c. diversidad cultural

d. cultura

e. familia extensa

f. griot

g. parentesco

h. linaje

i. trabajador migratorio

j. nacionalismo

k. familia nuclear

l. plantación

Spanish Support

CARTA PARA LA FAMILIA

CAPÍTULO 4

Exploremos África del Norte

La Línea Abierta de Ciencias Sociales

Querida familia:

Mientras continuamos con el estudio de África en nuestra clase de ciencias sociales, vamos a estudiar en más detalle cada una de las cuatro regiones africanas. Durante los próximos días vamos a estudiar dos países de África del Norte: Egipto y Argelia. En nuestro estudio, examinaremos el contraste entre la vida rural y la vida urbana de ambos países, veremos la importancia del islamismo y estudiaremos los dos grupos étnicos principales de Argelia: los árabes y los bereberes.

Uno de los aspectos más fascinantes de la vida en África del Norte es la manera en que tradiciones de miles de años existen junto con la vida moderna. A poca distancia de ciudades modernas existen aldeas de piedra y barro. Incluso dentro de las mismas ciudades, hay secciones que fueron construidas con cientos de años de diferencia. Para que su hijo o hija comprenda mejor eso, usted podría identificar los edificios más antiguos y los más modernos de su comunidad. También podría animar a su hijo o hija a que se imagine y hable de cómo pudo haber sido la vida en su comunidad hace mil años. ¿Cómo ha cambiado? ¿Cómo podría afectar la presión de la vida moderna a alguien que vive en una aldea tradicional en una zona rural cercana? ¿En qué se diferencia la vida rural de la vida urbana en los Estados Unidos?

Cuando lea o vea las noticias, esté pendiente de información sobre la vida moderna de Egipto y Argelia. Puede usar esos informes para iniciar diálogos con su hijo o hija sobre los estudios de nuestra clase. Si tiene acceso al *Internet*, puede tratar de hallar más información que sea relevante para nuestros estudios.

Espero que tanto usted como su hijo o hija disfruten de este estudio en detalle de África del Norte.

Atentamente,

Egipto: El llamado del islamismo

A. Durante la lectura

Instrucciones: A medida que vayas leyendo la Sección 1, escribe tus respuestas a las siguientes preguntas en los espacios en blanco.

1. ¿Qué hacen los musulmanes en el mes del Ramadan?

_____

2. ¿Qué creen los musulmanes del Corán?

_____

3. ¿Con qué frecuencia oran los musulmanes devotos?

_____

4. ¿Qué es el sharia y en qué se basa?

_____

5. ¿Qué ha creado desacuerdos entre los musulmanes egipcios? ¿Cómo afecta eso a las mujeres?

_____

6. ¿Cuál es la ciudad más grande de Egipto? ¿Cómo describirías la vida allí?

_____

7. ¿Dónde quedan la mayoría de las aldeas rurales de Egipto?

_____

8. ¿Cómo son las viviendas de los agricultores de las zonas rurales de Egipto?

_____

9. ¿Qué es lo que unifica a la mayoría de los habitantes de Egipto?

_____

B. Repaso de los términos clave

Instrucciones: Para completar cada oración, escribe el término correspondiente en el espacio en blanco.

10. Los _____ de Egipto creen que si renuevan su fe en el islamismo todos los días, eso les dará fortaleza para conservar sus valores tradicionales en el mundo moderno.

11. La mayoría de _____ no son propietarios de tierras.

12. En el Cairo, muchas personas van a comprar alimentos en _____ , o mercados al aire libre.

Spanish Support

EXAMEN DE LA SECCIÓN

Egipto: El llamado del islamismo

A. Términos y conceptos clave

Instrucciones: Completa los espacios en blanco de la Columna I con los términos de la Columna II. Escribe la letra correspondiente en cada espacio en blanco.

Columna I

_____ **1.** Durante la celebración de _____ , las personas ayunan desde el amanecer hasta el anochecer y piensan en todos aquellos que son menos afortunados que ellos.

_____ **2.** Las personas del Cairo todavía hacen sus compras de manera tradicional en un mercado al aire libre, o _____ .

_____ **3.** Las leyes del islamismo o _____ , se basan en el Corán y en las palabras y acciones de Mahoma.

_____ **4.** _____ es la capital y la ciudad más grande de Egipto.

_____ **5.** Los _____ son los agricultores de las zonas rurales de Egipto.

Columna II

a. bazar

b. Ramadan

c. sharia

d. felá

e. Cairo

B. Ideas principales

Instrucciones: En cada espacio en blanco, escribe la letra que mejor conteste la pregunta.

_____ **6.** La religión oficial de Egipto es
    a. el cristianismo.
    b. el budismo.
    c. el confucianismo.
    d. el islamismo.

_____ **7.** ¿Qué efecto ha tenido la religión en la vida diaria de los egipcios?
    a. Ahora ellos siguen las enseñanzas de Buda.
    b. La mayoría de las leyes nacionales concuerdan con las leyes del islamismo.
    c. Las leyes nacionales por lo general no concuerdan con las del sharia.
    d. Todos los habitantes siguen las leyes del islamismo en lugar de las leyes de Egipto.

_____ **8.** En un principio, el islamismo se esparció desde
    a. Egipto hasta Nigeria.
    b. Arabia Saudita hasta África del Norte.
    c. Egipto hasta África del Sur.
    d. Mesopotamia hasta el Cairo.

_____ **9.** ¿Por qué los egipcios se trasladan de las zonas rurales a las ciudades?
    a. Hay viviendas para todos.
    b. Quieren conseguir trabajo y una mejor educación.
    c. En las ciudades hay menos gente que en las aldeas.
    d. Es fácil conducir automóviles en las ciudades.

_____ **10.** ¿En qué parte de Egipto vive la mayoría de las personas de las zonas rurales?
    a. en el norte
    b. en los alrededores del Cairo o Alejandría
    c. a lo largo del Nilo o cerca del Canal de Suez
    d. en las montañas

CAPÍTULO 4
Exploremos
África del Norte

Argelia: La casba y el campo

A. Durante la lectura

Instrucciones: A medida que vayas leyendo la Sección 2, completa la siguiente tablacon información detallada de Argelia. Debajo de cada idea principal escribe dos oraciones que la apoyen.

Datos de Argelia

Bereberes	1. 2.
Árabes	3. 4.
La vida en el campo	5. 6.
La vida en la ciudad	7. 8.

B. Repaso de los términos clave

Instrucciones: Escribe las definiciones de los siguientes términos clave en el espacio en blanco correspondiente.

9. terraza _____

10. souq _____

11. casba _____

Spanish Support

EXAMEN DE LA SECCIÓN

Argelia: La casba y el campo

A. Términos y conceptos clave

Instrucciones: Empareja las definiciones de la Columna I con los términos de la Columna II. Escribe la letra correspondiente en cada espacio en blanco.

Columna I

_____ **1.** nombre del grupo étnico que ha vivido en África del Norte desde el año 3000 A.C.

_____ **2.** grupo social que incluye otros parientes, además de la madre, el padre y los hijos

_____ **3.** plataforma cortada en el lado de una montaña que se usa para cultivar

_____ **4.** nombre del grupo étnico que se esparció a lo largo de África del Norte en el siglo VII.

_____ **5.** mercado al aire libre

Columna II

a. árabes

b. bereberes

c. familia extensa

d. souq

e. terraza

B. Ideas principales

Instrucciones: En cada espacio en blanco, escribe la letra que mejor conteste la pregunta.

_____ **6.** En Argelia, es difícil vivir en más del 85 por ciento del territorio, porque
   a. es muy montañoso.
   b. está cubierto por el Sahara.
   c. está cubierto de bosque húmedo.
   d. está muy congestionado.

_____ **7.** Los dos principales grupos étnicos de Argelia son
   a. chinos y árabes.
   b. árabes y musulmanes.
   c. árabes y bereberes.
   d. musulmanes e hindúes.

_____ **8.** Los bereberes se adaptaron a las leyes árabes al seguir los mandatos del gobierno central y
   a. su cristianismo.
   b. de los gobernantes de sus aldeas.
   c. un estilo de vida agrícola.
   d. un estilo de vida urbano.

_____ **9.** ¿En qué se parecen los bereberes y los árabes?
   a. Ambos hablan francés.
   b. Ambos viven en grandes ciudades.
   c. Ambos viven en familias extensas.
   d. Ambos viven sólo en zonas rurales.

_____ **10.** ¿Cuál oración describe mejor las ciudades de Argelia?
   a. Los habitantes tienen muy poco en común entre sí.
   b. Todas sus ciudades han sido modernizadas.
   c. Muy pocos argelianos viven en las ciudades.
   d. Las ciudades son una mezcla de edificios modernos y plazas de mercado al aire libre tradicionales.

Exploremos África del Norte

Preguntas guía:

- ¿De qué manera han afectado los acontecimientos históricos las culturas y los países de África?
- ¿Qué factores afectan las maneras como los africanos se ganan la vida?

Egipto está ubicada en la parte este de África del Norte, separado de Arabia Saudita, donde comenzó el islamismo por el Mar Rojo. A los egipcios los une su fe en el islamismo. Los musulmanes egipcios, como muchos otros, rezan cinco veces al día. Las enseñanzas del Corán (el libro sagrado de los musulmanes) acentúa la importancia de la honestidad, el honor, la caridad, y el amor y respeto por la familia. Muchos musulmanes egipcios tratan de vivir cada día según la ley islámica o sharia para renovar su fe.

Cerca de la mitad de los egipcios viven en ciudades. El Cairo es la ciudad más grande de Egipto y está densamente poblada. Algunas partes de la ciudad tienen más de 1,000 años de antigüedad, mientras que otras cuentan con altos y modernos edificios. Muchos egipcios han migrado del campo a la ciudad en busca de trabajo. La mayoría de los que viven en las zonas rurales, viven a orillas del Río Nilo. Esos aldeanos son, en su mayoría, agricultores que viven en viviendas hechas de barro, ladrillo o piedra. Las tradiciones en las aldeas rurales han cambiado muy poco en los últimos 4,000 años.

Argelia está al oeste de Egipto y la mayoría de su territorio está en el Sahara. Argelia limita al norte con el Mar Mediterráneo. La mayoría de los argelinos viven en esa zona costera. Los dos grupos étnicos principales de Argelia son los bereberes y los árabes. Los bereberes han vivido allí por miles de años. La mayoría vive en aldeas rurales, donde cultivan y crían animales. La familia es muy importante para los bereberes. El gobierno de las aldeas está conformado por las cabezas de cada familia.

Los árabes llegaron al África del Norte en el siglo VII y trajeron consigo el islamismo a la región. Ese evento cambió el estilo de vida tradicional de los bereberes. Los árabes formaron un gobierno central cuya base es el islamismo. Con el paso de los años, los bereberes se han adaptado a conservar el gobierno de sus propias aldeas y al mismo tiempo cumplir las leyes del gobierno central. Los árabes que conquistaron África del Norte eran nómadas. Algunos berebere fueron influenciados por ellos y cambiaron su estilo de vida, de agricultores a nómadas. Los bereberes y los árabes que viven en las ciudades tienen mucho en común. Al igual que las ciudades egipcias, Argelia tiene sectores antiguos y sectores modernos.

Spanish Support

Nombre _____ Clase _____ Fecha _____

Exploremos África del Norte

Instrucciones: Empareja los términos clave de la tabla con las definiciones de abajo. Escribe la letra correspondiente en cada espacio en blanco. Luego escribe una oración que use el término o la forma plural del término en el espacio respectivo. Si es necesario, observa los términos en el glosario de tu libro de texto o fíjate cómo se usan en el Capítulo 4.

> **a.** bazar
> **b.** fellaheen
> **c.** terraza

_____ **1.** mercado al aire libre tradicional en África del Norte

_____

_____

_____

_____

_____ **2.** plataforma de tierra, cortada al lado de una montaña, que sirve para cultivar

_____

_____

_____

_____

_____ **3.** los campesinos agricultores de Egipto

_____

_____

_____

_____

© Pearson Education, Inc., publishing as Prentice Hall. All rights reserved.

42 ■ **Recursos del Capítulo y la Sección**   Exploremos África del Norte

Exploremos África Occidental

La Línea Abierta de Ciencias Sociales

Querida familia:

Ahora estamos estudiando las culturas de África Occidental. Durante los próximos días, aprenderemos acerca de Nigeria, Ghana y Mali. Aprendemos que África Occidental fue el centro del comercio de esclavos que trajo millones de africanos a los Estados Unidos y a otros lugares. Los habitantes de África Occidental trajeron consigo una rica herencia cultural de ideas, música e historias que han tenido mucha influencia en la cultura norteamericana.

Usted podría escuchar con su hijo o hija ejemplos de la influencia de la música africana, como el *jazz* y los *blues* (elementos que están presentes en la mayoría de la música popular). También podría leer *Uncle Remus Stories* de Joel C. Harris ó *The People Could Fly* de Virginia Hamilton (NY: Knopf, 1985). También podría tratar de hallar ejemplos de la música tradicional o música popular de África Occidental, como King Sunny Ade, Ali Farka Toure, Youson d'Nour y Baba Mal.

Cuando lea el periódico o vea las noticias, esté atento a informes sobre Nigeria, Ghana y Mali. Hable con su hijo o hija acerca de lo que aprenda y compare los aspectos políticos, sociales, del medio ambiente y otros aspectos que le interese con aspectos similares de los Estados Unidos.

En Mali, el problema del crecimiento del desierto, o desertificación, puede estimular una conversación sobre las reservas de agua en los Estados Unidos (en particular en el suroeste del país). O también pueden hablar de cómo cambiarían sus vidas si el clima o las condiciones de la tierra cambiaran repentinamente. ¿Qué sucedería si el suelo del estado donde viven se volviera inservible, si la temperatura promedio subiera o bajara cinco grados o si cambiara la cantidad de precipitación?

Usted recibirá más informes sobre nuestro estudio de África durante las próximas semanas, cuando estudiemos África Oriental, África Central y África del Sur. Espero que usted siga disfrutando de compartir lo que su hijo o hija está aprendiendo.

Atentamente,

Spanish Support

Nombre _____ Clase _____ Fecha _____

LECTURA DIRIGIDA Y REPASO

Nigeria: Un país con muchas identidades

A. Durante la lectura

Instrucciones: A medida que vayas leyendo la Sección 1, contesta las preguntas a continuación en los espacios asignados.

1. ¿Quién gobernó Nigeria antes de la llegada de los europeos?

_____

2. ¿Cuándo logró Nigeria su independencia y de quién?

_____

3. ¿Cómo cambió Nigeria de capital y por qué lo hizo?

_____

4. ¿Cómo hicieron los hausa-fulani para sobrevivir por cientos de años?

_____

5. ¿Cuál es la ciudad más antigua de África Occidental? ¿Por cuánto tiempo ha sido el principal centro de comercio de esa región?

_____

6. ¿Cuál es el nombre de la ciudad donde habita gran cantidad de yorubas? En el siglo XIX, ¿de qué era el centro principal?

_____

7. ¿Qué hacen los yoruba y los igbo para sobrevivir?

_____

8. ¿Cómo se gobiernan a sí mismos los igbo?

_____

9. ¿De qué manera fue inusual el censo de Nigeria de 1991?

_____

10. ¿Por qué fue el censo tan importante para los habitantes de Nigeria?

_____

B. Repaso de los términos clave

Instrucciones: En los espacios en blanco a continuación, escribe la definición de los siguientes términos clave.

11. multiétnico _____

12. censo _____

Nombre _____ Clase _____ Fecha _____

eXAMEN DE LA SECCIÓN

**Exploremos
África
Occidental**

Nigeria: Un país con muchas identidades

A. Términos y conceptos clave

Instrucciones: Lee las oraciones a continuación. Si una oración es verdadera, escribe V en el espacio en blanco. Si es falsa, escribe F. Vuelve a escribir las oraciones falsas para convertirlas en verdaderas.

_____ **1.** Nigeria es multiétnica, lo que significa que muchos grupos étnicos viven dentro de sus fronteras.

_____ **2.** En 1991, el gobierno de Nigeria decidió convertir a Lagos en su capital, ciudad que está localizada en el sur del país.

_____ **3.** Los hausa y los yoruba conforman juntos el 32 por ciento de la población de Nigeria.

_____ **4.** En Nigeria, un censo determina qué grupo étnico tiene más poder.

_____ **5.** Los igbo se gobiernan a sí mismos con un sistema de monarquía.

B. Ideas principales

Instrucciones: En cada espacio en blanco, escribe la letra que mejor conteste la pregunta.

_____ **6.** ¿Qué son los hausa, yoruba e igbo?
    a. las principales ciudades de Nigeria
    b. grupos étnicos de Nigeria
    c. los principales centros de mercado de Nigeria
    d. los ríos más importantes de Nigeria

_____ **7.** ¿Cuál enunciado es cierto acerca de Nigeria?
    a. Muy pocos grupos étnicos viven allí.
    b. Aproximadamente uno de cada cinco africanos vive allí.
    c. Es el país más pequeño de África.
    d. Nigeria ha sido habitada desde 1900.

_____ **8.** En el siglo XV, los portugueses llegaron por primera vez a Nigeria para comprar
    a. telas.   **c.** esclavos.
    b. alimento.   **d.** madera.

_____ **9.** La capital de Nigeria fue cambiada con el fin de que estuviera más cerca
    a. al Sahara.
    b. a un número mayor de grupos étnicos.
    c. a los principales ríos.
    d. a las principales rutas de comercio.

_____ **10.** Los hausa-fulani de Nigeria han sobrevivido durante cientos de años
    a. con la agricultura.   **c.** con la manufactura.
    b. con la minería.   **d.** con el comercio.

© Pearson Education, Inc., publishing as Prentice Hall. All rights reserved.

Spanish Support

Exploremos África Occidental   **Recursos del Capítulo y la Sección ■ 45**

Ghana: El primero en independizarse

A. Durante la lectura

Instrucciones: A medida que vayas leyendo la Sección 2, completa la siguiente tabla con cuatro ideas que apoyen cada idea principal a continuación.

Idea principal A
Kwame Nkrumah tuvo muchas ideas y metas para Ghana.

I. _____

_____

2. _____

_____

3. _____

_____

4. _____

_____

Idea principal B
La vida ha cambiado de muchas formas desde la independencia de Ghana.

5. _____

_____

6. _____

_____

7. _____

_____

8. _____

_____

B. Repaso de los términos clave

Instrucciones: Para completar cada oración, escribe el término correspondiente en el espacio en blanco.

9. Nigeria obtuvo su _____ , o su independencia política, en 1960.

10. El gobierno de Kwame Nkrumah fue derrocado por un _____ militar.

CAPÍTULO 5
Exploremos
África
Occidental

Ghana: El primero
en independizarse

A. Términos y conceptos clave

Instrucciones: Empareja las definiciones de la Columna I con los términos de la Columna II.
Escribe la letra correspondiente en cada espacio en blanco.

Columna I

_____ **1.** Muchos países africanos querían su ____ .

_____ **2.** El cacao fue un producto de ____ importante de la
Costa de Oro.

_____ **3.** El primer mandatario de Ghana fue derrocado por
un ____ militar.

_____ **4.** El primer presidente de Ghana fue ____ .

_____ **5.** En la decada de 1980, el presidente de Ghana,
____ , intentó reformar la economía y el sistema
político del país.

Columna II

a. golpe

b. exportación

c. Jerry Rawlings

d. Kwame Nkrumah

e. soberanía

B. Ideas principales

Instrucciones: En cada espacio en blanco, escribe la letra que mejor conteste la pregunta.

_____ **6.** Kwame Nkrumah animó a la población de su país a
   a. detener la importación de alimentos.
   b. expandir sus rutas comerciales con otros países.
   c. buscar la independencia de Gran Bretaña.
   d. convertirse en una potencia colonial.

_____ **7.** ¿Con qué objetivo los ingleses colonizaron la Costa de Oro?
   a. para controlar su economía   **c.** para controlar su vida religiosa
   b. para controlar su gobierno   **d.** para controlar su sistema educativo

_____ **8.** Los oficiales del ejército derrocaron a Nkrumah y lo acusaron de
   a. haber reformado el sistema político del país.
   b. haber causado los problemas económicos del país.
   c. haber ayudado a sus compatriotas.
   d. no haber intentado unificar el país.

_____ **9.** ¿Cómo cambió Jerry Rawlings la vida en Ghana?
   a. Animó a los ciudadanos a adoptar la cultura occidental.
   b. Construyó una gran represa.
   c. Trató de reformar la economía y el sistema político de Ghana.
   d. Construyó un gran centro de conferencias.

_____ **10.** Cuando los ingleses gobernaban la Costa de Oro, la población cultivó menos alimentos, porque
   a. los cultivos para la venta eran mejor negocio.
   b. la tierra no era lo suficientemente fértil.
   c. los agricultores dedicaron más tiempo a la artesanía.
   d. resultaba más económico importar alimentos.

Spanish Support

Nombre _____ Clase _____ Fecha _____

LECTURA DIRIGIDA Y REPASO

Mali: El desierto se aproxima

CAPÍTULO 5
**Exploremos
África
Occidental**

A. Durante la lectura

Instrucciones: A medida que vayas leyendo la Sección 3, completa la siguiente tabla con información detallada sobre Mali. Escribe por lo menos tres detalles importantes en los espacios correspondientes.

Datos sobre Mali

El medio ambiente	1.
	2.
	3.
El Sahel	4.
	5.
	6.
La desertificación	7.
	8.
	9.

B. Repaso de los términos clave

Instrucciones: Para completar cada oración, escribe el término correspondiente en el espacio en blanco.

10. A los habitantes del Sahel les afecta mucho _____ , o el proceso en el que la tierra fértil se convierte en desierto.

11. Algunos ecólogos creen que el crecimiento del Sahara se debe a muchos años de

_____ .

12. Muchas personas creen que cuando los animales pastan por mucho tiempo en una zona,

_____ esa zona.

CAPÍTULO 5
Exploremos
África
Occidental

Mali: El desierto se aproxima

A. Términos y conceptos clave

Instrucciones: Empareja las definiciones de la Columna I con los términos de la Columna II.
Escribe la letra correspondiente en cada espacio en blanco.

Columna I

_____ 1. la zona entre el desierto y el bosque que pasa por el medio de Mali

_____ 2. desgaste lento

_____ 3. el cambio de tierra fértil a tierra muy seca, o demasiado maltratada, para poder mantener plantas o animales

_____ 4. período largo de tiempo en el que cae muy poca o nada de lluvia

_____ 5. el desierto que cubre la mayoría de África Occidental

Columna II

a. desertificación

b. sequía

c. erosión

d. el Sahara

e. el Sahel

B. Ideas principales

Instrucciones: En cada espacio en blanco, escribe la letra que mejor conteste la pregunta.

_____ 6. El Sahara, el Sahel y la sabana son
    a. los ríos más importantes de Mali.
    b. las ciudades más importantes de Mali.
    c. las zonas de vegetación más importantes de Mali.
    d. los idiomas más importantes de Mali.

_____ 7. Las personas que viven en el Sahel se mantienen de
    a. la manufactura.   **c.** los tejidos.
    b. la ganadería.   **d.** la minería.

_____ 8. ¿Cuál es la mayor amenaza para la economía de Mali?
    a. el esparcimiento del Sahara
    b. el aumento en la cantidad de lluvia
    c. el cierre del comercio con otros países
    d. la inestabilidad del mercado de bienes que produce el país

_____ 9. ¿Cuál puede ser una explicación de la desertificación del Sahel?
    a. los largos períodos de lluvia   **c.** la falta de sol
    b. la cantidad de inundaciones   **d.** los largos períodos de sequía

_____ 10. El crecimiento del Sahara amenaza la forma de vida de los
    a. árabe sauditas.   **c.** tuaregs.
    b. bereberes.   **d.** egipcios.

Spanish Support

RESUMEN DEL CAPÍTULO

Exploremos África Occidental

Preguntas guía:

- ¿De qué manera han afectado los acontecimientos históricos las culturas y los países de África?
- ¿Qué factores llevaron a que en África surgieran gobiernos diferentes?

Hay 17 países en África Occidental y cientos de grupos étnicos e idiomas. Tres de esos países son: Nigeria, Ghana y Mali.

Nigeria es el más poblado de todos los países africanos. En Nigeria se hablan más de 400 idiomas. Los tres más comunes son hausa, yoruba e igbo, los idiomas de los tres principales grupos étnicos. Nigeria, como la mayoría de los países en África, fue creada por los europeos, e incluye grupos étnicos que estaban acostumbrados a gobernarse a sí mismos. Los hausa-fulani viven en el norte y se dedican al pastoreo y al comercio. Los yoruba viven cerca de la costa y cultivan su propia tierra. La ciudad de Lagos es por tradición una ciudad yoruba. Los igbo viven en el sureste, son agricultores y no tienen ciudades.

Los europeos gobernaron a Ghana, a la que llamaron por muchos años la Costa de Oro. Bajo el gobierno colonial, los ingleses fomentaron el cultivo del cacao como un cultivo para la exportación. Los habitantes cultivaron menos alimentos y se volvieron dependientes de los alimentos importados y de los productos manufacturados. Kwame Nkrumah fue un líder que trabajó en favor de la independencia de su país. En 1957, Ghana obtuvo su independencia y Nkrumah se convirtió en el líder del nuevo país. Nueve años más tarde, Nkrumah fue reemplazado por un gobierno militar. Durante la década de 1980, Jerry Rawlings lideró el país y acentuó los valores tradicionales africanos del trabajo duro y el sacrificio. Bajo su mandato, la economía se fortaleció y, al mismo tiempo, Ghana logró conservar su herencia cultural.

Mali está ubicada en la parte norte de África Occidental. Alrededor de una tercera parte del país está en el Sahara, donde viven muy pocas personas. Otra parte está en la región semiárida del Sahel y la parte restante en la sabana, la única zona que recibe lluvia suficiente para el cultivo de alimentos. La mayoría de los habitantes de Mali vive del comercio, la agricultura y el pastoreo. Sin embargo, el crecimiento del desierto (que se conoce como desertificación) amenaza la supervivencia de todas esas ocupaciones. Las llanuras del Sahel están desapareciendo poco a poco. Algunas personas creen que este fenómeno se debe a que ha habido demasiado pastoreo en esa zona. Otros creen que el problema se debe a las largas sequías que ha habido en la región. Hoy en día, el gobierno trabaja con las Naciones Unidas en busca de una solución al problema de la desertificación.

Exploremos África Occidental

Instrucciones: Lee las oraciones a continuación. Las palabras en negrilla hacen falsa cada oración. Vuelve a escribir cada oración para que sea verdadera. Si necesitas ayuda, usa tu libro texto. Los términos clave de tu libro texto están subrayados. Si es necesario, mira los términos equivalentes en inglés en el glosario de tu libro de texto.

1. Nigeria es un ejemplo de país <u>multiétnico</u>, porque allí viven muchos **tipos de plantas.**

_____

2. El <u>censo</u> se lleva a cabo para contar el número de **días que llueve cada mes.**

_____

3. En 1957, Gran Bretaña acordó otorgar <u>soberanía</u> a los habitantes de Ghana, a quienes les dio **dinero.**

_____

4. Después del <u>golpe</u> militar, el gobierno **siguió igual.**

_____

5. Durante muchos años, la <u>desertificación</u> ha ido cambiando **el deseirto en tierra fértil.**

_____

6. Los animales pueden ayudar a causar <u>erosión</u> en la tierra al **caminar sobre ella.**

_____

7. Un <u>grupo étnico</u> está formado por personas que tienen **diferentes idiomas y religiones.**

_____

8. La <u>sequía</u> ocurre cuando hay **exceso de lluvia.**

_____

Spanish Support

CARTA PARA LA FAMILIA

CAPÍTULO
6

Exploremos África Oriental

La Línea Abierta de Ciencias Sociales

Querida familia:

Para continuar con el estudio de África, nos vamos a enfocar en África Oriental. Estudiaremos en detalle tres países de la región que son: Etiopía, Tanzania y Kenia. Para empezar, vamos a aprender sobre la historia de Etiopía y cómo se desarrolló allí una forma especial de cristianismo. Luego veremos cómo Tanzania y Kenia han logrado mantener la paz, mientras confrontan retos políticos y económicos. Para finalizar, estudiaremos cómo está cambiando la vida en África Oriental, a medida que más y más personas migran del campo a las ciudades.

Si usted halla artículos de revistas sobre alguno de esos países, ellos le pueden servir de ayuda adicional para los estudios de su hijo o hija. Si los artículos tienen ilustraciones o fotografías, podría pedirle a su hijo o hija que las recorte para compartirlas con la clase.

Puede observar un mapa de esta región con su hijo o hija para iniciar una conversación sobre la influencia de la ubicación de una región en la forma de vida de sus habitantes. Puede observar las zonas costeras y decir cómo esa ubicación puede estimular el comercio e intercambio de ideas y costumbres.

A medida que su hijo o hija lea sobre el contraste entre la vida en el campo y la vida en las ciudades en África Oriental, usted podría hablar de ese mismo contraste en los Estados Unidos. Si usted o alguien que conozca se ha mudado recientemente, puede usar esa experiencia para comenzar una conversación sobre las dificultades de irse lejos de donde uno ha vivido.

En la siguiente sección, la última sobre África, aprenderemos más sobre África Central y África del Sur. Gracias por su ayuda y apoyo a nuestro programa.

Atentamente,

CAPÍTULO 6
Exploremos
África Oriental

Etiopía: Iglesias y mezquitas

A. Durante la lectura

Instrucciones: A medida que vayas leyendo la Sección 1, completa la tabla con información de Etiopía.

Información sobre Etiopía

Cristianismo	1.
	2.
	3.
Islamismo	4.
	5.
Lalibela	6.
	7.
	8.
Addis Abeba	9.
	10.

B. Repaso de los términos clave

Instrucciones: Para completar cada oración, escribe el término correspondiente en el espacio en blanco.

11. Cuando los jóvenes querían estudiar música o pintura en la antigua Etiopía, ellos podían ingresar a un

_____ cristiano.

Spanish Support

EXAMEN DE LA SECCIÓN

Etiopía: Iglesias y mezquitas

A. Términos y conceptos clave

Instrucciones: Lee las oraciones a continuación. Si una oración es verdadera, escribe V en el espacio en blanco. Si es falsa, escribe F. En otra hoja de papel, vuelve a escribir las oraciones falsas para hacerlas verdaderas.

_____ **1.** El lugar donde los sacerdotes viven, trabajan y estudian se llama mezquita.

_____ **2.** Uno de los idiomas más antiguos del mundo se llama geez.

_____ **3.** Somalia fue la capital de la Etiopía cristiana por cerca de 300 años.

_____ **4.** La capital de Etiopía es Eritrea.

_____ **5.** La mayoría de los etíopes viven en zonas rurales.

B. Ideas principales

Instrucciones: En cada espacio en blanco, escribe la letra que mejor conteste la pregunta.

_____ **6.** Los cristianos de Etiopía fueron aislados de los cristianos de otras partes del mundo, porque
    a. los separaba el Mar Rojo.
    b. comerciaban con Egipto.
    c. quedaron rodeados de países islámicos.
    d. vivían en zonas rurales.

_____ **7.** ¿Cómo fue afectada la cultura de Etiopía por los primeros comerciantes árabes?
    a. Algunos etíopes adoptaron las creencias musulmanas.
    b. Los etíopes asistieron a escuelas árabes.
    c. Todos los etíopes adoptaron el idioma árabe.
    d. Los etíopes conquistaron a los árabes.

_____ **8.** Hoy en día, las religiones que más practican los etíopes es
    a. el cristianismo y el islamismo.   **c.** el islamismo y el budismo.
    b. el judaísmo y el cristianismo.   **d.** el cristianismo y el budismo.

_____ **9.** Pocos habitantes de Lalibela tienen
    a. alimento.   **c.** autos.
    b. creencias religiosas.   **d.** tierras para cultivar.

_____ **10.** ¿Qué oración es verdadera acerca de la capital de Etiopía?
    a. Es muy similar a una aldea en el campo.
    b. La mayoría de sus habitantes viven de la manufactura de productos.
    c. La mayoría de los etíopes viven en la capital.
    d. Es una mezcla de formas de vida tradicionales y modernas.

Nombre _____ Clase _____ Fecha _____

CAPÍTULO 6
Exploremos
África Oriental

Tanzania: Cuando las personas cooperan

A. Durante la lectura

Instrucciones: A medida que vayas leyendo la Sección 2, contesta las preguntas a continuación en los espacios asignados. Si es necesario, usa una hoja de papel adicional.

1. ¿Cómo hizo Julius Nyerere para ayudar a que todos los grupos étnicos se sintieran parte de Tanzania?
_____

2. ¿Qué hizo Nyerere para evitar el conflicto entre los grupos étnicos en las elecciones? ¿Por qué?
_____

3. ¿Qué le dijo Nyerere a los habitantes de Tanzania sobre el significado de independencia? ¿Qué quería él decir con eso?
_____

4. ¿Qué es ujamaa? ¿Qué eran las aldeas ujamaa?
_____

5. ¿Cuáles fueron algunas cosas en las que Nyerere tuvo éxito?
_____

6. ¿Cómo terminó el programa de ujamaa?
_____

7. ¿Cómo cambiaron los nuevos líderes la manera de cultivar la tierra en Tanzania?
_____

8. ¿Cómo cambió el sistema electoral en Tanzania después que Julius Nyerere entregó el poder?
_____

B. Repaso de los términos clave

Instrucciones: Para completar cada oración, escribe el término correspondiente en el espacio en blanco.

9. Julius Nyerere se sintió orgulloso de aumentar la tasa de _____ de Tanzania.

10. Tanzania tiene una gran _____ , porque ha tenido que pedir dinero prestado.

11. Un país que tiene dos o más partidos políticos tiene una _____ .

Spanish Support

EXAMEN DE LA SECCIÓN

Tanzania: Cuando las personas cooperan

A. Términos y conceptos clave

Instrucciones: Empareja las definiciones de la Columna I con los términos de la Columna II. Escribe la letra correspondiente en cada espacio en blanco.

Columna I

_____ **1.** La mayoría del territorio de Tanzania era gobernado por los ingleses, quienes la llamaban _____ .

_____ **2.** La capital de Tanzania es _____ .

_____ **3.** Tanzania está trabajando para pagar su _____ o el dinero que debe a otros países.

_____ **4.** Una parte de Tanzania es una isla llamada _____ .

_____ **5.** El primer presidente de Tanzania fue _____ .

Columna II

a. Dar es Salam

b. deuda externa

c. Julius Nyerere

d. Zanzíbar

e. Tanganica

B. Ideas principales

Instrucciones: En cada espacio en blanco, escribe la letra que mejor conteste la pregunta.

_____ **6.** ¿Por qué Tanzania siempre ha sido un centro de comercio?
   a. El país está ubicado en la costa este de África Occidental.
   b. El país tiene un ejército poderoso.
   c. El país rodea al Río Nilo.
   d. El país está ubicado en la costa de África Oriental.

_____ **7.** El país de Tanzania se formó cuando Tanganica se unió con la isla de
   a. Kaliban.   **c.** Zanzíbar.
   b. Dar es Salam.   **d.** Zambia.

_____ **8.** ¿Cuál fue uno de los cambios que el primer presidente introdujo en el sistema político de Tanzania?
   a. Creó un sistema de gobierno con un partido único.
   b. Se negó a tener elecciones.
   c. Creó un sistema de gobierno con dos partidos políticos.
   d. Acabó con la monarquía.

_____ **9.** Para mejorar la economía del país, el presidente le pidió a los agricultores que se trasladaran a
   a. las grandes ciudades.   **c.** las aldeas ujamaa.
   b. la costa.   **d.** las montañas.

_____ **10.** ¿Qué hicieron los líderes de Tanzania para tratar de mejorar la economía del país?
   a. Aumentaron los impuestos.
   b. Pidieron dinero prestado a otros países.
   c. Les pidieron a los agricultores que no sembraran más cultivos de exportación.
   d. Se negaron a comerciar con otros países africanos.

CAPÍTULO 6
**Exploremos
África Oriental**

Kenia: Rascacielos en la sabana

A. Durante la lectura

Instrucciones: A medida que vayas leyendo la Sección 3, contesta las preguntas a continuación en los espacios asignados.

1. ¿Qué descendencia tienen los habitantes de Kenia?

_____

2. ¿Qué tienen en común los habitantes de Kenia?

_____

3. ¿Cuál es un ejemplo de harambee?

_____

4. ¿Quiénes forman la mayoría de los agricultores de Kenia?

_____

5. ¿Cuáles son algunas de las responsabilidades de los niños en una aldea agrícola de Kenia?

_____

6. ¿Qué hacen los niños de las aldeas para divertirse?

_____

7. ¿Cómo está cambiando la vida en Kenia?

_____

8. ¿Quiénes tienden a migrar a las ciudades? ¿Cuáles son las consecuencias de esas migraciones?

_____

9. ¿Cómo se ayudan las mujeres entre sí en la Kenia rural?

_____

10. En las ciudades, ¿qué hacen los miembros de un mismo grupo étnico por el otro?

_____

11. ¿Qué dijo Moses Mpoke sobre quién era él?

_____

B. Repaso de los términos clave

Instrucciones: Para completar la oración, escribe el término clave en el espacio en blanco.

12. La palabra swahili que significa "trabajemos juntos" es _____ .

Spanish Support

EXAMEN DE LA SECCIÓN

Kenia: Rascacielos en la sabana

A. Términos y conceptos clave

Instrucciones: Empareja las definiciones de la Columna I con los términos de la Columna II.
Escribe la letra correspondiente en cada espacio en blanco.

Columna I

_____ **1.** granja pequeña cultivada y administrada por una
familia de Kenia

_____ **2.** la montaña más alta de Kenia

_____ **3.** palabra en swahili que significa "trabajemos juntos"

_____ **4.** el primer presidente de Kenia

_____ **5.** la capital de Kenia

Columna II

a. harambee

b. Jomo Kenyatta

c. Monte Kenia

d. Nairobi

e. shamba

B. Ideas principales

Instrucciones: En cada espacio en blanco, escribe la letra que mejor conteste la pregunta.

_____ **6.** La mayoría de los habitantes de Kenia trabajan como
  a. comerciantes.   **c.** agricultores.
  b. educadores.   **d.** fabricantes.

_____ **7.** ¿Cuál enunciado es cierto sobre los habitantes de Kenia?
  a. Pertenecen sólo a dos grupos étnicos.
  b. Pertenecen a muchos grupos étnicos.
  c. Hablan un solo idioma.
  d. La mayoría son de descendencia europea.

_____ **8.** ¿Qué oración es verdadera acerca de los habitantes de Kenia?
  a. La mayoría de las mujeres migran a aldeas más grandes en busca de trabajo.
  b. La mayoría de los hombres y las mujeres abandonan las zonas rurales.
  c. Muchos hombres se migran a las ciudades en busca de trabajo.
  d. Muchos hombres ahora se encargan del cuidado de los niños.

_____ **9.** Para poder resolver los problemas de la comunidad, las mujeres de las zonas rurales de toda
Kenia trabajan en grupo para formar
  a. grandes granjas.   **c.** nuevos mercados al aire libre.
  b. centros educativos.   **d.** grupos de ayuda mutua.

_____ **10.** La mayoría de los recién llegados a las ciudades reciben la bienvenida de
  a. educadores de las escuelas locales.   **c.** oficiales del gobierno.
  b. trabajadores sociales.   **d.** miembros del mismo grupo étnico.

Exploremos África Oriental

Preguntas guía:

- ¿Cómo han afectado los acontecimientos históricos las culturas y los países de África?
- ¿Qué factores afectan la manera de supervivencia de los africanos?

El área que hoy en día es Etiopía, antes comprendía los países de Eritrea, Yibuti y Somalia. Etiopía es una de las fuentes del Río Nilo. Durante siglos, su historia ha sido registrada por monjes. Etiopía fue un antiguo centro de comercio y los egipcios cristianos esparcieron su religión por todo el país. Unos 200 años más tarde, los árabes conquistaron África del Norte, excepto Etiopía. Con el tiempo, los comerciantes musulmanes controlaron el comercio de la región y se establecieron a lo largo de la costa de Etiopía. Los cristianos quedaron cada vez más aislados, a medida que se iban internando en el país. Los cristianos y musulmanes etíopes han vivido juntos y en paz durante la mayor parte de su historia. Lalibela fue la capital de la Etiopía cristiana por cerca de 300 años. Lalibela es un pueblo rural sin electricidad ni acueducto. Addis Abeba es la capital y la ciudad más grande de Etiopía con comodidades modernas.

Tanzania, al sur de Etiopía, ha sido durante mucho tiempo un centro de comercio. Tanzania se independizó en 1961. Su presidente, Julius Nyerere, trabajó para ayudar a que Tanzania se convirtiera en un país autosuficiente. Proclamó el swahili como el idioma oficial para que todos los grupos étnicos se sintieran parte del nuevo país. Para evitar problemas con los grupos étnicos, Nyerere insistió en que hubiera un solo partido político. Conservó la paz en Tanzania y mejoró la educación. Sin embargo, Nyerere no pudo mejorar la economía. Los nuevos líderes cambiaron algunos de sus programas y crearon un sistema político multipartidista.

Kenia está cambiando rápidamente hoy en día. Ubicada en el centro de África Oriental, cuenta con buenas zonas para la agricultura, pastos secos y desiertos. La mayoría de los habitantes son agricultores y viven en aldeas rurales. El país cuenta con más de 40 grupos étnicos diferentes, que son en su mayoría cristianos o musulmanes. Los habitantes de Kenia valoran mucho la tierra y la familia. En las aldeas agrícolas, la mayoría de las mujeres cultivan alimentos, mientras los hombres siembran cultivos para la venta. Sin embargo, muchos hombres migran a las ciudades con el propósito de buscar empleo. Las mujeres que se quedan en las aldeas tienen que trabajar el doble. Las mujeres en las zonas rurales han iniciado grupos de ayuda mutua en los que se ayudan unas a otras para resolver los problemas de su comunidad. Por lo general, los hombres en las ciudades viven con parientes, amigos o miembros de su mismo grupo étnico. Sus amistades les permiten llevar vidas placenteras fuera de casa.

Spanish Support

ACTIVIDAD DE VOCABULARIO

Exploremos África Oriental

Instrucciones: Las palabras subrayadas en los pasajes a continuación son términos importantes del capítulo 6. Escribe tu propia oración que use el término o la forma plural del término en el espacio respectivo. Si es necesario, observa los términos en el glosario de tu libro de texto.

1. Iyasus Moa ingresó a un <u>monasterio</u> en Etiopía para aprender sobre arte y para convertirse en un monje cristiano.

_____

_____

_____

2. El swahili es la <u>lingua franca</u> de Tanzania. Dos personas cuyo primer idioma es diferente, se pueden comunicar en swahili entre sí.

_____

_____

_____

3. Muchos países piden dinero prestado a otros países y crean una <u>deuda externa</u>.

_____

_____

_____

4. <u>Harambee</u> fue una campaña que inició Jomo Kenyatta para ayudar a unificar a todos los habitantes de Kenia.

_____

_____

_____

5. Las primeras elecciones de Tanzania bajo el sistema <u>multipartidista</u> ocurrieron en 1995.

_____

_____

_____

Exploremos África Central y África del Sur

La Línea Abierta de Ciencias Sociales

Querida familia:

A medida que completamos el estudio de África en nuestra clase de ciencias sociales, vamos a explorar dos países: la República Democrática del Congo y Suráfrica (uno ubicado en la región central y el otro en la región sur del continente). Vamos a aprender acerca de la importancia de la minería en el Congo, de la manera en que el país logró su independencia y de lo que ha sucedido desde ese entonces. En Suráfrica, aprenderemos acerca de la influencia europea, en particular la de los colonos holandeses, o afrikaneros, y los ingleses. También estudiaremos cómo la población blanca, que es muy pequeña, tenía todo el poder y creó el sistema de segregación racial (*apartheid*). Para finalizar, veremos cómo la segregación racial llegó a su fin al comienzo de la década de los 90.

Los cambios que ocurren en el Congo y Suráfrica son noticia casi a diario. Buscar y hablar sobre esas noticias con su hijo o hija puede ser de mucha utilidad para nuestras exploraciones. Una visita a la biblioteca también podría servir para que su hijo o hija halle más información sobre esa región africana. Si tiene acceso al *Internet,* allí también podría hallar noticias y otra información interesante para complementar nuestros estudios.

A medida que obtengan información, anime a su hijo o hija a comparar la vida de su propia comunidad con lo que están aprendiendo acerca de esa región africana. ¿En qué se parecen? ¿En qué se diferencian? También podrían hablar de los cambios que están ocurriendo actualmente en esos dos países. ¿Cuáles son algunas razones que hacen que esos cambios sean tan difíciles?

Ahora que vamos a terminar nuestra exploración de África, espero que tanto usted como su hijo o hija hayan disfrutado aprender más sobre este continente tan diverso y fascinante.

Atentamente,

Spanish Support

LECTURA DIRIGIDA Y REPASO

La República Democrática del Congo: Rica pero pobre

A. Durante la lectura

Instrucciones: A medida que vayas leyendo la Sección 1, completa la siguiente tabla con información acerca del Congo.

Información sobre el Congo

La minería	1.
	2.
	3.
Las características físicas	4.
	5.
Los recursos naturales en su historia	6.
	7.
	8.
El gobierno desde la independencia	9.
	10.

B. Repaso de los términos clave

Instrucciones: Para completar cada oración, escribe el término correspondiente en el espacio en blanco.

11. Cuando Mobutu llegó al poder en el Congo, estableció un gobierno _____ , en el que él sólo tenía el poder para gobernar.

12. Una de las maneras que empleó Mobutu para eliminar todos los lazos con el pasado colonial del Congo fue _____ las industrias extranjeras.

CAPÍTULO 7
Exploremos
África Central y
África del Sur

La República Democrática del Congo: Rica pero pobre

A. Términos y conceptos clave

Instrucciones: Lee las oraciones a continuación. Si una oración es verdadera, escribe V en el espacio en blanco. Si es falsa, escribe F. En otra hoja de papel, vuelve a escribir las oraciones falsas para convertirlas en verdaderas.

_____ **1.** El Congo tiene depósitos muy grandes de cobre en la provincia sur de Swahili.

_____ **2.** El Rey Leopoldo II de Bélgica fue un gobernante cruel del Congo.

_____ **3.** El Congo ganó su independencia de Francia en 1960.

_____ **4.** En un gobierno democrático, un solo líder tiene todo el poder.

_____ **5.** En el Congo, las industrias que pertenecían a empresas extranjeras fueron nacionalizadas.

B. Ideas principales

Instrucciones: En cada espacio en blanco, escribe la letra que mejor conteste la pregunta.

_____ **6.** A pesar de que la mayoría de los habitantes del Congo son agricultores, la mayoría de la riqueza proviene de
    a. el cultivo de bosques.
    b. los textiles.
    c. la minería.
    d. la manufactura.

_____ **7.** Los europeos llegaron por primera vez a lo que hoy en día es el Congo, porque querían
    a. el oro del país.
    b. el cacao del país.
    c. la historia cultural del país.
    d. los bosques del país.

_____ **8.** ¿Qué le sucedió al Congo cuando el precio del cobre cayó de manera drástica a finales de la década de los setenta?
    a. La deuda externa del país disminuyó.
    b. Aumentó el precio de muchos productos de exportación.
    c. El país obtuvo más dinero por la venta de su exportación más importante.
    d. La economía del país sufrió un colapso.

_____ **9.** ¿Qué hizo el presidente del Congo cuando hubo protestas por las alzas del gobierno?
    a. Renunció a su cargo.
    b. Encarceló a sus enemigos.
    c. Pidió que se repitieran las elecciones.
    d. Cambió las políticas del gobierno.

_____ **10.** A medida que muchos habitantes del Congo se fueron empobreciendo, algunas personas de la clase media decidieron que
    a. se irían del país.
    b. formarían un nuevo partido político.
    c. dejarían de pagar impuestos.
    d. establecerían una monarquía.

Spanish Support

LECTURA DIRIGIDA Y REPASO

Suráfrica: El fin de la segregación racial

A. Durante la lectura

Instrucciones: A medida que vayas leyendo la Sección 2, contesta las preguntas a continuación en los espacios asignados.

1. ¿Cuándo se establecieron por primera vez en Suráfrica los antepasados de la mayoría de los habitantes negros de esa región?

_____

2. ¿Qué nombre usaron los colonizadores holandeses para referirse a sí mismos? ¿Qué idioma hablaban ellos?

_____

3. ¿Cuál fue el resultado de las guerras entre los holandeses y los ingleses para controlar Suráfrica?

_____

4. ¿Qué se estableció en el Acta de los Territorios (*Natives Land Act*) de 1913?

_____

5. ¿Quién creó el sistema de segregación racial?

_____

6. ¿Qué efecto tuvo la segregación racial en la población negra?

_____

7. Cuando la población negra protestaba de manera pacífica, ¿cuál era la reacción de la policía?

_____

8. ¿Qué líder apoyó las leyes que terminaron con el sistema de segregación racial? ¿Quién se convirtió en el primer presidente electo de Suráfrica?

_____

9. Después de que terminó la segregación racial, ¿cómo eran los trabajos de los blancos comparados con los de los negros?

_____

B. Repaso de los términos clave

Instrucciones: En otra hoja de papel, escribe la definición de los siguientes términos clave.

10. segregación racial (*apartheid*)

11. discriminar

12. *homeland*

CAPÍTULO 7
Exploremos
África Central y
África del Sur

Suráfrica: El fin de la segregación racial

2

A. Términos y conceptos clave

Instrucciones: Empareja las definiciones de la Columna I con los términos de la Columna II. Escribe la letra correspondiente en cada espacio en blanco.

Columna I

_____ **1.** el sistema político en el que la discriminación racial es legal en Suráfrica se llama _____ .

_____ **2.** Cuando una persona trata a otra de manera injustacon base en su raza, religión o sexo, se dice que una persona es _____ contra la otra.

_____ **3.** Un territorio en Suráfrica donde los negros fueron obligados a vivir, se conoce como _____ .

_____ **4.** En 1990, el presidente de Suráfrica, _____ , ayudó a cambiar su sistema político.

_____ **5.** El 5 de Mayo de 1994, los surafricanos de todas las razas eligieron a _____ como presidente.

Columna II

a. segregación racial

b. discrimina

c. F. W. de Klerk

d. *homeland*

e. Nelson Mandela

B. Ideas principales

Instrucciones: En cada espacio en blanco, escribe la letra que mejor conteste la pregunta.

_____ **6.** Los afrikaneros son los descendientes de
    a. los colonos portugueses de Suráfrica.
    b. los colonos americanos de Suráfrica.
    c. los colonos holandeses de Suráfrica.
    d. los colonos ingleses de Suráfrica.

_____ **7.** ¿Qué sucedió cuando descubrieron oro y diamantes en Transvaal?
    a. Los afrikaneros empezaron a minar esa zona.
    b. Los ingleses que eran rastreadores de minas sacaron a los afrikaneros de sus tierras.
    c. Los americanos se establecieron en Suráfrica.
    d. Suráfrica se convirtió en colonia de Gran Bretaña.

_____ **8.** Después de 1910, leyes aprobadas por el gobierno blanco de Suráfrica pretendían
    a. preservar el dominio blanco sobre la tierra y las riquezas.
    b. ayudar a los suráfricanos negros a obtener mejores ingresos por su trabajo.
    c. dividir la tierra de manera equitativa entre los ciudadanos blancos y negros.
    d. mejorar las condiciones de vida de todos los trabajadores del país.

_____ **9.** ¿Cómo afectaron al país las leyes aprobadas por el Partido Nacional en 1948?
    a. Aumentaron el poder de los ciudadanos negros.
    b. Hicieron que la discriminación fuera ilegal.
    c. Dividieron a Suráfrica en categorías raciales.
    d. Volvieron ricos a los surafricanos negros.

_____ **10.** El gobierno de Nelson Mandela terminó con
    a. la discriminación racial legal.
    b. la discriminación económica
    c. el sistema político de Suráfrica.
    d. las leyes comerciales

Spanish Support

RESUMEN DEL CAPÍTULO

Exploremos África Central y África del Sur

Preguntas guía:

- ¿Qué factores llevaron a que en África surgieran diferentes tipos de gobiernos?
- ¿Qué factores han afectado la forma de sobrevivencia de los africanos?

La República Democrática del Congo, ubicada en el oeste de África Central, es el tercer país más grande de África y una de las principales fuentes de cobre del mundo. Congo se divide en cuatro regiones físicas: la cuenca del Congo, las tierras elevadas del norte, las montañas del este y las tierras elevadas del sur. El territorio incluye bosques con fuertes lluvias, sabanas y zonas con diferentes tipos de árboles. Cerca de las dos terceras partes de la población del Congo vive de la agricultura, aunque los mayores ingresos y la riqueza de la nación provienen de la explotación de las minas de cobre, oro y diamantes. Durante cientos de años, los europeos (en particular los belgas) controlaron el país, explotaron sus recursos y obtuvieron grandes ganancias. En 1960, el Congo se convirtió en un país independiente. Después de cinco años de problemas políticos y luchas internas, Mobutu Sese Seko tomó el control del país. Para hacerlo, él estableció un gobierno autoritario y cambió el nombre del país a Zaire. Mobutu nacionalizó la industria extranjera. La mala administración y la caída mundial del precio del cobre, causó el colapso en la economía del Congo a finales de la década de 1970. El gobierno recortó los gastos, lo cual afectó sobre todo a los pobres.

Suráfrica está localizado en la punta sur de África. Los antepasados de los surafricanos negros llegaron por primera vez a esa zona hace unos 1,500 años. En 1652, los colonizadores holandeses se establecieron en Ciudad del Cabo. Se autodenominaron afrikaneros. Más tarde, llegaron otros europeos que lucharon contra los africanos negros y los holandeses. A finales del siglo XIX, los europeos habían logrado sacar a los surafricanos de las mejores tierras. En 1910, los ingleses obtuvieron control del país y la declararon nación independiente. El gobierno de la nueva nación era todo de raza blanca.

En 1948, los afrikaneros tomaron el control del país e iniciaron un sistema de segregación racial o "separación" (*apartheid*). Las leyes dividieron a las personas en categorías raciales. La discriminación racial se volvió legal. La segregación racial negaba casi todos los derechos a los negros. Durante las décadas de 1950 y 1960, los negros protestaron. Muchos de los protestantes fueron asesinados o encarcelados. Las protestas continuaron. Otros países se unieron al movimiento en contra de la segregación racial. En 1994, todos los surafricanos obtuvieron el derecho de votar. La mayoría votó por Nelson Mandela como presidente. Mandela es un surafricano negro que pasó 28 años en prisión por luchar contra la segregación racial. La discriminación legal fue abolida. Sin embargo, los cambios reales avanzan lentamente. Los blancos aún controlan la mayor parte de los negocios más grandes del país. Los surafricanos tienen que enfrentar un gran reto: dar a los negros igualdad a la vez que aseguran a los blancos que en el proceso no perderán sus derechos.

Exploremos África Central y África del Sur

CAPÍTULO
7

Instrucciones: Empareja los términos clave de la tabla con las definiciones de abajo. Escribe la letra correspondiente en cada espacio en blanco. Luego escribe una oración que use el término o la forma plural del término en el espacio respectivo. Si es necesario, observa los términos en el glosario de tu libro de texto o mira cómo se usan en el capítulo 7.

a. segregación racial	**c.** discriminar	**e.** nacionalizar
b. autoritario	**d.** *homeland*	

_____ **1.** zona en las partes más secas y menos fértiles de Suráfrica, donde los negros eran forzados a vivir

_____

_____

_____ **2.** controlado por un líder o un grupo pequeño

_____

_____

_____ **3.** poner bajo el control del gobierno

_____

_____

_____ **4.** el sistema surafricano en el que los grupos raciales vivían separados y la discriminación racial era legal

_____

_____

_____ **5.** tratar a la gente de manera injusta con base en su raza, religión o sexo

_____

_____

Glosario

A

apartheid
segregación racial sistema sudafricano en el que los grupos raciales vivían separados y la discriminación racial era legal

authoritarian
autoritario algo controlado por una persona o por un grupo pequeño

B

bazaar
bazar tradicional mercado oriental al aire libre, formado por hileras de tiendas o puestos

boycott
boicot rehusar comprar o usar ciertos productos o servicios

C

casbah
casba antigua sección nativa de una ciudad en África del Norte

cash crop
cultivo para la exportación una cosecha que se cultiva con el propósito de ser vendida

cataract
catarata cascada o salto rocoso de un río

census
censo el registro de los habitantes de un país

city-state
ciudad-estado ciudad que controla la mayor parte de las tierras que la rodean y que tiene su propio gobierno

civilization
civilización sociedad con ciudades, un gobierno y clases sociales; la arquitectura, la escritura y el arte también caracterizan a una civilización

clan
clan grupo de linajes

colonize
colonizar establecerse en una región y tomar el poder o crear un gobierno

commercial farming
agricultura industrial producción agrícola para la venta en gran escala, como la producción de café, cocoa o plátanos

coup
golpe de estado la toma de poder de un gobierno, que por lo general lo lleva a cabo las fuerzas militares

Glosario

cultural diffusion
difusión cultural la transmisión de costumbres e ideas de una cultura a otra

cultural diversity
diversidad cultural una gran variedad de culturas

culture
cultura forma de vida de un grupo de personas que comparte costumbres y creencias similares

D

democracy
democracia forma de gobierno en la que los ciudadanos tienen poder por medio de representantes que ellos eligen

desertification
desertificación la transformación de tierra fértil en tierra que es demasiado seca para producir cosechas

discriminate
discriminar tratar a la gente de manera injusta en base a su raza, religión o sexo

diversify
diversificar añadir variedad; un país puede producir más productos para diversificar su economía

domesticate
domesticar criar plantas y animales para nuestro uso

drought
sequía un período largo de tiempo en el que cae muy poca o nada de lluvia

E

economy
economía todas las cosas que la gente hace para ganarse la vida en un lugar en particular

elevation
elevación la altura de la tierra sobre el nivel del mar

erode
erosión desgaste lento del suelo

escarpment
acantilado risco empinado de por lo menos unos 100 pisos de altura

ethnic group
grupo étnico grupo de personas que comparte un mismo lenguaje, religión, lazos de familia y costumbres

extended family
familia extensa unidad familiar que incluye otros parientes además de los padres e hijos

Spanish Support

Glosario

F

fellaheen
felá campesinos o trabajadores agrícolas en un país árabe

fertile
fértil que puede producir muchas plantas; productivo

foreign debt
deuda externa dinero que un país debe a otros países

G

griot
griot un narrador africano de cuentos

H

harambee
harambee la palabra swahili que significa 'trabajemos en harmonía'; campaña en Kenia iniciada por el presidente Jomo Kenyatta en 1963, después que el país se independizó

homeland
homeland tierras en Sudáfrica donde los negros eran forzados a vivir; las partes más secas y menos fértiles del país

hunter-gatherer
cazador y recolector persona que sobrevive de la recolección de alimentos silvestres y la caza de animales

hybrid
híbrida planta que es una combinación de dos o más tipos de una misma planta

I

irrigate
irrigar regar artificialmente las cosechas

K

kinship
parentesco una relación de familia

L

life expectancy
promedio de vida el promedio de años que se puede esperar que una persona viva

Glosario

lineage
linaje grupo de familias con un antepasado en común

literacy
alfabetismo la habilidad de leer y escribir

M

migrant worker
trabajador migratorio persona que viaja de un lugar a otro en busca de trabajo

migrate
migrar mudarse de un lugar a otro

monastery
monasterio lugar donde los monjes o las monjas viven, trabajan y estudian

multiethnic
multiétnico que contiene muchos grupos étnicos

N

nationalism
nacionalismo sentimiento de orgullo por la tierra natal; la identidad de un grupo de personas como miembros de una nación

nationalize
nacionalizar poner una industria privada bajo el control nacional

nomad
nómada persona que se muda constantemente y pastorea animales, comercia, caza o recolecta alimentos para sobrevivir

nuclear family
familia nuclear unidad familiar que incluye los padres y los hijos

O

oasis
oasis lugar fértil en el desierto donde hay agua y vegetación

P

Pan-Africanism
Panafricanismo movimiento que hace énfasis en la unidad entre todos los africanos

pilgrimage
peregrinación viaje religioso; para los musulmanes, el viaje a la Meca

Glosario

plantation
plantación granja grande donde se cultivan cosechas para la venta

plateau
meseta zona plana y extensa que se eleva por encima del terreno a su alrededor

Q

Quran
Corán el libro sagrado de la religión del Islam

R

rift
grieta zanja profunda; una hendidura en la tierra

S

silt
sedimento trozos de roca y lodo en el fondo de los ríos

souq
souq mercado al aire libre

sovereignty
soberanía independencia política

subsistence farming
agricultura de subsistencia cultivo de cosechas para sostener a una familia

surplus
excedente más cantidad de una cosa o producto de lo que se necesita

Swahili
swahili idioma africano que es una mezcla de palabras árabes y africanas

T

terrace
terraza plataforma cortada en el lado de una montaña para cultivar en lugares empinados

tributary
tributario arroyo o río pequeño que desemboca en un río principal

Respuestas

Capítulo 1

Sección 1   Lectura dirigida y repaso

1. porque la mayoría del terreno africano es elevado
2. el Gran Valle del Rift
3. el Nilo, el Congo, el Níger y el Zambeze
4. porque los ríos son interrumpidos por cataratas, o saltos rocosos
5. una meseta
6. la elevación
7. un acantilado
8. una grieta
9. una catarata
10. el sedimento
11. fértil
12. un tributario

Sección 1   Examen

1. V
2. F; A través de África, la elevación, o la altura bajo el nivel del mar, es relativamente alta.
3. F; Cuando la tierra es fértil, muchas plantas crecen allí.
4. V
5. V
6. c
7. a
8. a
9. c
10. a

Sección 2   Lectura dirigida y repaso

1. la latitud o la distancia a la línea ecuatorial
2. la elevación
3. la distancia a grandes extensiones de agua y accidentes geográficos
4. bosques tropicales húmedos
5. la sabana tropical
6. desiertos
7. irrigar
8. un oasis
9. nómadas

Sección 2   Examen

1. c
2. d
3. b
4. a
5. e
6. a
7. b
8. a
9. c
10. d

Sección 3   Lectura dirigida y repaso

1. el cacao, el café, la cebada, el trigo, el dátil, el ñame, la yuca, el maíz, el arroz, el té, árboles de madera dura
2. el petróleo, el oro, el cobre, la plata, el uranio, el titanio, los diamantes
3. granjeros
4. economías
5. extranjeras
6. fábricas
7. el cultivo de cosechas para alimentar a una familia
8. una cosecha que se cultiva para la exportación

Sección 2   Examen

1. b
2. e
3. d
4. c
5. a
6. b
7. d
8. d
9. c
10. b

Actividad de vocabulario

1. i
2. j
3. a
4. e
5. p
6. k
7. n
8. b
9. g
10. l
11. f
12. h
13. d
14. o
15. c
16. m

Capítulo 2

Sección 1   Lectura dirigida y repaso

1. de la caza de animales y la recolección de alimentos silvestres
2. la agricultura y la cría de animales, la domesticación de plantas y animales

Respuestas

3. la civilización egipcia y la nubia
4. Grupos de personas que hablaban el idioma bantú se mudaron de África Occidental a África Central y África del Sur en busca de terrenos nuevos.
5. La introducción de herramientas de hierro, la agricultura y cría de animales, y el idioma bantú a las regiones a donde fueron.
6. un cazador-recolector
7. domesticar
8. un excedente
9. una civilización
10. migrar
11. grupo étnico

Sección 1   Examen

1. V
2. F; Cuando las primeras comunidades producían excedentes de alimentos, tenían más alimento del necesario.
3. F; Con el tiempo, muchos grupos de agricultores de la Edad de Piedra se convertieron en civilizaciones, las cuales se caracterizan por set sociedades con ciudades, gobernantes y clases sociales.
4. F; Grupos de personas que hablaban el edioma bantú decidieron migrar, o irse, de África Occidental.
5. F; Las personas que comparten un mismo idioma, religión y costumbres forman grupos étnicos.
6. c
7. b
8. c
9. b
10. d

Sección 2   Lectura dirigida y repaso

1. el critianismo
2. el oro y el sal
3. Muchos musulmanes viajaron allí e introdujeron la religión islámica.
4. el comercio
5. el Océano Índico
6. Corán
7. peregrinación
8. swahili
9. ciudades-estado

Sección 2   Examen

1. F; El Corán es el libro sagrado de la religión islámica.
2. V
3. V
4. F; El idioma swahili, desarrollado en África Occidental, es una mezcla de palabras árabes y africanas.
5. F; Una ciudad que tiene un gobierno y que contrala la mayoría de sus alrededores es una ciudad-estado.
6. b
7. b
8. d
9. b
10. d

Sección 3   Lectura dirigida y repaso

Las oraciones pueden variar. Damos ejemplos de respuestas.
1. la vela latina, el astrolabio
2. Los comerciantes europeos establecieron centros de comercio y comerciaron en oro, marfil y otros productos en Ghana, Mali, África Oriental y otras regiones de la costa africana.
3. Los europeos esclavizaron a los africanos y los obligaron a trabajar en las colonias del continente americano.
4. Los trabajadores africanos más jovenes, fuertes y capaces fueron arrebatados de su tierra natal.
5. Los europeos se llevaron recursos africanos para enriquecerse.
6. Los europeos no dejaron que los africanos participaran en su propio gobierno.
7. Los europeos colonizaron la mayoría del continente y se quedaron con las mejores tierras.
8. Los europeos obligaron a los africanos a trabajar para ellos. Los europeos causaron conflictos al cambiar las fronteras políticas, ya que dividieron algunos grupos étinicos y mezclaron a otros en una misma zona.
9. establecerse en un área y derrocar un gobierno existente o crear un gobierno nuevo

Respuestas

Sección 3   Examen

1. d
2. a
3. e
4. b
5. c
6. b
7. a
8. b
9. d
10. b

Sección 4   Lectura dirigida y repaso

1. Las fronteras forzaron a algunos antiguos grupos rivales a vivir en un mismo país.
2. Que era necesario establecer un espíritu de cooperación entre todos los grupos.
3. un movimiento político que empezó en la década de 1920, que fomentaba la unidad entre todos los africanos
4. Después de haber luchado por la independencia en Europa, querían obtener la independencia en sus propios países.
5. Ganaron una guerra contra Francia que duró ocho años.
6. Los colonizadores rara vez dejaban que los africanos participaran en el gobierno, lo cual significó que los nuevos líderes no estaban preparados para gobernar.
7. nacionalismo
8. panafricanismo
9. un boicot
10. democracia

Sección 4   Examen

1. d
2. e
3. a
4. b
5. c
6. b
7. d
8. c
9. d
10. a

Sección 5   Lectura dirigida y repaso

1. Muchos países dependían de la exportación de uno o dos productos; muchos países tienen poca industria; algunos países pueden tener dificultad para alimentar a sus poblaciones.
2. Los países están diversificando sus economías y ayudando a los agricultores a mejorar sus cultivos.
3. Muchos niños tienen que trabajar para ayudar a sus familias; no siempre hay suficiente dinero para construir escuelas; con frecuencia hay demasiados estudiantes para la capacidad

de las escuelas.
4. Muchas familias sacrifican otras cosas para que los niños pueden ir a la escuela; muchas familias ayudan en la construcción de nuevas escuelas; los alumnos se turnan para atender clases.
5. El desierto se está creciendo, los bosques se están disminuyendo y hay mucha erosión del subsuelo.
6. Muchos países están sembrando árboles y verduras, desarrollando proyectos de irrigación y probando nuevas cosechas.
7. la agricultura de subsistencia
8. la agricultura industrial
9. híbrida
10. el alfabetismo
11. el promedio de vida

Sección 5   Examen

1. F; La producción a gran escala de productos como café, cacao y plátano se llama agricultura industrial.
2. V
3. F; Los agricultores obtienen una planta híbrida cuando combinan dos o más tipos de la misma planta.
4. V
5. V
6. b
7. c
8. b
9. c
10. c

Actividad de vocabulario

Las oraciones pueden variar. Damos ejemplos de respuestas.
1. Los ciudadanos enojados montaron un boicot para que nadie comprara productos del extranjero.
2. Hubo varias poderosas ciudades-estado en África Oriental que controlaron grandes extensiones de tierra.
3. Hace unos 5000 años, una civilización con ciudades y un gobierno surgió a lo largo del Río Nilo.
4. Durante el siglo XIX, los europeos creían que tenían el derecho de colonizar, es decir, de

Respuestas

apoderarse de las tierras africanas.

5. En la agricultura industrial a menudo se producen cosechas como el plátano, el cacao y el café para la exportación.

6. Muchos países africanos tienen largas historias de democracia, mientras que otros no permiten muchos derechos a sus ciudadanos.

7. Cuando los seres humanos aprendieron a domesticar plantas y animales, nació la agricultura.

8. En África, hay centenas de grupos étnicos que comparten idiomas, religiones y costumbres.

9. Los primeros seres humanos eran cazadores-recolectores que no habían aprendido a cultivar la tierra.

10. Los científicos tratan de ayudar a los agricultores al desarrollar plantas híbridas que incrementan la producción.

11. El promedio de vida varía, dependiendo del país en que uno viva, de la atención médica disponible y de las condiciones de vida.

12. El nivel de alfabetismo de Tanzania ha aumentado dramáticamente, ya que muchos de sus habitantes han aprendido a leer y a escribir.

13. Las personas pueden migrar a otro lugar en busca de una vida mejor.

14. Muchos africanos desarrollaron un fuerte sentido de nacionalismo cuando estuvieron bajo el dominio europeo.

15. El eslogan del movimiento del panafricanismo durante la década de 1920 era: "África para los africanos".

16. Una peregrinación a la Meca es una de las cinco partes importantes del islamismo.

17. La ley musulmana se basa en las enseñanzas del Corán.

18. Los agricultores pueden vender o intercambiar el excedente de sus cosechas.

19. Muchas personas en África Oriental hablan el swahili hoy en día.

Capítulo 3

Sección 1   Lectura dirigida y repaso

1. Más del 95 por ciento de la población de África de Norte es musulmana.

2. Las leyes del islamismo, que están basadas en el Corán, gobiernan todos los aspectos de la vida musulmana, incluyendo la vida familiar, el comercio, los negocios y el gobierno.

3. La mayoría de la población es árabe; otros grupos étnicos incluyen los bereberes.

4. Las ideas culturales se transmitan a través de los viajeros y de la conquista.

5. Dada su ubicación en la costa mediterránea, África del Norte es un centro importante de comercio y por eso ha sido influenciada por las culturas de Europa, Asia y África.

6. cultura

7. el Corán

8. un grupo étnico

9. la difusión cultural

Sección 1   Examen

1. c		6. b	
2. b		7. c	
3. d		8. c	
4. e		9. c	
5. a		10. b	

Sección 2   Lectura dirigida y repaso

Las oraciones pueden variar. Damos ejemplos de respuestas.

Puede aceptar todas las respuestas bien pensadas y basadas en información obtenida.

1. África Occidental consta de 17 países y cientos de grupos étnicos distintos.

2. Hay varias religiones e idiomas en África Occidental.

3. Muchas personas de África Occidental viven en familias extensas y trabajan con ellas.

4. Muchas familias de África Occidental tienen antepasados en común y lazos de parentesco con otros clanes y linajes.

5. diversidad cultural

6. parentesco

7. familia nuclear

8. familia extensa

Respuestas

9. linaje
10. clan
11. griot

Sección 2 Examen

1. b
2. e
3. c
4. d
5. a

6. b
7. c
8. a
9. c
10. d

Sección 3 Lectura dirigida y repaso

1. su ubicación, porque al estar ubicado a lo largo de la costa del Océano Índico, es un centro que conecta a los árabes y asiaticos
2. Son africanos con antepasados bantúes y árabes; viven en la costa de África Oriental, a lo largo de Somalia y Mozambique.
3. Su idioma es el segundo idioma de millones de habitantes de África Oriental y el idioma oficial de Kenia y Tanzania.
4. porque están intentando preservar su herencia africana
5. el islamismo y el cristianismo
6. Usaban la tierra, pero no eran dueños de ella; nadie compraba ni vendía tierra.
7. los colonizadores europeos
8. Fueron divididas y vendidas a africanos.
9. Tienen un fuerte lazo sentimental con sus hogares natales.
10. La mayoría nombraría la aldea de su familia o clan.
11. plantaciones

Sección 3 Examen

1. e
2. d
3. c
4. b
5. a

6. c
7. a
8. d
9. b
10. c

Sección 4 Lectura dirigida y repaso

1. Migran a Suráfrica para trabajar en las minas.
2. Luchan por el gobierno de la mayoría.
3. Viven de la caza y recolección en algunas zonas rurales; trabajan en fábricas, oficinas y hoteles.
4. Viven en ciudades.
5. la identidad de un grupo de personas como miembros de una nación en particular
6. persona que se muda de un lugar a otro en busca de trabajo

Sección 4 Examen

1. F; Un partido político importante de Suráfrica es el Congreso Nacional Africano (ANC).
2. F; El país de Suráfrica ha tenido mucha influencia en la región.
3. V
4. F; Las personas que se mudan de lugar a lugar para trabajar se conocen como trabajadores migratorios.
5. F; El país del Congo, en África Central, tiene muchos grupos étnicos.
6. b
7. b
8. b
9. c
10. d

Actividad de vocabulario

1. h
2. k
3. j
4. a
5. l
6. b

7. g
8. c
9. e
10. f
11. d
12. i

Capítulo 4

Sección 1 Lectura dirigida y repaso

1. Ayunan desde el amanecer hasta el anochecer, piensan en quienes son menos afortunados que ellos y se esfuerzan por no enojarse cuando las cosas no salen bien.
2. que contiene las palabras de Dios, las cuales fueron reveladas a Mahoma en el mes de Ramadan
3. cinco veces al día
4. El Sharia es la ley islámica; se basa en el Corán, en las palabras y las acciones de Mahoma y en comentarios escritos por eruditos y legisladores musulmanes.

Spanish Support

Respuestas

5. En Egipto, hay desacuerdo entre los musulmanes sobre si todas o sólo la mayoría de las leyes del país deben concordar con la ley islámica. Por ejemplo, algunas personas creen que la ley islámica requiere que las mujeres se velen la cara y otras personas no lo creen.
6. El Cairo; es una ciudad densamente poblada con mucho tráfico y escasez de vivienda; dada la escacez de vivienda, algunas personas viven en campamentos, en botes de remos en el Río Nilo y otras viven en grandes cementerios.
7. a orillas del Río Nilo
8. La mayoría son pequeñas, de entre una a tres habitaciones, construidas de ladrillos de barro o piedras, y con el techo plano.
9. su fe en el islamismo
10. musulmanes
11. Fellaheen
12. un bazar

Sección 1   Examen

1. b
2. a
3. c
4. e
5. d
6. d
7. b
8. b
9. b
10. c

Sección 2   Lectura dirigida y repaso

Las oraciones pueden variar. Damos ejemplos de respuestas. Puede aceptar todas las respuestas bien pensadas y basadas en información obtenida.
1. La mayoría vive en familias extensas en aldeas rurales.
2. Los bereberes son agricoltores y pastores, su gobierno se basa en familias y suelen constuir terrazas.
3. Llegaron a África del Norte en el siglo VII A.C. y poco a poco conquistaron la región.
4. Viven en familias extensas, tienen un gobierno central islámico y fueron nómadas en su mayoría.
5. Algunos son agricultores y algunos son nómadas.
6. Hay una mezcla de bereberes y árabes; la mayoría son musulmanes; algunos bereberes han mantenido sus costumbres tradicionales, mientras que otros han mezclado la religión islámica con otras religiones africanas.

7. Los bereberes y los árabes urbanos tienen bastante en común.
8. Hay mesquitas y mercados (es decir, *souqs*); los barrios viejos de las ciudades se llaman *casbahs* y tienen calles estrechas y curvas; también hay vecindarios modernos.
9. plataforma de tierra cortada en el lado de una montaña, para cultivar en lugares empinados
10. souq o mercado al aire libre
11. partes más viejas de las ciudades

Sección 2   Examen

1. b
2. c
3. e
4. a
5. d
6. b
7. c
8. b
9. c
10. d

Actividad de vocabulario

Las oraciones pueden variar. Damos ejemplos de respuestas.
1. a; En Egipto, mucha gente va al bazar a comprar alimentos y ropa.
2. c; En Argelia, los agricultores de las zonas montañosas cultivan en terrazas.
3. b; Algunos fellaheen cultivan terrenos alquilados pequeños, mientras que otros labran los terrenos de los terratenientes adinerados.

Capítulo 5

Sección 1   Lectura dirigida y repaso

1. muchos grupos étnicos, entre ellos los hausa, los fulani, los yoruba y los igbo
2. en 1960; de Gran Bretaña
3. La capital se trasladó de la ciudad de Lagos en el sur, a Abuja en la zona central del país. La nueva ubicación estaba más cerca a un número mayor de grupos étnicos; el gobierno intentaba unificar el país.
4. con el comercio y la cría de ganado y caballos
5. Kano; por más de mil años
6. Lagos; del comercio de esclavos con Europa
7. Trabajan en la agricultura.
8. con un concilio democrático de ancianos

Respuestas

9. Durante tres días, nadie podía entrar o salir del país, o salir de su vecinidad entre las 7 a.m. y las 7 p.m.
10. Porque el grupo minoritario con mayor población tiene la mayoría del poder político.
11. que tiene muchos grupos étnicos
12. el registro de todos los habitantes de un país

Sección 1   Examen

1. V
2. F; En 1991, el gobierno de Nigeria cambió la capital de Lagos en el sur, a Abuja en la zona central del país.
3. F; Los hausa y los fulani conforman juntos el 32 por ciento de la población de Nigeria.
4. V
5. F; Los igbo se gobiernan a sí mismos con un concilio democrático de ancianos.
6. b
7. b
8. c
9. b
10. d

Sección 2   Lectura dirigida y repaso

Las oraciones pueden variar. Damos ejemplos de respuestas. Puede aceptar todas las respuestas bien pensadas y basadas en información obtenida.

1. Creía en la independencia de Gran Bretaña.
2. Pensaba que los habitantes de Ghana se debían beneficiar de su propia riqueza.
3. Pensaba que los habitantes de Ghana se podían gobernar a sí mismos.
4. Guió a su pueblo a la independencia.
5. Se han introducido tecnologías nuevas.
6. Ha habido cambios políticos.
7. Han surgido problemas económicos seguidos de un crecimiento de la economía.
8. Ha habido renovación de la cultura tradicional.
9. Se ha establecido la soberanía.
10. Hubo un golpe de estado.

Sección 2   Examen

1. e
2. b
3. a
4. d
5. c
6. c
7. a
8. b
9. c
10. a

Sección 3   Lectura dirigida y repaso

Las oraciones pueden variar. Puede aceptar todas las respuestas bien pensadas y basadas en información obtenida.

1. El desierto del Sahara cubre una tercera parte del territorio de Mali.
2. El desierto está creciendo.
3. Pocas personas viven en el desierto del Sahara, unas cuantas en el Sahel y muchas en las llanuras de la sabana.
4. la zona entre el desierto y la sabana que pasa por el medio de Mali y por otros 12 países africanos
5. Por miles de años, sus llanuras han permitido que muchos animales pasten allí.
6. Es el hogar para el centro de comercio de caravanas de sal en la ciudad de Tombouctou.
7. posiblemente a causa de que muchos animales pastan por largo tiempo, a causa de las sequías, o a causa de ambos factores
8. erosión destruye tierras cultivables
9. obliga a la gente a dejar su tierra natal y a cambiar su manera de sobrevivir
10. la desertificación
11. sequía
12. erosionan

Sección 3   Examen

1. e
2. c
3. a
4. b
5. d
6. c
7. b
8. a
9. d
10. c

Actividad de vocabulario

1. Nigeria es un ejemplo de un país multiétnico, porque allí viven muchos grupos étnicos.
2. El censo se lleva a cabo para contar el número de habitantes que tiene un país.

Spanish Support

Respuestas

3. En 1957, Gran Bretaña acordó otorgar soberanía a los habitantes de Ghana, a quienes les dio su independencia.
4. Después del golpe militar, el gobierno cambió de dirigentes.
5. Durante muchos años, la desertificación ha ido cambiando la tierra fértil en desierto.
6. Los animales pueden ayudar a causar erosión en la tierra al pastar por mucho tiempo.
7. Un grupo étnico está formado por personas que tienen el mismo idioma y religión.
8. La sequía ocurre cuando hay muy poca o nada de lluvia.

Capítulo 6

Sección 1   Lectura dirigida y repaso

Las oraciones pueden variar. Damos ejemplos de respuestas. Puede aceptar todas las respuestas bien pensadas y basadas en información obtenida.

1. se esparció por Etiopía proveniente de la iglesia egipcia cóptica
2. aislada del cristianismo del resto del mundo
3. se convirtió en una forma única de cristianismo
4. Los árabes no invadieron Etiopía, pero conquistaron sus alrededores.
5. Los comerciantes árabes llegaron a Etiopía e introdujeron el islamismo.
6. Fue la capital de la Etiopía cristiana por cerca de 300 años.
7. No hay electricidad ni teléfonos.
8. Los habitantes viven de la agricultura, la ganadería y la pesca.
9. la actual capital de Etiopía
10. una ciudad moderna con mezcla de tradiciones rurales
11. monasterio

Sección 1   Examen

1. F; El lugar donde los sacerdotes viven, trabajan y estudian se llama monasterio.
2. V
3. F; Lalibela fue la capital de la Etiopía cristiana por cerca de 300 años.
4. F; La capital de Etiopía es Addis Abeba.
5. V

6. c
7. a
8. a
9. c
10. d

Sección 2   Lectura dirigida y repaso

1. Convirtió el swahili en el idioma oficial.
2. Creó un sistema de gobierno con un partido único para todas las elecciones, para así evitar que se formaran partidos en base a los grupos étnicos.
3. que era "libertad y trabajo"; que un país puede acabar con la pobreza, sólo a través del trabajo duro
4. La palabra ujamaa significa "estar unidos" o "en familia". Las aldeas ujamaa fueron parte del plan de autosuficiencia propuesto por Nyerere. Se les pidió a muchas familias que se trasladaran de sus hogares esparcidos en el campo a aldeas donde era más fácil para el gobierno darles educación y agua potable.
5. Conservó la paz en Tanzania y mejoró la educación.
6. Los nuevos líderes de Tanzania lo eliminaron.
7. Ellos dijeron que los agricultores deberían esforzarse más en cultivar productos de exportación.
8. se convirtió en un sistema político multipartidista
9. alfabetismo
10. deuda externa
11. sistema multipartidista

Sección 2   Examen

1. e
2. a
3. b
4. d
5. c

6. d
7. c
8. a
9. c
10. b

Sección 3   Lectura dirigida y repaso

1. La mayoría son de descendientes africanos de más de 40 grupos étnicos distintos (cada uno con su propia cultura e idioma). La mayoría de los habitantes de Kenia son cristianos o musulmanes. Muy pocos son de descendencia europea o asiática.

Respuestas

2. La importancia que le dan a la tierra y a la familia.

3. El gobierno paga una parte de la educación de los niños, pero la comunidad trabaja junta para construir y apoyar las escuelas.

4. las mujeres

5. traer agua, ordeñar las vacas y cabras, y limpiar sus casas antes de ir a la escuela

6. juegan fútbol y a la pelota, hacen autos de juguete, muñecas y otros juguetes, y de vez en cuando ven una película

7. Muchas personas están migrando del campo a las ciudades en busca de trabajo.

8. los hombres; una vez en las ciudades se sienten mal y extrañan sus hogares y a sus seres queridos; las mujeres que se quedan en casa tienen que trabajar el doble

9. con la creación de grupos de ayuda mutua; las mujeres cosechan cultivos de exportación además de los cultivos para su sustento; ellas usan el dinero en efectivo para llevar a cabo proyectos comunales, como guarderías, instalación de tuberías de agua y préstamos.

10. Por lo general ofrecen sus bienvenidas, comparten sus cuartos y se ayudan mutuamente.

11. que era tanto un hombre de la ciudad como un hombre del campo; que se puede sentir bien en ambos lugares; que la ciudad no ha hecho que él deje de ser quien es: un maasai.

12. harambee

Sección 3   Examen

1. e		6. c	
2. c		7. b	
3. a		8. c	
4. b		9. d	
5. d		10. d	

Actividad de vocabulario

Las oraciones pueden variar. Damos ejemplos de respuestas.

1. Los estudiantes de Lyasus Moa construyeron monasterios y escuelas en toda Etiopía.

2. La lingua franca les permite comunicarse a las personas que hablan distintos idiomas primarios.

3. Con el propósito de mejorar la economía, los líderes de Tanzania han creado una gran deuda externa.

4. Parte de la propuesta de harambee, es que el gobierno pagaba parte de la educación de cada niño y las personas ayudaban a construir escuelas.

5. Después de que el gobiernó inició el sistema político multipartidista, hubo candidatos de diez partidos en las elecciones.

Capítulo 7

Sección I   Lectura dirigida y repaso

Las oraciones pueden variar. Damos ejemplos de respuestas. Puede aceptar todas las respuestas bien pensadas y basadas en información obtenida.

1. La explotación de las minas de cobre empezó hace mucho tiempo.

2. El Congo se ha convertido en una de las principales fuentes de cobre del mundo.

3. El Congo también explota oro y diamantes.

4. El Congo es el tercer país más grande de África.

5. Las cuatro regiones principales son: la cuenca del Congo (bosque húmedo), las tierras elevadas del norte (sabana), las montañas del este (sabana y bosques) y las tierras elevadas del sur (llanuras y zonas con árboles)

6. El poder de los antiguos reinos se basaba en su habilidad para trabajar el hierro.

7. Los belgas los obligaron a cultivar caucho para el enriquecimiento de los propios belgas.

8. Más adelante, los belgas explotaron el cobre y los diamantes.

9. Mobutu fue un líder militar que estableció un gobierno autoritario y nacionalizó las industrias.

10. Después de años de problemas económicos comenzó una rebelión y se estableció un gobierno nuevo.

11. autoritario

12. nacionalizar

Spanish Support

Respuestas

Sección I   Examen

1. F; El Congo tiene depósitos muy grandes de cobre en la provincia sur de Katenga.

2. V

3. F; El Congo se independizó de Bélgica en 1960.

4. F; En un gobierno autoritario, un sólo líder o un grupo pequeño de líderes tiene todo el poder.

5. V

6. c   **7.** a   **8.** d   **9.** b   **10.** a

Sección 2   Lectura dirigida y repaso

1. hace 1,500 años

2. afrikaneros; afrikaans

3. Inglaterra ganó y en 1910, declaró a Suráfrica un país independiente.

4. Los habitantes de raza negra podían vivir sólo en el 8 por ciento del territorio total del país; también podían trabajar en las zonas de los habitantes blancos con unos salarios muy bajos, pero no podían comprar tierras allí.

5. el partido político de los afrikaneros, el Partido Nacional

6. Restringió las zonas en las que podían vivir los habitantes negros; les negó el derecho de ciudadanía y de voto; los mantuvo con salarios bajos y escuelas inferiores; y les negó acceso a instituciones "blancas", como escuelas, hospitales y restaurantes.

7. La policia mató a cientos de hombres, mujeres y niños, y encarceló a miles más.

8. F.W. de Klerk; Nelson Mandela

9. Personas de raza blanca todavía controlaban la mayoría de los grandes negocios y periódicos; la población blanca tenía mejores trabajos y más propiedad.

10. sistema surafricano en el que los grupos raciales eran separados

11. tratar injustamente a alguien en base a su raza, religión o sexo

12. las regiones más secas y menos fértiles de Suráfrica, donde los habitantes de raza negra fueron obligados a vivir

Sección 2   Examen

1. a   **6.** c
2. b   **7.** b
3. d   **8.** a
4. c   **9.** c
5. e   **10.** a

Actividad de vocabulario

Las oraciones pueden variar. Damos ejemplos de respuestas.

1. d; Los surafricanos de raza blanca oligaron a los de raza negra a vivir en 10 *homelands* localizadas en todo el país.

2. b; Mobutu Sese Seko fue un líder poderoso congolés que estableció un gobierno autoritario.

3. e; Mobutu Sese Seko logró nacionalizar todas las industrias en el Congo que pertenecían a compañías extranjeras.

4. a; El sistema de segregación racial de Suráfrica ya no existe.

5. c; Bajo el sistema de segregación racial en Suráfrica era legal discriminar con base en en la raza de una persona.